ALEXANDER PUŠKIN

*A Symposium on the 175th
Anniversary of His Birth*

EDITORS:

ANDREJ KODJAK
New York University

KIRIL TARANOVSKY
Harvard University

New York · New York University Press · 1976

Copyright © 1976 by New York University
Library of Congress Card Number: 75-39776
ISBN: O-8147-4562-8

Library of Congress Cataloging in Publication Data

Puškin Symposium, New York University, 1974.
  Alexander Pušhkin: a symposium on the 175th
anniversary of his birth.

  (New York University Slavic papers; v. 1)
  English or Russian.
  1. Puškin, Aleksandr Sergeevič, 1799–1837
Criticism and interpretation— I. Kodjak,
Andrej. II. Taranovski, Kiril. III. Title.
IV. Series: New York University. New York University
Slavic papers; v. 1.
PG3356.P88   1964   891.7 1 3   75-39776
ISBN: 0-8147-4562-8

Manufactured in the United States of America

NEW YORK UNIVERSITY
SLAVIC PAPERS

Volume I

EDITORS' NOTE

This volume consists of papers presented at the Puškin Symposium at New York University on November 16–17, 1974, in commemoration of the 175th anniversary of Alexander Puškin's birth. The organization of the volume reflects that of the symposium: the first part devoted to Puškin's poetry, the second to his prose, and the third to his narrative poetry and drama.

The Slavic Department of New York University suggested that the papers presented at the symposium deal with the artistic aspects of Puškin's works. This is why the reader of this volume will not find any studies of biographical or textual problems.

Unfortunately the contribution of Professor Kiril Taranovsky of Harvard University, "Puškin's Lyric Iambic Tetrameter of the Mixajlovskoe Period (1824–26)" and of Professor J. Thomas Shaw of the University of Wisconsin, "Puškin''s 'The Stationmaster' and the New Testament Parable," could not be included in this collection.

Thanks to Roman Jakobson's assistance, an article from Professor Riccardo Picchio of Yale University was received after the symposium and has been included in the first part of this volume.

The Slavic Department of New York University is grateful to all the contributors to the Puškin Symposium for their cooperation and assistance.

The editorial work on this volume was kept to a minimum. Since this volume consists of articles dealing for the most part with specific works of Puškin, it was felt that an index was unnecessary.

All the quotations from Puškin's works are taken from the seventeen-volume edition of the Academy of Science 1937–1959 and appear in the footnotes as "P" or "П" followed by volume, part, and page.

CONTENTS

PART I
Puškin's Poetry

Роман Якобсон (M.I.T. and Harvard University)
Стихи Пушкина о деве-статуе, вакханке и смиреннице   3

Vadim Liapunov (New York University)
Mnemosyne and Lethe: Puškin's "Vospominanie"   27

Riccardo Picchio (Yale University)
Dante and J. Malfilâtre as Literary Sources of Tat'jana's
Erotic Dream   42

Elisabeth Stenbock-Fermor (Stanford University)
French Medieval Poetry as a Source of Inspiration for
Puškin   56

Walter Vickery (University of North Carolina at Chapel Hill)
"Arion": An Example of Post-Decembrist Semantics   71

PART II
Puškin's Prose

Andrej Kodjak (New York University)
"The Queen of Spades" in the Context of the Faust Legend   87

Krystyna Pomorska (M.I.T.)
Structural Peculiarities in "Putešestvie v Arzrum"   119

Леонид Ржевский (New York University)
Структурная тема «Египетских ночей» Пушкина   126

Светлана Умрихина
(State University of New York at New Paltz)
Заметки об эпистолярном стиле Пушкина   135

PART III
Puškin's Narrative Poetry and Drama

Walter Arndt (Dartmouth College)
"Ruslan i Ljudmila": Notes from Ellis Island   155

Victor Erlich (Yale University)
Puškin's Moral Realism as a Structural Problem   167

Richard Gregg (Vassar College)
The Eudaemonic Theme in Puškin's "Little Tragedies"   178

William Harkins (Columbia University)
The Place of "Domik v Kolomne" in Puškin's Creation   196

Victor Terras (Brown University)
Puškin's "Feast During the Plague" and Its Original:
   A Structural Confrontation   206

PART ONE
Puškin's Poetry

СТИХИ ПУШКИНА О ДЕВЕ-СТАТУЕ, ВАКХАНКЕ И СМИРЕННИЦЕ

Роман Якобсон
M.I.T. and Harvard University

I ЦАРСКОСЕЛЬСКАЯ СТАТУЯ

Урну с водой уронив, об утес ее дева разбила.
Дева печально сидит, праздный держа черепок.
Чудо! не сякнет вода, изливаясь из урны разбитой;
Дева, над вечной струей, вечно печальна сидит.

Малые формы в творчестве Пушкина поражают необыкновенной концентрацией художественных средств. Четверостишие на статую работы П. П. Соколова, сочиненное первого октября 1830г., тематически отличается от других надписей Пушкина: здесь девушка над разбитой урной, там юноши, играющие в свайку или в бабки. Из 14 стихотворений, сложенных элегическим дистихом, единственно «Царскосельская статуя» наделена всецело женской фабулой. Глубоко пушкинская символика стертой границы между изваянием и жизнью (ср. Якобсон 1937) нигде, кроме названного четверостишия, не включает статуи женской. В «Царскосельской статуе», разделяющей целый ряд выразительных штрихов с другими

---

* The author preserves the right to reproduce the paper "Stixi Puškina o deve-statue, vakxanke i smirennice" in his *Selected Writings*.

элегическими дистихами автора, в то же время таится немало ярко индивидуальных особенностей и в звуковой фактуре, и в строе стиха, и в художественном претворении словаря и грамматики.

В обоих элегических дистихах «Царскосельской статуи» (ЦС) распределение ударных гласных между шестью иктами каждой строки подчинено череде законов. Предварительно напомним: в русском пятифонемном вокалическом треугольнике внутри каждой из двух пар фонем ($U{:}I = O{:}E$) гласные различаются, на перцептивном уровне, по темной и светлой тональности; гласный A, компактный по складу акустического спектра, яркий в соответственных терминах звукового восприятия, противопоставлен всем прочим гласным, т.е. паре диффузных по складу спектра, перцептивно блеклых фонем U и I, а также фонемам O и E, гласным пониженной компактности и пониженной диффузности, в терминах восприятия полуярким и заодно полублеклым.

И в начале, и в конце стиха репертуар ударных фонем сводится к гласным, участвующим в тональном, темно-светлостном противопоставлении. Начальный гласный обоих гекзаметров, темное и диффузное U, отличается обеими дифференциальными чертами (distinctive features) от начального гласного обоих пентаметров, светлого и пониженно диффузного E: ₁Ýрну—₂Дéва—₃Чýдо—₄Дéва.

Примечателен факт, что гласный шестого, конечного икта неизменно отличается и притом всего одной дифференциальной чертой от гласных предшествующего и следующего за ним начального икта. Из двух дифференциальных черт, находящих себе здесь применение, назовем противопоставление диффузных и пониженно диффузных гласных первичным (primary opposition), а тональное противопоставление темных и светлых гласных вторичным (secondary opposition). Шестые икты всех стихов неизменно пользуются первичным противопоставлением. Если за конечным иктом следует икт начальный, то первичное противопоставление применяется к расподоблению шестого и дальнейшего начального ударного гласного; если же конечный икт принадлежит последней строке четверостишия, то первичное противопоставление применяется к расподоблению шестого и первого из ее собственных ударных гласных. Во всех остальных случаях, т.е. в первых трех стихах, расподобление первого и шестого ударного гласного каждой строки построено на вторичном противопоставлении.

Члены обоих противопоставлений образуют в цепи стихов регулярную альтернацию направлений. Первичное противопоставление: I—E ($_1$разбила.—$_2$Дева), O—U ($_2$черепок.—$_3$Чудо!), I—E ($_3$разбитой;—$_4$Дева), E—I ($_4$Дева—$_4$сидит.). Таким образом на обоих переходах от гекзаметра к пентаметру конечное диффузное I противопоставлено следующему начальному, пониженно диффузному E. Вторичное противопоставление: U—I ($_1$Урну—разбила), E—O ($_2$Дева—черенок), U—I ($_3$Чудо—разбитой). Таким образом в обоих гекзаметрах начальное темное U противопоставлено конечному светлому I. Можно было бы также отметить, что начальное темное U противопоставлено конечному светлому I всего четверостишия ($_1$Урну—$_4$сидит).

Ударное I появляется только под иктами, замыкающими полустишие, и доминирует в этой роли над прочими гласными; в строках последнего дистиха ударным I кончается второе полустишие, $_3$разбитой—$_4$сидит), а в науальном дистихе либо првое ($_2$сидит),либо оба полустишия ($_1$уронив—разбила). Характерно, что конечное полустишие второго пентаметра повторяет почти текстуально начальное полустишие первого ченстаметра и воспроизводит все его ударные гласные (E—A—I): , Дева печально сидит . . .—$_4$. . . вечно печальна сидит. Соответственно второй пентаметр замыкает ударным O начальное полустишие (струей), обратно первый пентаметр заканчивает ударным I начальное, а ударным O конечное полустишие (черепок).

В русском стихе волнообразная регрессивная диссимиляция (ср. Якобсон 1960, 362) склонна усилить каждый второй икт, начиная обратный счет с предпоследнего икта; соответственно в шестииктовом стихе сильны четные икты. В ЦС оба четных икта, принадлежащих внутренней части стиха, т.е. второй и четвертый, связаны одинаковым—либо пониженно диффузным, либо компактным—гласным: $_1$с водой—об утёс, $_2$печально—праздный, $_3$не сякнет—изливаясь, $_4$над вечной—вечно, причем оказываются сопоставлены две разновидности одной и той же грамматической категории: в первой строке существительные женского и мужского рода, в третьей финитная

форма и деепричастие, а в обоих пентаметрах имя прилагательное сближено с адъективным наречием.

Вышеотмеченная тесная связь между текстом и особенно
вокалическим строем обоих пентаметров встречает дальней-
шее выражение в том обстоятельстве, что оба раза прину-
дительное совпадение гласных под вторым и четвертым
иктом находит себе одинаковую поддержку в смежном удар-
ном гласном: ₂*печа́льно сиди́т, пра́здный держа́ черепо́к—*
₄*Де́ва над ве́чной струёй ве́чно.*

Любопытно распределение фонемы *A,* самой частой среди
ударных гласных ЦС: она представлена в тексте семью примерами. Из восьми внутренних (т.е. неначальных и неконечных)
иктов, принадлежащих внутренним (т.е. второй и третьей)
строкам стихотворения, шесть приходятся на фонему *A* и по
одному на диффузные гласные *U* и *I* при полном отсутствии
O и *E.* Обратно, из восьми внутренних иктов, принадлежащих
внешним (т.е. первой и четвертой) строкам стихотворения,
шесть примеров приходятся именно на *O* и *E* (2 *O,* 1 *E* в первой,
2*E,* 1*O* во второй строке), и всего по одному на *A* и на *I.* Здесь
сказывается прежде всего отпор против совместного появле-
ния гласных компактных с гласными пониженной компактности.

В ЦС нет «замен дактиля хореем», наблюдаемых у Пушкина,
согласно выкладкам Б. И. Ярхо (стр. 83), в 60% гекзаметров
и в 14% пентаметров, написанных после 1825 года. По месту
своего ударения слова под иктом разделяются в ЦС всего на
две категории—окситонные (с ударением на конечном слоге)
и парокситонные (с ударением на предпоследнем слоге).
Каждое из этих слов содержит не менее двух слогов. Моно-
силлабы и пропарокситоны отсутствуют, тогда как в прочих
«анфологических эпиграммах» Пушкина, сложенных элегическими дистихами в том же 1830г., такие акцентовки обыч-
ны: в двустишии «На перевод Илиады»—*умо́лкнувший зву́к
боже́ственной э́ллинской речи, ста́рца вели́кого те́нь;* в четверостишии «Отрок»—*студёного мо́ря;* в шестистишии «Труд»
—*ми́г вожделе́нный, тру́д многоле́тний, непоня́тная гру́сть,
молчали́вого спу́тника но́чи;* в восьмистишии «Рифма»—
*бессо́нная ни́мфа, стра́стию к не́й, пло́д понесла́, влюблённого
бо́га, ме́ж говорли́вых, ми́лую до́чь, ма́тери чу́ткой, па́мяти*

строгой. Равно не чуждаются ни пропарокситонов, ни моносиллабов позднейшие пушкинские надписи на статуи, напр. «На статую играющего в бабки» (1836): *юноша; меткую кость; прицелился . . . прочь; врозь расступись*. Ввиду отсутствия ударных моносиллабов, всем падающим на икты словесным ударениям предоставлена независимая фонологическая роль и равная ритмическая сила (ср. Якобсон, 1973); кроме того, в результате исключения пропарокситонов и моносиллабов из ритмического словаря «Царскосельской статуи» явление начального ударения ограничивается первым слогом стиха в гекзаметрах и первым слогом обоих полустиший в пентаметрах, т.е. в общей сложности шестью примерами на протяжении всего стихотворного текста.

К шести примерам принудительно конечного ударения, падающего на последний слог первого полустишия во всех четырех строках и на последний слог второго полустишия в обоих пентаметрах, ЦС прибавляет всего три окситонных слова, все три в первом дистихе ($_1$*с водой—об утёс,* $_2$*держа*) и ни одного во втором. Оба внутренних икта полустиший, т.е. второй и пятый икт стиха, неизменно падают во втором дистихе на середину трехсложных словесных единиц («амфибрахиев»): $_3$*не сякнет . . . из урны,* $_4$*над вечной . . . печальна*. В первом же дистихе такие «амфибрахии» представлены всего одним примером ($_2$*Дева печально сидит*). Закономерный, принудительный словораздел, разверстывающий безударные слоги между первым и вторым иктом во всех строках обоих дистихов, находит себе последовательное распространительное применение в тексте финального дистиха, отделяющего тем же способом второй икт от третьего и пятый от обоих окрестных иктов, тогда как начальный дистих, вводя окситонные слова, трижды отступает от такого рода симметрических сечений.

Текст ЦС, слагающийся из 24 полноударных слов, насчитывает всего 16 лексически раздельных единиц. Слово $_{1,2,4}$*дева*, сперва служившее подлежащим начального гекзаметра, вслед затем поочередно открывает оба пентаметра, сочетаясь в обеих строках с одним и тем же сказуемым $_{2,4}$*сидит*. Фигуры, построенные на морфологических вариациях одного и того же корня, связывают оба гекзаметра ($_1$*урну с водой . . .*

разбила—₃*вода . . . из урны разбитой*), затем оба пентаметра (₂*дева печально сидит*—₄*дева . . . печальна сидит*) и заодно оба полустишия заключительного пентаметра (₄*над вечной струёй, вечно печальна*). С каждой строкой число лексически новых слов убывает: 6 в первой, 5 во второй, 3 в третьей и 2 в четвертой (₄*вечной струёй*).

Каждая строка содержит по одному «двусказуемому» предложению, деепричастному в первых трех стихах, адъективному в четвертом (ср. Шахматов, §§265 sqq.). Полное отсутствие союзов в ЦС придает еще бо́льшую осязательность параллелизму синтаксического состава строк. Предложения конечного дистиха отделены от начального восклицательным ₃«*Чудо!*»—Каждое предложение разнится от трех остальных порядком своих основных членов—подлежащего (П) и сказуемых (С), главного (C^1) и побочного (C^2),—и их распределением между полустишиями: ₁C^2/ПC^1—₂ПC^1/C^2—₃C^1П/C^2—₄П/C^2C^1.

Каждое последующее предложение отличается от предыдущего одной единственной перестановкой в порядке названных членов предложения, а именно второй стих от первого—конечным положением побочного сказуемого, третий от второго—начальным положением главного сказуемого, а четвертый от третьего конечным положением главного сказуемого. Второй гекзаметр по сравнению с первым характеризуется полной инверсией, т.е. зеркальной симметрией в порядке всех трех членов. Оба пентаметра отличаются от гекзаметров начальным положением подлежащего в стихе и смежностью обоих сказуемых. Во внешних, т.е. в начальной и в последней, строках четверостишия два из трех членов принадлежат второму, а в обеих внутренних строках первому полустишию; внешние строки в противоположность внутренним помещают главное сказуемое после побочного.

Урна в винительном уничтожаемого объекта (₁*Урну . . . разбила*), открывает гекзаметры ЦС, а затем, в отделительном генитиве, замыкает гекзаметры ЦС. Это имя в значении кувшина для воды непривычно ни пушкинским стихам, ни русскому словоупотреблению вообще. Достаточно рассмотреть материал, собранный в *Словаре языка Пушкина* (Виноградов, IV, 727), чтобы бросилась в глаза неразрывная ассоциация этого слова с образом пресеченной жизни. Большей частью оно выступает непосредственно в похоронной обстановке: «Ворами со столбов отвинченные урны, Могилы склизкие, которы также тут Зеваючи жильцов к себе на утро ждут, Такие смутные мне мысли всё наводит, Что злое на меня уныние находит»; «Придешь ли, дева красоты, Слезу пролить над ранней урной»; «Твоя краса, твои страданья Исчезли в урне гробовой»; «И, может быть, об участи моей Она вздохнет над урной гробовою». Но и вне кладбищенского контекста *урна* остается, как например в «Египетских ночах», явственно погребальной эмблемой: «И ложе смерти их зовет. Благословенные жрецами, Теперь из урны роковой Пред неподвижными гостями Выходят жребии чредой.» Помимо «праздных урн» публичного кладбища, тем же эпитетом, сочетающим семантику порожнего и бесцельного, оказываются одарены и пиршественные сосуды в стихах Кривцову (1817), размышляющих над «гроба близким новосельем»: «Смертный миг нам будет светел, И подруги шалунов Соберут их легкий пепел В урны праздные пиров.» В круг символики вековечных утрат входит также «праздный черепок» разбитого кувшина, намеренно переименованного в урну.

Трехфонемный корень с начальным темным U в сопровождении двух смежных сонорных RN малообычен, явственно экспрессивен и выделен парономазией *уронив*, а также тройственной аллитерацией начальных гласных: ₁*Урну—уронив—утёс*. Из четырех сонорных (если оставим в стороне различие между их мягкими и твердыми разновидностями) M вовсе не встречается в четверостишии, L ровно по разу на каждую строку, а R и N, т.е. сонорные корня *урн-* выступают неукоснительно пять раз в каждом стихе, причем в первом дистихе преобладает R (в обеих строках по 3 R и по 2 N), а во втором, как бы вторя анаграмматически порядку сочетания RN, подсказанному траурным словом дистихов, за счет R учащается N (2 R, 3 N в третьей, 1 R, 4 N в четвертой строке).

Драматическое сообщение о несчастном происшествии, втиснутое в первую строку ЦС, отличается от дальнейшего повествования прошедшим временем перфективных глаголов, между тем как три прочих стиха знают только настоящее время и только несовершенный вид. Только в первой строке нет непереходных глаголов, и только эта строка полнится тремя аккузативами в противоположность единственному аккузативу следующей строки и полному отсутствию винительного падежа в финальном дистихе.

Вторая строка—«живая картина» непосредственных последствий состоявшегося злоключения. Категория прошедшего исчезает вместе с видовой категорией завершения. Настоящее время и несовершенный вид до самого конца четверостишия овладевают глаголами. Помимо смены видов и времен, следует отметить существенную разницу в характере лексических значений между глаголами обеих строк. Если в гекзаметре глаголы обозначали перемену, динамику процесса ($_1$*уронив . . . разбила*), то в пентаметре они уступают место глаголам, отображающим статическую неизменность ($_2$*сидит . . . держа*).

Героиней первого дистиха была дева, разбившая лепную урну и в печали застывшая с праздным черепком в руках. В пентаметре цепкая связь образов подчеркнута аллитерацией наречия $_2$*печально* с прилагательным *праздный* и искусной парономазией $_2$печа*льно*—череп*ок*. Это слово, последнее в дистихе, перечит своим темным *О* светлой тональности ударных *I* в клаузуле окрестных стихов и остро контрастирует семантически с чудом, предпосланным обоим предложениям второго дистиха, между тем как аллитерация сливает конец и начало смежных дистихов: $_2$*черепок.—$_3$Чудо!*

Изумленный пушкинской поэтической мифологией чудотворных изваяний, я в свое время сопоставил воспетое поэтом торжество воображенной подвижности над косностью материи с обратным, в свою очередь скульптурным дивом—вечно недвижной материей, преодолевающей призрачность эфемерных движений. Поэту почудилось—*Чудо!* в том, как *урну с водой уронив, . . . дева, над вечной струей, вечно печальна сидит.* «Внутренний дуализм знака снят: недвижность статуи воспринимается как недвижность девы, противоположение знака и предмета исчезает, недвижность налагается на реальное время и осознается как вечность» (Якобсон 1937, 19).

В то время как единственное число безраздельно господствует во всем четверостишии, между дистихами есть заметная разница в распределении грамматических родов. Рядом с

женским родом, занимающим доминирующее положение (по
четыре имени в каждом дистихе), два образчика мужского
рода, фактор и результат разбития урны, ₁*утес* и ₂*праздный
черепок*, включены в драматический словарь первого дистиха;
во втором же дистихе средним родом выделен вступительный
возглас, за которым до конца стихотворения следуют имена
одного лишь женского рода.

Второй дистих превращает в изваяние деву вместе с урной,
ею разбитой. Капризному ритму первого дистиха и в особен-
ности первого стиха приходит на смену неуклонно единообраз-
ная разверстка словоразделов на протяжении двух последних
строк. В противоположность первой строке с ее тремя аккузативами и двумя переходными глаголами, а также второй
строке начального дистиха, удержавшей в своем, синтаксически побочном полустишии деепричастие переходного
глагола и одно существительное в винительном падеже,
второй дистих отменяет переходные глаголы и не знает ни
прямых, ни косвенных дополнений; действия теряют направ-
ленность; *вода* из предложного дополнения (₁*с водой*) становится во втором гекзаметре самостоятельным подлежащим вместо
субъекта *дева*, управлявшего первым гекзаметром, и согласные
обоих подлежащих взаимно перемещаются: ₁*дева*—₃*вода*.
Главное сказуемое, замыкавшее первый гекзаметр, переходный глагол ₁*разбила*, превращается в конце второго гекзаметра
в отглагольное прилагательное *разбитой*, причем и связь, и
контраст обеих метрически сходных строк, скреплены парал-
лелизмом двух предлогов, обрамленных приставками: ₁*уронив, об утес . . . разбила*—₃*изливаясь из урны разбитой* (с
тремя *Z* в конце предлога и префиксов).

Если в первом дистихе глагольные формы гекзаметра про-
тивопоставляли динамическую семантику статическому ха-
рактеру сказуемых пентаметра, снова то же лексическое
соотношение обнаруживается во втором дистихе с тою лишь
разницей, что второй пентаметр, подхватив главное сказуемое
первого (₄*сидит*), упраздняет глагольность побочного сказуемого, а именно сменяет деепричастия первых трех строк на
предикативное прилагательное (₄*печальна*), бездейственное
по самому своему грамматическому значению, а глагольные
формы второго гекзаметра в своей собственной семантике
соответствуют глаголам первого гекзаметра, т.е. сами по себе

они выражают действительно переменный характер процессов (₃*сякнет . . . изливаясь*), но контекст и прежде всего отрицательная частица *-не-* сводит на нет процесс иссякания и обращает мотив неустанного излияния в дурную, мертвенную бесконечность.

Словесное воплощение зловещей магии ваяния, превратившего разбитую, праздную урну в источник неисчерпаемого, праздного потока, строится Пушкиным на троекратном—в каждой из внутренних строк—повторении ударного *A*, наиболее вокального среди всех гласных, самого сильного, длительного и выпуклого особенно на несхожем звуковом фоне:

₂печа́льно . . . пра́здный держа́

₃не ся́кнет вода́, излива́ясь

Слова по оба конца этой цепи связала строка цветистой реплики Дон Гуана Доне Анне в «Каменном госте», написанном в ту же пору: Печа́ли *ва́шей во́льно* излива́ться.

Конечным пентаметром завершается скульптурный миф Пушкина. Казалось бы незначительная, к слову сказать—неслышная замена прозвучавшего в первом пентаметре наречия ₂*печально* предикативным прилагательным женского рода *печальна* досказывает метаморфозу девы живой в деву-статую. ₂*Дева печально сидит*—₄*Дева, над вечной струёй, вечно печальна сидит*. Обособленное, взятое в запятые обстоятельство—*над вечной струёй*—перекликается во-первых с синонимическим инструменталом начального полустишия—₁*Урну с водой уронив*, где и синтаксически, и фактически вода оставалась подчинена урне. Близость подчеркнута парономастической инверсией: ₁*с водой уронив*—₄*струёй* (*OJUR—RUJO*). Во-вторых, внутри второго дистиха весть гекзаметра о неиссякающей воде уже подсказывает слова пентаметра о вечности струи, и тесная связь между темами воды и девы, единственных двух и притом чередующихся подлежащих в четверостишии, позволяет прочесть в первых стопах последней строки прихотливую парономастическую инверсию: ₄*Дева, над вечной* (*D'ÉVA-ADV'É*). Наконец, эпитет струи из прилагательного ₄*вечной* преображается в заключительном полустишии в наречие ₄*вечно* при сказуемом ₄*печальна*, ставшем, как раз наоборот прилагательным из наречия ₂*печально*.

Неутолимая печаль по утраченной урне, навеки охватившая недвижную, окаменелую деву и пришедшая на смену казалось бы, лишь врéменному, мимолетному переживанию той же героини «в бытность человеком», причудливо сплетена с фантасмагорией вечной струи, обреченной без конца и попусту изливаться из разбитого сосуда.

Что осталось в обсуждаемых дистихах от их литературного первоисточника, басни «La laitière et le pot au lait» подсказавшей скульптору Соколову его статую «Молочница», на которую Пушкин ответил своей «анфологической эпиграммой». В басне Лафонтена молочница Перетта несет в город кувшин с молоком и в мечтах о выручке и последующей цепи хозяйственных операций неосторожно подскакивает от восторга: "Le lait tombe; adieu veau, vache, cochon, couvée; La dame de ces biens, quittant d'un oeil marri Sa fortune ainsi répandue, Va s'excuser à son mari En grand danger d'être battue." Трудно опознать oeil marri злополучной Перетты в вечно печальной деве пушкинских строк. В царскосельском фонтане под названьем «Молочница», вторя эротической символике, взлелеянной Ж.-Б. Грёзом в его «Cruche cassée», полуобнаженная бронзовая девушка с осколком в руке обаятельно горюет на утесе пьедестала, а у ее ног из расколотого кувшина бежит струя прозрачной ключевой воды (см. Петров, 88, и альбомные страницы 66, 67). Утес, печально сидящая дева, черепок, неиссякаемая струя воды из разбитого сосуда переняты у скульптора пушкинскими стихами, но все эти аксессуары испытали при пересадке глубокую метаморфозу в своей мотивировке и особенно в сюжетном осмыслении самых основ ваяния и парковой архитектуры.

Это было в том самом месяце, когда автор сжег десятую главу Онегина и закончил «Домик в Коломне», где в одной из не вошедших в печатный текст строф поэт коснулся гекзаметра: «о с ним я не шучу: Он мне невмочь.» Надпись на Царскосельскую статую была сложена Пушкиным 1 октября 1830г. в селе Болдине, далеком и от Царского села, и от Москвы, где невеста ждала поэта. Днем раньше, 30 сентября, он писал ей: "Notre mariage semble toujours fuir devant moi, et cette peste avec ses quarantaines n'est-elle pas la plus mauvaise plaisanterie que le sort ait pu imaginer.» В следующем к ней же письме от 11 октября он сетует на болдинское заключение и сравнивает Болдино с «окруженным утесами островом». Вспомним роковой утес первого стиха ЦС. В начале ноября засевший всё в том же Болдине Пушкин уведомляет свою поверенную, Прасковью Александровну Осипову: "Je suis l'athée du bonheur; je n'y crois pas."

II НЕТ, Я

1   Нет, я не дорожу мятежным наслажденьем,
2   Восторгом чувственным, безумством, исступленьем,
3   Стенаньем, криками вакханки молодой,
4   Когда, виясь в моих объятиях змией,
5   Порывом пылких ласк и язвою лобзаний
6   Она торопит миг последних содроганий!

7   О, как милее ты, смиренница моя!
8   О, как мучительно тобою счастлив я,
9   Когда, склонняяся на долгие моленья,
10   Ты предаешься мне нежна без упоенья,
11   Стыдливо-холодна, восторгу моему
12   Едва ответствуешь, не внемлешь ничему
13   И оживляешься потом всё боле, боле—
14   И делишь наконец мой пламень поневоле!

Всё стихотворение слагается из двух восклицательных фраз, отделенных пробельной строкой и отталкивающихся друг от друга тематической антитезой и глубоким несходством в грамматическом составе. У каждой из двух частей своя героиня—она и ты. $_6$*Она* замыкает начальную фразу; $_{7,10}$*Ты*—грамматический субъект следующей, конечной фразы, начиная с ее первого стиха. *Она* выступает под прозвищем $_3$*вакханки молодой*, оброненным в качестве приименного генитива, подчиненного шестерке творительных форм, управляемых в свою очередь отрицательным сказуемым $_1$*не дорожу*. За «сердечным»—согласно пушкинскому определению—подлежащим *ты* непосредственно следует приложение или, вернее, обращение: $_7$*ты, смиренница моя!* «Вакханка» первой фразы и «смиренница» второй—единственно личные из двадцати имен всего текста. Каждое из этих двух обозначений со своим постпозитивным определением—$_3$*вакханки молодой* и $_7$*смиренница моя*—симметрично занимает вторую половину первого в данной фразе мужского стиха.

Подстрочный перевод всего стихотворения, например, у Henri Troyat (II, 228), предположим, éclaire avec exactitude les rapports physiques de Pouchkine et de sa femme (?), но в то же время убедительно показывает и во французской, и еще нагляднее в английской версии (стр. 448), что отнюдь не в самóй протокольной регистрации двух противоположных эротических переживаний таится захватывающее искусство речей о ней и к тебе. Единичные стертые тропы, два-три слова в трафаретно переносном значении—$_4$*виясь змией,* $_5$*язвою лобзаний,* $_{14}$*мой пламень*—не возмещают недостатка метафорики. Между тем, в русском подлиннике эти семь двустиший развивают необычную художественную силу прежде всего грамматическими средствами, виртуозно использованными.

Действенность мастерства требует строгого отбора пущенных в ход словесных категорий. Так например репертуар получивших доступ в стихи глагольных разрядов ограничен несовершенным видом, настоящим временем и единственным числом. Имена существительные неодушевленные чуждаются пространственных, предметных слов; исключений нет: переносное значение обеспредмечивает слова, как «язва» или «пламень». В обеих фразах выразительность притяжательных местоимений повышается их неуклонной принадлежностью к одному лишь говорящему лицу: $_4$*в моих объятиях,* $_{11}$*восторгу моему,* $_{14}$*мой пламень.* Подлежащими ни в той, ни в другой фразе не могут быть имена, а одни только личные местоимения: $_{1,8}$*я,* $_{7,10}$*ты,* $_6$*она.*

В основе обеих фраз с внеположным восклицанием—отрицательным в приступе к первой фразе, $_1$*Нет,* экспрессивно-утвердительным в приступе ко второй, $_{7,8}$*О* (ср. Виноградов 1947, 752)—лежат контуры явственного параллелизма:

$_1$*Нет, я не дорожу . . . наслаждением,*

$_4$*Когда, виясь в моих объятиях*

$_6$*Она торопит миг последних содроганий!*

$_{7,8}$*О, как . . .* $_8$*тобою счастлив я,*

$_9$*Когда, склоняяся на долгие моленья,*

$_{14}$*И делишь наконец мой пламень по неволе!*

ными, в общей сложности четырьмя. В противоположность
начальной фразе с ее девятью именами существительными
в приглагольном творительном и четырьмя в приименном
родительном падеже, имена существительные конечной фразы
не знают ни творительного падежа, ни беспредложного генитива. Обратно дательный падеж существительных имен и
местоимений, чуждый начальной фразе, трижды засвидетель-
ствован в конечной фразе при трех глаголах, требующих этого
падежа: $_{10}$*Ты предаешься мне,* $_{11}$*восторгу моему* $_{12}$*Едва
ответствуешь, не внемлешь ничему.* Все четыре примера
приименного генитива выделены отличием в грамматическом
числе и роде от смежного управляющего имени, причем тот
же принцип расподобления родов и особенно чисел распрост-
раняется и на прочие имена существительные той же строки:
$_3$*Стенаньем* (ед., ср.), *криками* (мн., м.) *вакханки* (ед., ж.);
$_5$*Порывом* (ед., м.) *пылких ласк* (мн., ж.) *и язвою* (ед., ж.) *лобзаний* (мн., ср.); $_6$*миг* (ед., м.) *последних содроганий* (мн., ср.).
В этой фразе соотношение между грамматическими числами
и «объемными» (квантифицирующими) падежами, т.е. генитивом и локативом (ср. Якобсон 1971, 148-153 и 158), допус-
кает еще более обобщенную формулировку. Здесь имя в
объемном падеже неизменно отличается числом от смежных
имен. Помимо приведенных генитивных примеров, отметим
соседство локатива с инструменталом: $_4$*в моих объятиях*
(мн., ср.) *змией* (ед., ж.). Легкий количественный шарж в
изображении вакханки последовательно прибегает к контрасту
единства и множественности.

Любопытно, что именно вокруг начального набора творительных форм приобретает заметно сгущенный характер
звуковая фактура. Таково повторение звонкого шипящего в
трех смежных словах первого стиха—$_1$*дорожу мятежным
наслажденьем,* в то время как во всем остальном тексте
фонема Ž попадается всего два раза ($_{10}$*нежна,* $_{13}$*оживляешься*). Первое двустишие отличается от всех дальнейших
скоплением пятнадцати носовых. Ср., в частности, звуковую
спайку первого инструментала с прилегающим эпитетом:
мятежным (T'ÉŽN,M) *наслажденьем* (ŽD'ÉN',M). Серий-
ность инструментальных дополнений подчеркнута навязчиво
повторной группировкой одинаковых согласных: $_2$*Восторгом*

(*V.ST*) *чувственным* (*STV*), *безумством* (*STV*), *исступленьем* (*ST*), ₃*Стенаньем* (*ST'*). Именно вторичному появлению узлового слова *восторг* в конечной фразе сопутствует рецидив того же звукового окружения: ₁₁*стыдливо* (*ST*) . . . *восторгу* (*V.ST*), ₁₁*ответствуешь* (*STV*). На краю начальной фразы развязка узлового мотива вторит его звукоряду: ₂*Восторгом—* ₆*содроганий* (*ST.RG.M—S.DR.G.N'*). Словосочетание ₃*криками вакханки* приковывает внимание своими четырьмя *K*, а деепричастная конструкция ₄*виясь в моих объятиях змией* шестикратным появлением фонемы *J* при отсутствии подобных повторов в других стихах, Губной в сочетании со звонким свистящим и прочие броские созвучия сплели этот стих со следующим: ₄*виясь* [*V'IJÁS*] . . . *объятиях* [*ABJÁT'IJAX*] *змией* [*ZM'IJÓJ*]—₅*пылких* [*PYLK'IX*] *ласк* [*LÁSK*] *и язвою* [*IJÁZVAJU*] *лобзаний* [*LABZÁ*].

Не может быть и речи о случайном стечении пятнадцати имен существительных, в том числе девяти приглагольных творительных форм и четырех приименных генитивов, на протяжении шестистрочной фразы, насчитывающей всего три глагольных формы, и явственно преднамерен контраст между этими шестью строками и последующим восьмистишием с его десятком основных и побочных сказуемых и с их одиннадцатью наречными атрибутами. Конечная фраза нарочито противопоставляет полное отсутствие имен в инструментале и беспредложном генитиве их разительному изобилию в первой, притом менее пространной фразе. С другой стороны, первая фраза не менее четко отличается от второй отсутствием имен в дативе и существительных местоимений в каких бы то ни было косвенных падежах.

Особенно показательно расхождение обеих фраз в отборе и употреблении падежей. Девяти случаям именного, неизменно приглагольного творительного падежа в начальной фразе конечная фраза отвечает одной единственной местоименной творительной формой при предикативном прилагательном, ₈*тобою счастлив я*. Ср. пример из *Соборян* Лескова, «Я женою моею счастлив», цитируемый и комментируемый в *Синтаксисе* Шахматова (§451): «Значением творит. падежа здесь является выражение завершенности, удовлетворённости пассивного признака, соответствующего прилагательному.» В начальной фразе нет ни дательного, выступающего в трех смежных стихах конечной фразы, ни предложных конструкций с винительным ($_9$*склоняяся на долгие моленья*) и родительным ($_{10}$*нежна без упоенья*), связывающих рифмой предпоследнее двустишие. Отличие конструкций с инструменталом, генитивом и дативом в конечной фразе усугублено зависимостью этих падежных форм от морфологических категорий, несвойственных начальной фразе, т.е. от предикативных прилагательных и второго лица глаголов.

Глубокое несходство в грамматическом профиле обеих фраз находит себе красноречивое подтверждение в морфологически разнородном составе рифм: трем инструменталам и трем генитивам шести имен существительных и прилагательных в рифмах начального шестистишия рифмовка второй фразы противопоставляет четыре местоименных формы в номинативе и дативе, две предложных конструкции с именами существительными и, наконец, наречия в обеих заключительных строках. Таким образом первую фразу, в прямую противоположность второй, характеризует репертуар рифм из склоняемых слов *лексического* характера, непосредственно управляемых или согласуемых.

Сравнительная таблица нескольких особенностей, противополагающих обе фразы (I и II), наглядно показывает широту их художественного контраста:

	I	II
Творительный имен существительных и прилагательных:	11	—
Косвенные падежи существительных местоимений:	—	3
Родительный приименный:	7	—
Местный:	1	—
Дательный:	—	4
Беспредложные атрибутивные прилагательные:	5	—
Предикативные прилагательные:	—	4
Наречия:	—	11
Глаголы первого лица:	1	—
второго лица:	—	5
третьего лица:	1	—

Из этой таблицы явствует, что в стихотворении по меньшей мере пятьюдесятью тремя примерами представлены грамматические разряды слов, находящие себе место всего в одной из двух фраз и отсутствующие в другой.

Дополнения и их согласуемые атрибуты в падежах, лишенных признака направленности, т.е. в инструментале, генитиве и локативе (см. Якобсон 1971, 158), представлены двадцатью примерами в начальной и всего двумя в конечной фразе ($_8$*тобою,* $_{10}$*без упоенья*), тогда как в «направленных» падежах, т.е. в аккузативе и дативе, они насчитывают восемь примеров в конечной фразе и только один в начальной, а именно в ее последнем стихе ($_6$*миг*). Приглагольные члены предложения во всех трех «периферийных» падежах строго размежеваны: во второй фразе единственно датив с его признаком направленности (три примера), а в первой исключительно падежи, лишенные этого признака, т.е. девять инструменталов и один локатив ($_4$*в моих объятиях*).

Конечная фраза чуждается слов-названий, как свидетельствует перевес шести существительных местоимений над пятью именами, тогда как начальная фраза при наличии пятнадцати имен уделяет место всего двум существительным местоимениям. Вышеотмеченному обилию основных и побочных сказуемых и их наречных атрибутов в конечной фразе (21 пример) начальная фраза противопоставляет только три примера ($_1$*дорожу*, $_6$*торопит*; $_4$*виясь*). Иными словами, глубоко расхождение между установкой конечной фразы на череду и смену предицируемых явлений и упорной склонностью начальной фразы к субстантивации и резкому ракурсу всех составных мотивов, превращаемых в ассортимент одновременных подробностей.

К словам Стерна о том, что «живейшее из наших наслаждений кончится содроганием почти болезненным», Пушкин приписал: «Несносный наблюдатель! Знал бы про себя; многие того не заметили б.» Покойного пушкиноведа Альфреда Людвиговича Бема стихи «Нет, я» восхищали необычной отвагой. Их смелость, повторяю, таится в превращении всей системы грамматических категорий в язык страстей, в символику любовных состязаний. Поэтика контрастов сопоставляет две фразы и два женских образа, *ее* под знаком удаления и *тебя,* желанную соучастницу диалога и действия. На первый, поверхностный взгляд, поражает парадоксальность нарочито статического подхода к стихийному «порыву ласк» исступленной вакханки, обезглаголенная фраза, обросшая вереницей отягчающих рассказ именных и адъективных привесков, противоположенная сполна предикативному,—я сказал бы—кинематографическому образу стыдливо-холодной смиренницы. Однако в действительности именно замедленный темп позволяет развернуть и гармонически расчленить временную последовательность подневольного воспламенения, искусно сочетая отпор с приятием натиска. Недаром единственный эпитет второй фразы—$_9$*долгие моленья*—подсказывает *andante*. Все три предложения с дативными, по Шахматову, «приближающе косвенными дополнениями» (§415), вносящими идею направленности, чуждую творительным формам первой фразы, в то же время задерживают движение либо ограничительными, либо отрицательными оговорками: $_{10}$*без упоенья*, $_{11}$*Едва ответствуешь, не внемлешь ничему*. Скопление шести наречий при двух глаголах заключительного двустишия—$_{13}$*потом всё боле, боле*, $_{14}$*наконец . . . по неволе*—служит последним приёмом *ritardando* и внятно истолковывает «несносный» оксюморон—$_8$*О, как мучительно тобою счастлив я, Когда . . .* Обратно, стремглав убыстренный темп событий начальной фразы с ее заключительным уторопленным мигом последних содроганий противится временно́й сегментации и обрывисто пресекает любовное действо, сведенное к синтаксической низке периферийных, инструментальных значений. Единственно в сцене оргазма, т.е. в конечном стихе каждой из двух фраз, всплывает переходный глагол и при нем аккузативное дополнение, но прямолинейная развязка первой фразы ведет от глагола попросту к аккузативу—$_6$*торопит → миг*, тогда как во второй фразе с расширенным тематическим охватом ее объекта и предиката ход действия, напротив, поступает от первого к последнему: $_{14}$*делишь наконец ← мой пламень*.

Сходство в развитии двух контрастирующих тем скреплено звуковыми повторами: *иссту*ПЛЕН*ьеМ* вакханки предсказан *Миг Пос*ЛЕ*дН*их *содроганий*, а узловым словам второй фразы —*Мо*ЛЕН*ья . . . Не* ВНЕМ*Лешь*—в эпилоге отвечает *П*Ла*МеНь По НеВоЛе*!

При всем разнообразии в распорядке рифм целостное сочетание четырнадцати ямбических стихов принадлежит в поэзии Пушкина к его излюбленным композиционным единицам. Сюда принадлежит и сонет, и онегинская строфа, и стихотворения в четырнадцать строк с семью различно расположенными рифмами, как, например, уже в 1821 г. «Муза» и «Умолкну скоро я». Часть этих стихотворений синтаксически подражает строфике сонета. Таковы стихи «Из письма к Вяземскому» 1825 г., разделенные на два четверостишия с заключительным шестистишием, и в том же году стихотворение «Я был свидетелем златой твоей весны» из семи рифмованных двустиший с синтаксической схемой: 4 + 4 + 3 + 3. В более поздних стихотворениях шестистишие предшествует восьмистишию, по примеру опрокинутых сонетов, облюбованных маринизмом. К настоящему разбору, надеюсь, мне вскоре удастся присоединить и стихи об одалиске—«Вчера у В., оставя пир»—захватывающий отрывок из Альбома Онегина, сложенный по схеме (AAb + bCC) + (dEEd + FgFg). Композиционная основа Элегии 8 сентября 1830 г., «Безумных лет угасшее веселье»,—aaBBcc + (DDee + FFgg) совпадает с разверсткой рифмованных двустиший стихотворения о вакханке и смиреннице, точно так же отмечающего пробельной строкой границу между третьим и четвертым двустишием, но в то время как в Элегии грамматически разграничены только обе половинки конечного восьмистишия, в стихах «Нет, я» четко размежеваны еще и оба начальных трехстишия.

Первые четыре строки конечной фразы построены, во-первых, на альтернации собственно личных местоимений в качестве подлежащих, во-вторых на поочередном противопоставлении обоих местоимений в ролях подлежащего и косвенного дополнения: $_7$*ты,* $_8$*тобою* . . . *я* в главном и $_{10}$*Ты* . . . *мне* в придаточном предложении. В заключительном четверостишии соположных предложений личные местоимения эллиптически исчезают. В контрасте двух половин фразы—одной с личными местоимениями и другой без таковых—начальная фраза сходствует с конечной: на подлежащем *я* построено предложение первых трех строк, тогда как дальнейшие три строки, образующие второе, в данном случае придаточное предложение, лишены существительных местоимений первого и второго лица, т.е. собственно личных, непосредственно относящихся к адресанту и адресату речи. Подлежащим здесь служит анафорическое местоимение $_6$*Она.* В последних половинках шестистишия и восьмистишия, готовящих финальный аккорд обеих фраз, исчезают прямые ссылки на собеседников, как бы утверждая тем самым независимо эпический характер повествования, и только притяжательное местоимение продолжает напоминать об участии говорящего лица в ходе действия: ₄*в моих объятиях*, ₁₄*мой пламень*.

Между обеими половинками шестистишия наблюдается существенная разница в контекстуальных значениях падежных форм. В тексте стихотворения все восемь примеров творительного падежа при личных глагольных формах, обозначают, согласно шахматовскому обзору (§445), «проявления физических органов», с тою разницей, что в последнем предложении начальной фразы с его двумя факультативными творительными конструкциями, ₅*порывом пылких ласк и язвою лобзаний*, при переходном глаголе ₆*торопит*, подлежащее *она* обозначает производителя названных действий, между тем как в первом предложении, где шесть соположных форм того же падежа следуют за принудительно требующим творительного дополнения глаголом ₁*дорожу*, подлежащее отнюдь не называет «деятеля». Так как творительный сравнения ₄*виясь . . . змией* относится к тому же подлежащему ₆*она*, как и последующие творительные «отвлеченного орудия» (ср. Станишева, 80 сл.), то следует отметить, что наличие и отсутствие внутренней связи творительного дополнения с подлежащим служит различительной чертой между обоими трехстрочными предложениями, из которых слагается начальная фраза. Синтаксическое значение приименного генитива в свою очередь расподобляет оба предложения. Здесь творительный орудия постоянно выступает в сопровождении приименного генитива. Но в первом предложении все шесть творительных, начиная ₁*наслажденьем* и кончая ₃*криками*, соотнесены с родительным субъекта ₃*вакханки*, тогда как во втором предложении и творительным формам, и аккузативу сопутствует «родительный отношения» в его различных разновидностях (ср. Шахматов, §420): ₅*порывом пылких ласк и язвою лобзаний*; ₆*миг последних содроганий*.

Несмотря на значимые различия в архитектонике обеих фраз и их сегментов, неменьшая роль в художественной структуре всего стихотворения принадлежит инвариантам. У каждой фразы два героя—первое лицо и соучастница (*она* в начальной фразе, *ты* в конечной). Падежи приглагольных (точнее—присказуемостных) дополнений последовательно распределены между обоими героями. Творительный падеж—как именной, так и местоименный ($_8$*тобою*)—при всем разнообразии своих частных, контекстуальных значений—неизменно отнесен к соучастнице, а дательный к говорящему лицу: $_{10}$*мне*, $_{11}$*восторгу моему*, $_{12}$*не внемлешь ничему* (исходящему от меня). Винительный падеж—как в беспредложном употреблении, так и в предложной конструкции—характеризует моменты дуэта, вовлекающие обоих участников: $_7$*Она торопит миг последних содроганий*; $_{14}$*И делишь наконец мой пламень*; $_9$*склоняяся на долгие моленья*, $_{10}$*Ты предаешься мне.*

Лексика строк о смиреннице странным образом перекликается с давними стихами Пушкина про Цыган, «смиренной вольности детей» и про их урок—«Ты для себя лишь хочешь воли»—в укор тому, кто требует, чтобы смиренница делила его «пламень поневоле». Слова *мучительно тобою счастлив я* словно пытаются оксюмороном снять противоречие, запечатленное в эпилоге Цыган «Но счастья нет . . . Живут мучительные сны».

Как ни уточнять датировку стихов «Нет, я не дорожу мятежным наслажденьем, Восторгом чувственным . . .», и как ни отнестись к хронологической помете в дошедших копиях, «19 января 1830 г.», всё-же трудно предполагать слишком длительный интервал между этими стихами и сонетом 7 июля 1830 г.—«Поэт, не дорожи любовию народной, Восторженных похвал пройдет минутный шум». Та же тема «лучшей», царственной свободы, еще раз вложенная в александрийские стихи, всплывет в 1836 г. в мнимом подражании итальянцу Пиндемонти—«Не дорого ценю я громкие права», в третий раз с однородным зачином. «Ты царь», заговорное противопоставление своего, высшего суда и восторга минутному шуму и назойливым восторгам вакханки и толпы нашло себе здесь продолжение в заклятии против угод не то царскому, не то народному самовластию и в умысле служить «себе лишь самому . . .По прихоти своей . . .Трепеща радостно в восторгах умиленья, Вот счастье!»** Между тем в стихах 1823 года «Кто, волны, вас остановил» поэту изгнаннику был дорог «поток *мятежный*», лейтмотив начальной строфы, а заключительная строфа звала «грозу—символ свободы» промчаться «поверх *невольных* вод.»

P.S. Настоящая статья была уже в печати, когда автор познакомился с увлекательным обзором С. Г. Бочарова «'Свобода' и 'счастье' в поэзии Пушкина», сборник *Проблемы поэтики и истории литературы*—К 75-летию со дня рождения и 50-летию научно-педагогической деятельности Михаила Михайловича Бахтина (Мордовский гос. университет имени Н.П. Огарева, Саранск, 1973). Не могла не порадовать близость в выборке и сопоставительной трактовке пушкинских афоризмов.

ИСТОЧНИКИ ССЫЛОК

В. В. Виноградов, *Русский язык* (Учпедгиз, Ленинград, 1947).

В. В. Виноградов и др. (ред.), *Словарь языка Пушкина,* I-IV (Академия Наук СССР, Москва, 1956-1961).

А. Н. Петров, *Пушкин. Дворцы и парки* (Ленинград, 1969).

Д. С. Станишева, «Творительный инструментальный», *Творительный падеж в славянских языках* (АН СССР, Москва, 1958).

H. Troyat, *Pouchkine,* II (Albin Michel, Paris, 1946). Англ. перевод, *Pushkin* (Doubleday, New York, 1970).

А. А. Шахматов, *Синтаксис русского языка* (Учпедгиз, Ленинград, 1941).

Р. Якобсон, "Socha v symbolice Puškinově", *Slovo a slovesnost, III* (Praha, 1937).—Франц. перевод в Questions de poétique того же автора (Editions du Seuil, Paris, 1973). Английский перевод, *Puškin and His Sculptural Myth* (Mouton, The Hague-Paris, 1975).

———, "Linguistics and Poetics," *Style in Language* (M.I.T. Press, 1960).

———, *Selected Writings* II (Mouton, The Hague-Paris, 1971).

———, «Об односложных словах в русском стихе», *Slavic Poetics: Essays in honor of Kiril Taranovsky* (Mouton, The Hague-Paris, 1973).

R. Jakobson & M. Halle, "Phonology and Phonetics," *Fundamentals of Language* (Mouton, The Hague-Paris, 1971).

Б. И. Ярхо и др., *Метрический справочник к стихотворениям Пушкина* (Academia, Москва-Ленинград, 1934).

MNEMOSYNE AND LETHE: PUŠKIN'S "VOSPOMINANIE"

Vadim Liapunov
New York University

Puškin's contribution to *Severnye Cvety* for 1829 comprised an excerpt from "a historical novel" and sixteen poems, among them the following:[1]

ВОСПОМИНАНИЕ

Когда для смертного умолкнет шумный день
   И на немые стогны града
Полупрозрачная наляжет ночи тень
   И сон, дневных трудов награда,
В то время для меня влачатся в тишине
   Часы томительного бденья:
В бездействии ночном живей горят во мне
   Змеи сердечной угрызенья;
Мечты кипят; в уме, подавленном тоской,
   Теснится тяжких дум избыток;
Воспоминание безмолвно предо мной
   Свой длинный развивает свиток:
И с отвращением читая жизнь мою,
   Я трепещу и проклинаю,
И горько жалуюсь, и горько слёзы лью,
   Но строк печальных не смываю.

This text appeared again, at the end of June 1829, in the second volume of Puškin's collected poems.[2]

While the poem is generally recognized as one of Puškin's most memorable poetic feats, the question of what is at issue in the poem remains unsettled.[3] There are two possible reasons for this: (1) interference with the integrity of the published poem from the černovoj avtograf and (2) insufficient clarification of the basic linguistic structure of the poem.

1. There is no belovoj avtograf of the published text of the poem. There is only an untitled černovoj avtograf in which one can distinguish two parts.[4] The first part corresponds to the published poem and records the various stages of the process of composition and recomposition that resulted in the final version published in Severnye Cvety.[5]

Following the first part of the černovoj avtograf there is a second part (with "19 May" at the end) which represents, in Tomaševskij's words, "očen' zaputannyj i nedorabotannyj černovik"[6] from which, after strenuous efforts, a coherent text of twenty lines has been reconstructed.[7] This twenty-line text, the result of efforts aimed to produce the fullest possible "final" version from the "očen' zaputannyj i nedorabotannyj černovik," is an unfinished text. It is unfinished not only in the sense that lacunae and uncertainties remain within the body of the reconstructed text, but also in the sense that, in the absence of an actual final version, we have no way of knowing where the process of composition and recomposition might have ultimately led.

Yet it is precisely this hypothetical and unfinished text that has been repeatedly used as a decisively relevant point of reference for understanding the sense of the pubished poem even though the reconstructed text presents peculiar semantic obscurities of its own. The result is that one tends to deprive the ending of the published poem of its finality. The published poem begins to assume the character of a proem to a larger composition, and one falls into the habit of calling the hypothetical twenty-line text a "continuation" of the completed poem, i.e., one judges the completed text from the perspective of an uncompleted text. A more reasonable procedure, it seems to me, would be to begin with the published poem and determine it as a whole with its own beginning, middle, and end. Conjectures about possible connections of the reconstructed, twenty-line text with the text of the completed poem are outside the scope of my paper. What I hope to make clear, however, is this: whatever the poem combining the published and the reconstructed texts might have been, it would have been an entirely different poem from the one published. It is quite likely, after all, that what Puškin excluded from the poem he published, he excluded in order to produce the poem he meant to produce and did.

2. The linguistic structure of the poem presents a problem which was formulated by Ščerba in 1923: Затруднительным представляется понимание и чтение стиха 16. Спорным является, *не хочет* или *не может* автор смыть печальные строки. Я решаю его в первом смысле и в соответствии с этим делю стих на две части—психологического подлежащего и психологического сказуемого, считая, что сознание при этом как бы останавливается сначала на созерцании «печальных строк» в их целом, а затем на несколько неожиданном нежелании их всё же вычеркнуть из истории своего я, из истории своей личности. Один из моих бывших слушателей, С. М. Бонди, человек, обладающий очень тонким чутьём языка, понимал дело иначе, ссылаясь на то, что форма настоящего времени в русском языке может иметь модальное значение: *я не говорю по-французски* значит: «я не могу, не умею говорить.» Однако это модальное значение, по-моему, является лишь оттенком общего значения: «я вообще не говорю (не только в настоящее время).» Между тем приписать словам *не смываю* в данном случае общее значение решительно невозможно. Я полагаю, что для выражения невозможности смыть печальные строки надо было бы употребить оборот с *не смывается* или что-либо в этом роде.[8] Levkovič agrees with Ščerba but does not go beyond the simple assertion that "ne smyvaju" is to be understood as "ne xoču smyt'."[9] If we consider, however, that reading the last line of the poem as "ne xoču smyt'" rather than "ne mogu smyt'" has decisive consequences for our understanding of the entire text, the linguistic "basis" of the poem's "ideological superstructure" should be worked out as definitely as possible.

The text of the poem on the syntactic level represents a single correlative construction initiated by a two-predicate *kodga*-construction and followed by a five-predicate *v to vremja* (= *togda*)-construction, which is extended by way of an adverbial-participle clause ("i . . . čitaja žizn' moju") by an additional group of five predicates:

Kogda
  umolknet den'
  i naljažet noči ten' i son,
v to vremja
  vlačatsja časy bden'ja
  gorjat ugryzen'ja
  mečty kipjat
  tesnitsja dum izbytok
  vospominanie razvivaet svitok,
i čitaja žizn' moju,
  ja trepešču
    i proklinaju
    i žalujus'
    i slëzy l'ju
  no strok ne smyvaju.

The two predicates of the *kogda*-clause are perfective nonpreterit verbs. All other predicate verbs in the poem are imperfective nonpreterit. A similar construction with a combination of perfective and imperfective predicates was examined in 1891 by L. Razmusen.[10] Razmusen pointed out that the Russian perfective nonpreterit ("nastojaščee vremja soveršennogo vida") often assumes the meaning of an action which precedes every manifestation of another repeatedly occurring action, namely: in dependent clauses after temporal conjunctions, in conditional clauses, and in indefinite-concessive clauses. When the perfective nonpreterit is used in this way, there is always some indication that the form does not have the meaning of *future*; this indication may consist in the use of an imperfective nonpreterit verb alongside the perfective nonpreterit form: "Kogda xlor *uletučitsja*, ja *nalivaju* rastvor v banku." The imperfective verb in this case designates the repetition of an action conceived as perfective in aspect ("povtorenie dejstvija, predstavljaemogo v *soveršennom* vide"). "Nalivaju" (in the sense of perfective nonpreterit about something usual) instead of "nal'ju" is necessary in order to show that the perfective nonpreterit does not relate to the future. Cf. "Kogda xlor *uletučilsja*, ja *nalival* rastvor v banku" ("ja nalival" in the sense of "ja byvalo nal'ju"). For contrast, cf.: Kogda xlor *uletučilsja*, ja *nalivaju* rastvor v banku," "Kogda xlor *uletučilsja*, ja *nal'ju* rastvor v banku," "Kogda xlor *uletučilsja*, ja *nalil* rastvor v banku." If in the latter examples the volatilization is represented as entirely prior to the action of pouring (whether the pouring occurs once or several times), in "kogda xlor uletučitsja, ja nalivaju rastvor v banku," we are dealing with the recurrence of the combination of the two actions.

If we relate Razmusen's observations to the syntax of Puškin's poem, we could sum up its syntactic contexture as follows: "*Whenever* the day falls silent and night descends, *this* is what befalls me during the time when the rest of the world is in semidarkness, silent and asleep (i.e., when the world is in the state which results from the day's falling silent and the night's descent), and *this* is what I do then (i.e., within the time when that state is in force)." The construction initiated with *kogda* states the periodic events ("umolknet den' i naljažet noči ten'—i son") which result in the specific setting or occasion of the "action" unfolded in the correlative construction initiated with *v to vremja*. The construction which unfolds the "action" is distributed continuously over three quatrains: the "action" begins with exclusion—with the exclusion of the outside environment as well as with the exclusion of the "ja" (cf. *dlja smertnogo/dlja menja*) from participation in the "life" of the City.[11] The City is dominated by the imposed "*poluprozračnaja*[12] ten' noči" and "son, dnevnyx trudov *nagrada*" (cf. the implicit analogy of *son = nagrada* and *bden'e = [nakazanie]*). The exlusion of and from the City gives rise to interiorization: *dlja menja* ("dlja menja vlačatsja v tišine . . .") is transformed into *vo mne* ("v bezdejstvii nočnom . . . gorjat vo mne . . . ," the first pronoun in rhyming position).[13] The activation of interior life set off by and from the surrounding unconsciousness and inertness is continued and developed by *predo mnoj, žizn' moju*, and finally—*ja* as the agent-subject. Thus, in juxtaposition with the first quatrain, the second quatrain (lines 5–8) might be said to establish the *interior setting*, the foundation of the happening enacted in the next quatrain (lines 9–12): "mečty kipjat," "v ume tesnitsja dum izbytok," *culminating* in "vospominanie . . . razvivaet svitok."[14] The culmination consists in the compelled confrontation of the "ja" with its own self in its entirety,[15] and elicits a *responding* movement enacted in the fourth and closing quatrain ("ja trepešču i proklinaju, i gor'ko žalujus', i gor'ko slëzy l'ju"), *culminating* in—"no strok pečal'nyx ne smyvaju."

The single complex construction which constitutes the poem syntactically operates with twelve verbs performing the function

of predicates and two additional verbs in the function of participles
("podavlennyj," "čitaja"):

den'	umolknet	dlja smertnogo
noči ten' i son	naljažet	na stogny grada
časy bden'ja	vlačatsja	dlja menja
ugryzen'ja	gorjat	vo mne
mečty	kipjat	
izbytok dum	tesnitsja	v ume, *podavlennom* toskoj
vospominanie	razvivaet	svitok: i *čitaja* žizn' moju
ja	trepešču	
	proklinaju	
	žalujus'	
	l'ju slëzy	(= *pláču*)
	ne smyvaju	strok

Of the twelve predicate verbs only two function as *transitive* verbs
as opposed to ten predicate verbs used intransitively: "vospominanie
razvivaet svitok" and "no (ja) ne smyvaju pečal'nyx strok" (where
the genitive case is a transform of the accusative "pečal'nye stroki").
That is, the transitive constructions occur only at the points of
culmination: the culmination of the movement marked by the four
predicates, *vlačatsja—gorjat—kipjat—tesnitsja*, and the culmination of the answering countermovement marked by the four predicates, *trepešču—proklinaju—žalujus'—slëzy l'ju*. In all the other
instances where the verb could function transitively the explicit
transitive formulation is avoided: by transformation into participles
("v ume, podavlennom toskoj," "čitaja žizn' moju"), by leaving the
direct object unformulated ("ja trepešču i proklinaju, i . . ."),[16] or
by formulating an "artificial" direct object ("l'ju slëzy," i.e., an
equivalent of "pláču" with an "accusative of content"). This results
in the confrontation of two self-active agents performing purposive
or "target-directed" actions, or actions *sensu stricto*, as opposed to
"activities." The action of *vospominanie* renders manifest what lay
coiled up and hidden from the consciousness of the "ja," and afflicts
the "ja" with a poignant feeling of obscure guilt.[17] The answering
action of the "ja" is aimed directly at what was rendered manifest
by *vospominanie*: "vospominanie bezmolvno predo mnoj/svoj
dlinnyj razvivaet svitok"—"no strok pečal'nyx ne smyvaju."
It should be noted in particular that the closing sentence of the

syntactic group initiated with the *čitaja žizn' moju* clause is linked to the preceding sentences by the conjunction *no*. Except for this instance, only one type of conjunction is used in the poem—the conjunction *i*—and only in the first and last quatrains. In the first quatrain it occurs twice,[18] while in the last it cumulates to four, followed directly by the conjunction *no*: "*i . . . čitaja žizn' moju, ja trepešču i proklinaju, i žalujus', i slëzy l'ju, no strok pečal'nyx . . . .*" In terms of the addresser/addressee relationship the conjunction *no* could be described here as involving two presuppositions: (1) the addresser anticipates that the addressee expects him to wash away the lines, and (2) there is no prior understanding between the addresser and the addressee that the preceding predicates and the predicate *ne smyvaju* exclude one another. Thus the conjunction of the last sentence signals new information which is *both* unexpected for the addressee and contrary to the likelihood set up by what went before, i.e., contrary to the expectation that the addresser was going to obliterate the lines.

The verb *smyvat'* in the last line is a secondary imperfective derived from the specifically *resultative* perfective verb *smyt'*.[19] This is to say that it is specific for *smyt'/smyvat'* to be used, as a rule, in the perfective aspect with an indication of the result accomplished, while the use of its derived imperfective form designates, as a rule, the reiteration of producing a result rather than "being in the act of producing a result." In the context of the poem it is clear that the verb is to be taken in the sense which it carries in the code of the moral domain: "to make clean or free from guilt, dishonor, shame, etc., by taking appropriate action"; "to expiate"; "to justify oneself." Two established contexts for the use of the verb in this sense should be taken into account: (1) "smyt' s sebja pozor," "smyt' svoë besčestie poedinkom," "Vy ne smoete vsej vašej čërnoj krov'ju poèta pravednuju krov'" (Lermontov, "Smert' poèta"); cf. French "laver un affront/une injure dans le sang"; (2) "pokajanie," "tainstvo pokajanija"; cf. French "laver ses taches/ses péchés par des pleurs/dans les pleurs" (make them disappear by way of repentance, penance), for example: "Le bain sacré de la pénitence où il venait laver les souillures de son âme . . ." (Massillon, *Oraison fun. Villars*). The latter context, that of the Sacrament of Penitence, seems to me to be particularly relevant, albeit negatively. The Sacrament of Penitence, with its systematized structure (cf. the complex components of Penitence—contrition, confession, satisfaction) and its administration by the Church, provides a well-defined background which (1) enables us to identify the distinctive configuration of "penitence" in the poem and (2) enables us to see that this "penitence" proceeds in the absent presence of the Church. This point might become clearer, if the reader considers the 1836 poem of the obscure poet Mencov reproduced in Appendix IV.[20] Mencov's poem shows how the theme of anguished conscience could have been treated in distinctly ecclesiastic terms, and in this respect the poem recalls the response of Filaret, Metropolitan of Moscow, to Puškin's poem "Dar naprasnyj, dar slučajnyj . . ." (written a week after "Vospominanie"): "Ne naprasno, ne slučajno/Žizn' ot Boga mne dana,/Ne bez voli Boga tajnoj/I na kazn' osuždena. . . ." The possibility which one could formulate in Mencov's words as "smyt' grexi svoi pred Gospodom slezoju pokajan'ja"—this possibility exists, at least in the City of that time, but it is excluded by what the "ja" does in the end.

What the "ja" *does* in answer to memory's act of accusation is stated by "ne smyvaju pečal'nyx strok."[21] That is, the subjectum performs an *act of negation*, the content of which is defined by the refusal to perform the act negated, i.e., "ja smyvaju pečal'nye stroki." The act designated by *smyt' pečal'nye stroki* aims "to make something disappear," and thus the act designated by *ne smyt' pečal'nyx strok* could be read as negating the negation of *pečal'nye stroki* (the consequences of the *subjectum*'s life, cf. "i . . . čitaja žizn' moju . . ."). Instead of "making disappear," the *subjectum* chooses "to make endure" the "grievous lines" (cf. the variant considered prior to the choice of *pečal'nyx*—"No strok *zavetnyx* ne smyvaju").[22] In either case the issue at stake concerns the consequences for the self of what the self does, and it is by considering the implicit consequences of the act chosen and the act refused that we gain access to the meaning of "no strok pečal'nyx ne smyvaju."

For to accept the possibility of revocation of what I have done would, after all, have consequences for what I do and will do: my present and future action will be divested of its ultimate decisiveness and thus of its peculiar dignity. To refuse this possibility is to choose the burden of guilt. This choice, however, should be understood in full: it is not only an act of negation but also an act of position, just as the act of choosing relief from guilt is an act of position as well as of negation. The *subjectum* of the poem chooses to bear the burden of guilt, but he chooses to bear it not for the sake of guilt, but for the sake of an easily forgotten dimension of guilt: the recognition of one's guilt is the recognition of one's "authorship," of one's status as originator or creator. Memory reveals to the *subiectum* of the poem the consequences of his life, and in doing so, it compels him into a situation in which he *must* exercise his *freedom*: recognize his own guilt as his own and condemn himself, and in doing so— retain, "make endure," his status as originator or creator. In the final analysis, the situation memorialized in the poem is not a situation which issues in some sort of reconciliation but a situation of relentlessly recurrent confrontation with the necessity of choosing the anguish of guilt in order to continue being free.

NOTES

1. For the contents of *Severnye Cvety na 1829 god* (passed by the censor December 27, 1828) see N. Smirnov-Sokol'skij, *Russkie literaturnye al'manaxi i sborniki XVIII-XIX vv* (Moscow, 1965), pp. 135–136. Smirnov-Sokol'skij fails to indicate that the author of the poem, "Portret" ("S svoej pylajuščej dušoj . . ."), is Puškin. The excerpt from "a historical novel" is the first published fragment from the novel which came to be known after Puškin's death as *Arap Petra Velikogo*.

2. *Stixotvorenija Aleksandra Puškina. Vtoraja Čast'.* (Sanktpeterburg, 1829), pp. 127–128: IX *Vospominanie*.

3. Cf. the following specific discussions of the poem: L. V. Ščerba, "Opyty lingvističeskogo tolkovanija stixotvorenij. I. 'Vospominanie' Puškina," in his *Izbrannye raboty po russkomu jazyku* (Moscow, 1957), pp. 26–44 (originally published in *Russkaja Reč'*, I., Petrograd, 1923); V. V. Veresaev, "Stixi nejasnye moi," in Veresaev's *V dvux planax* (Moscow, 1929), pp. 123–129; N. L. Stepanov, *Lirika Puškina* (Moscow, 1959), pp. 364–374; Ja. L. Levkovič, "Vospominanie," in N. V. Izmajlov, ed., *Stixotvorenija Puškina 1820–1830-x godov* (Leningrad, 1974), pp. 107–120. Cf. also the brief remarks in D. D. Blagoj, *Tvorčeskij put' Puškina (1826–1830)* (Moscow, 1967), pp. 171–172, and the situating of the poem within certain thematic or "ideological" contexts in M. Geršenzon, *Mudrost' Puškina* (Moscow, 1919), pp. 78–79, in S. L. Frank, *Ètjudy o Puškine* (Munich, 1957), pp. 117–118, and in E. A. Majmin, "Filosofskaja poèzija Puškina i ljubomudrov," in *Puškin. Issledovanija i materialy,* VI (Moscow-Leningrad, 1969), pp. 101–110.

4. For a description of the *černovoj avtograf* see Levkovič, op. cit., pp. 108–110.

5. The stages of this process have been reconstructed and published in volume III ₂, pp. 651–653, of the "Bol'šoe Akademičeskoe izdanie." The starting point of the process may have been, as Izmajlov has suggested, an almost complete text which can be reconstructed on the basis of consistent "fair çopy" handwriting. See N. V. Izmajlov, "A. S. Puškin. Neizdannye teksty stixotvorenij," *Novyj Mir*, No. 1, 1937, pp. 7–8. See Appendix I of the present article.

6. B. V. Tomaševskij, *Pisatel' i kniga* (Leningrad, 1928), p. 174.

7. See P., 3, II, p. 651 for the reconstructed text (see Appendix II) and P., 3, II, pp. 653–655 for the variants from which the text was reconstructed. Izmajlov, op. cit., p. 8, proposes, again on the basis of "fair copy" handwriting, a reconstruction of the earliest version of the reconstructed "final" version. See Appendix III.

8. Ščerba, op. cit., pp. 33–34. See Note 3.

9. Levkovič, op. cit., pp. 111. See Note 3.

10. L. Razmusen, "O glagol'nyx vremenax i ob otnošenii ix k vidam v russkom, nemeckom i francuzskom jazykax," *Žurnal Ministerstva Narodnogo Prosveščenija*, Čast' 275 (maj 1891), pp. 410–411.

11. Ščerba, op. cit., p. 42, remarks that *stogny grada* is a clearly obsolete expression for us: "*stogny* prosto daže neponjatno, no i *grada* vmesto *goroda* ne motivirovano." The archaism of *stogny grada* would be quite motivated, however, if one reads *grad* as meaning more than just a particular urban center (Petersburg), i.e., if *grad*, reinforced by the even more archaic *stogny*, were read as an equivalent of the French *Cité*, "the state, the nation" (cf. "les lois de la cité"). See Horst Baader "Einige Bemerkungen zur Geschichte der Wörter *cité, ville* und *ètat*," in H. Stimm/J. Wilhelm, eds., *Verba et vocabula. Ernst Gamillscheg zum 80. Geburtstag*. (Munich, 1968), pp. 35–48.

12. Note that the adjective *poluprozračnyj* is unique in Puškin's works: it occurs only in this poem. The "semitransparency" of the "shadow" cast by the night is a significant constituent of the setting: neither darkness nor light but a transitional, intermediate state. Cf. L. S. Vygotskij's observations on the distinctive qualities of morning twilight and evening twilight ("Večernie sumerki ... *polu*svet i *polu*t'ma, to est' *ni* svet, *ni* t'ma, a smes' ...") in his *Psixologija iskusstva* (Moscow, 2nd edition, 1968), pp. 362ff. and Note 82, p. 527.

13. Cf. P. Ja. Caadaev in a letter to Puškin (March–April 1829): "Mon voeu le plus ardent, mon ami, est de vous voir initié au mystère du temps. Il n'y a pas de spectacle plus affligeant dans le monde moral que celui d'un homme de génie méconnaissant son siècle et sa mission. Quand on voit celui qui doit dominer les esprits, se laisser dominer lui-même par les habitudes et routines de la populace, on se sent arrêté dans sa marche; on se dit, pourquoi cet homme m'empêche-t-il de marcher, lui qui doit me conduire?/..../Si vous n'avez pas la

patience de Vous instruire de ce qui se passe dans le monde, rentrez en vous-même et tirez de votre propre intérieur la lumière que se trouve immanquablement dans tout âme faite comme la vôtre./ . . . /" (XIV, 44). In regard to "ugryzenija *gorjat*," cf. such expressions as "rana gorit," "žgučaja bol'," "žgučee raskajanie," "žgučij styd," "raskajanie, sožalenie žžёt." Cf. also the French *cuisant* (as opposed to *adoucissant*): "Je sens au fond du coeur mille remords cuisants . . ." (Corneille, *Cinna*, III, 2). Note also that the choice of "gorjat," instead of some form of *žeč'*, for example, makes possible a double opposition: hot/cold (active/inert) and dark/illuminated.

14. Note the shift from plural to singular in the verbs: from agitated multiplicity to concentrated unity.

15. "Žizn' moja" comprises the past life of the self in its continuity with the self's present life. What is called to mind in the act of remembering (an act in the present) is the self in its continuity and integrity. Note in this regard the importance of the consistent imperfective non-preterit verb predicates: it is the given present intermediating between the past and the uncertain future that will decide the continuity or discontinuity of the self.

16. Note the difference between, for example, *ja perepisyvaju* and *ja perepisyvaju pis'mo*. One may want to read *proklinaju* as implying *proklinaju moju žizn'*, but this does not change the point about the distinctive function of explicit formulation as opposed to implication. Moreover, a more immediate implied connection could be argued on the basis of the only verb rhyme in the poem: ". . . i proklinaju—no strok pečal'nyx ne smyvaju."

17. The word *ugryzenie* occurs seven times in Puškin. In four cases it is used in combination with *sovest'*: "urgryzenie sovesti" occurs twice in *Pikovaja Dama*, once in the unpublished fragment "Učast' moja rešena," and once in *Poltava*—"No gde že getman? gde zlodej?/Kuda bežal ot ugryzenij/Zmeinoj sovesti svoej?" In the unpublished fragment "Gosti s"jezžalis' na daču," there is one instance of "ugryzenija samoljubia." The "zmei serdečnoj ugryzen'ja" of our poem has its closest analogue in the "toska serdečnyx ugryzenij" of *Evgenij Onegin* (VI, stanza 35): "V toske serdečnyx ugryzenij,/Rukoju stisnuv pistolet,/Gljadit na Lenskogo Evgenij./"Nu, čto ž? ubit," rešil sosed./Ubit! . . ."; "vospominan'e gryzёt serdce" in the 1830 poem "Kogda poroj vospominan'e/Gryzёt mne serdce v tišine/I otdalёnnoe stradan'e/Kak ten' opjat' bežit ko mne . . ."; and in *Evgenij Onegin* (I, stanza 46): "Kto žil i myslil, tot ne možet/V duše ne prezirat' ljudej;/Kto čuvstvoval, togo trevožit/Prizrák nevozvratimyx dnej:/Tomu už net očarovanij,/Togo *zmeja vospominanij*,/Togo *raskajan'e* gryzёt . . . ." In analyzing the various meanings of *zmejá/zmijá* in Puškin (the word occurs twenty-seven times), one should take into

account the interaction of two sources of the symbolic meanings of the word: the Bible and classical mythology, namely the serpents of the goddesses of retribution—the Erinyes or Furies. Cf. in French classical literature: "Hé bien! filles d'enfer, vos mains sont-elles prêtes?/Pour qui sont ces serpents qui sifflent sur vos têtes?" (Racine, *Andromaque*, V, 5); "Tes remords te suivront comme autant de furies" (Racine, *Britannicus*, V, 6). Cf. also in G. R. Deržavin's "Evgeniju. Žizn' Zvanskaja" (stanza 5): "Projdja minuvšuju i ne našedši v nej,/Čtob čërnaja zmija mne serdce ugryzala. . . ."

18. Of the two instances of *i* in the first quatrain, the second one connects two subjects.

19. The verb occurs in Puškin only in this poem.

20. I owe the reference to Mencov's poem to Majmin's article, loc. cit., p. 106 (see Note 3). Majmin also points out the thematic and situational similarity of Mencov's poem to Puškin's.

21. Note the difference between "strok pečal'nyx" and the otherwise possible accusative "stroki pečal'nye" ("no stroki pečal'nye ne smyvaju"): "strok pečal'nyx" involves the entire text, while "stroki pečal'nye" could be taken as meaning: "I don't wash away particular lines of the text, namely the ones specified as being *pečal'nye*."

22. In the *černovoj avtograf*, Puškin's "find" of the definitive version of the last line is marked with three exclamation marks (P., 3, II, p. 653).

APPENDIX I

Умолкнул шумный день—и тихо налегла
   Немая ночь на стогны града.
Полупрозрачная нисходит с нею мгла
   И сон, дневных забот отрада.
Но сон меня бежит—влачатся в тишине
   Часы томительного бденья—
И грустно бодрствую—живей горят во мне
   Змеи сердечной угрызенья—
В уме, подавленном/   /тоской
   Теснится горьких дум избыток.
Воспоминание, зачем ты предо мной
   Свой мрачный развиваешь свиток?
И я минувшую читаю жизнь мою,
   И содрогаюсь и/   /
И стону жалобно, и горько слёзы лью
   Над/   /строками.

(*Novyj Mir*, No. 1, 1937, p. 8)

APPENDIX II

Я вижу в праздности, в неистовых пирах,
    В безумстве гибельной свободы,
В неволе, бедности, в гоненьи ⟨?⟩ [и] в степях
    Мои утраченные [годы].
Я слышу вновь друзей предательский привет
    На играх Вакха и Киприды,
Вновь сердцу   наносит хладный свет
    [Неотразимые обиды].
Я слышу   жужжанье клеветы
    Решенья глупости лукавой
И шопот зависти и лёгкой суеты
    Укор весёлый и кровавый—
И нет отрады мне—и тихо предо мной
    Встают два призрака младые,
Две тени милые—две данные судьбой
    Мне ангела во дни былые—
Но оба с крыльями, и с пламенным мечом—
    И стерегут—и мстят мне оба—
И оба говорят мне мёртвым языком
    О тайнах счастия и гроба.
(P., 3, II, p. 651)

APPENDIX III

Я вижу в праздности, в безумстве и пирах
    Свою потопленную младость,
В изгнаньи, в бедности, под стражей и в степях
    /   /
Я слышу вновь /   / жужжанье клеветы
    Я вижу смех и /   /ропот
Измены гнусные, и лёгкой суеты
    Укор жестокий и кровавый
Я слышу вновь друзей предательский привет
    /Мне сердце жгут его обиды/
Измену /   / вновь наносит лёгкой свет
    Неотразимые обиды.
И нет отрады мне—и тихо предо мной
    Встают два призрака младые,

Две тени милые, два данные судьбой
  Мне Гении во дни былые—
Но оба с крыльями, и с пламенным мечом,
  И стерегут—и мстят мне оба—
И мёртвую любовь сменила /в н/их огнём
  Неумирающая злоба—

(*Novyj Mir,* No. 1, 1937, p. 8)

APPENDIX IV

Je répandrai mon âme au seuil du sanctuaire,
Seigneur, dans ton nom seul je mettrai l'espoir,
Mes cris t'éveilleront et mon humble prière
S'élevera vers toi comme l'encens du soir.

Lamartine.*

Когда стеснит твою внезапно грудь
Мысль тяжкая о прежних заблужденьях,
От горести не сможешь ты вздохнуть,
И совести почуешь пробужденье;
Когда вся жизнь твоя и повесть дел твоих
В унылой пред тобой представится картине,
И дух Божественный от помыслов земных
Вдруг повлечёт тебя к высокому—к святыне;
Когда почувствуешь ты совести укор
И жажду чистых дум и чистых помышлений,
Тебя покинувших, забывших с давних пор,
Высоких чувств, высоких вожделений,—
Молись, молись! Усердною мольбой
Врачуются душевные страданья.
Молись, молись! и доблестно омой
Грехи свои слезою покаянья!
Смывает всё пред Господом она,
Смывает всё, и вопль отверженной любови,
Роптанье—бред болезненного сна,—
Отчаянье, и даже пятна крови!

* The opening stanza of A. de Lamartine's "Chants lyriques de Saül. Imitation des Psaumes de David" in the *Premières Méditations Poétiques.*

Ты сознаёшь грехи свои,
Ты сознаёшь, сколь низок ты и грешен;
Но до конца надежду сохрани,
Не будь отчаян, слаб и безутешен!
И на земле великое не прах,
И на земле раскаянье не тщетно;
Так пред Творцом святым на небесах,
Пребудет ли святое безответно?
Всевышний Бог слезу твою узрит
И тронется горячими мольбами,
Отпустит грех, и грешника простит,
И осенит защитными крылами.
Тогда души минувшим не тревожь,
Не вспоминай о жизни беззаконной—
И, с Небом и с самим собою примирённый,
Ты жизнью новою прекрасно процветёшь!

Менцов.

«Московский Наблюдатель», Часть 8, 1836, стр. 250-251.

DANTE AND J. MALFILÂTRE AS LITERARY SOURCES OF TAT'JANA'S EROTIC DREAM (NOTES ON THE THIRD CHAPTER OF PUŠKIN'S *EVGENIJ ONEGIN*)

Riccardo Picchio
Yale University

Puškin wrote the third chapter of *Evgenij Onegin* between February 8 and October 2, 1824. The first part (up to "Tat'jana's Letter") was written in Odessa, the second part was completed in Mixajlovskoe. In the front page of one of the manuscripts, which is preserved in the Moscow Public Library,[1] the text of this chapter is preceded by an epigraph consisting of the following two citations from Dante's *Inferno* (V, 118–120) and Jacques Malfilâtre's poem *Narcisse dans l'île de Vénus* (first edition, 1768), respectively:

> Ma dimmi: nel tempo di dolci sospiri
> A che e come concedette [*a conoscer*] amore
> Che conosceste i dubiosi desiri?
> *Dan*[te][2]

> Elle était fille, elle était amoureuse
> *Malfilâtre*[3]

As to the first citation, Puškin's first writing "*a conoscer*" (to know), and then correcting this line apparently after checking the right wording (i.e., "A che e come concedette amore") suggests that he knew this famous episode of the *Inferno* by heart. In the final

42

version of the third chapter of *Evgenij Onegin*, which was printed in 1827,[4] the citation from Dante's *Inferno* is omitted and only that from Malfilâtre's *Narcisse* was preserved as a thematic clue.

One does not know whether Puškin's first intention was to use both citations with reference to two coexisting motifs in his own poetic text. Nor can one say whether the citation from Malfilâtre represented a final substitution for a Dantesque motif which the poet may have abandoned in the process of describing Tat'jana's passion. In any case it is clear that Puškin considered both Dante and Malfilâtre as important models for his Russian love story.

To establish the importance of this epigraph, or motto, for the making of Onegin III, one should define the general function of epigraphs in the context of this poetic novel. Can one interpret all the epigraphs to each of the eight chapters of *Evgenij Onegin* as thematic guidelines intended to help the reader decode a poetic message conveyed by an extremely allusive text?

The first citation which opens the poem and precedes the dedication is taken from a "private letter."[5] It underlines the dominant features of Onegin's personality, namely: vanity, pride, indifference, and haughtiness: "Pétri de vanité *il avait encore plus de* cette espèce d'orgueil *qui fait avouer avec la même* indifférence *les bonnes comme les mauvaises actions, suite d'un* sentiment de superiorité, *peut-être immaginaire.*"[6] All these faults may be interpreted as lack of love. In the subsequent chapters they will result in the spiritual disease (spleen/*toska*) of the romantic hero.

The original draft of Chapter 1 contained two epigraphs which are no longer extant in the final version: (1) "*Sobran'e plamennyx zamet/Bogatoj žizni junyx let*" (Baratynskij); and (2) "Nothing is such an ennemy to accuracy of judgment as a coarse discrimination" (Burke).[7] Puškin was apparently looking for quotations that would have applied by analogy to the emotional and intellectual bewilderment of his main character. Neither the words of Baratynskij nor those of Burke could render the essence of this psychological problem. The first chapter, in fact, introduces the main character by describing his human condition and by adding to this description some general statements that the narrator supplies directly to the reader. The central theme is represented by the vain effort of contemporary man to overcome individual alienation and enjoy love. In spite of his awareness of having behaved as a "stupid and mute" man in several erotic experiences (*No ja, ljubja, byl glup i nem*),[8]

Puškin/Onegin is still longing for a different type of love. His dream represents a vital necessity as well as a literary ambition. In the language of Puškin's poetic allusiveness this ambition aims at reaching the level of the great age of Italian literature, in particular that of Petrarch's erotic poetry.[9] Onegin, as a new romantic hero, is yearning after joy of living and spiritual excitement. The motto from Vjazemskij that appears in the final version of Chapter 1 (*I žit' toropitsja i čuvstvovat' spešit*) calls the reader's attention precisely to this leitmotiv.

The Latin-Russian pun in the epigraph which opens Chapter 2 ("*O rus/O Rus'*") represents a thematic and stylistic introduction to the description of Russian country life. The Latin citation refers to an idyllic dream expressed in Puškin's narrative by the infatuation of both Tat'jana and her mother with sentimental literature. The Russian reading of the same words refers, on the other hand, to the dreary reality of the Russian countryside. Olga-Lenskij's pseudo-idyllic love affair is a poor Russian variation (*Rus'*) on the Horatian theme of *rus*.

The thematic pertinence of the epigraphs that open the remaining chapters of *Evgenij Onegin* can also be proved. This will represent a solid point of departure for our study of Chapter 3.

In Chapter 4 the spiritual alienation of Onegin and Lenskij from their country partners, Tat'jana and Olga, proves that there is no abstract rule of moral behavior. This idea is rendered at the beginning of the chapter by the motto, "*La morale est dans la nature des choses*" (Necker).[10]

Not too many words should be spent to show how pertinent the citation from a famous ballade by Žukovskij (*O, ne znaj six strašnyx snov/ty, moja Svetlana*")[11] appears to be in connection with the content and the poetic intonation of Chapter 5. Tat'jana's dream and sufferings represent a variation on the same set of symbolic themes that Žukovskij had developed in Russian literature under the influence of Bürger.

Chapter 6 describes the senseless killing of Lenskij. Petrarch's voice is used in the motto to indicate the traditional contempt for human life in Russia-Scythia: "*Là sotto i giorni nubilosi e brevi/ Nasce una gente a cui morir non duole.*"[12]

As to the cluster of quotations from Dmitriev, Baratynskij, and Griboedov that introduce Tat'jana's migration to Moscow[13] in Chapter VII, one can observe that the concluding lines (*Gde ž lučše?/Gde nas net*) contain a skeptical response to an optimistic literary myth. Once more it is the initial epigraph that tells the reader how to interpret the events which take place in the poetic novel: there is no hope—the poet means to say—in either the Russian countryside or Moscow.

This profession of despair is eventually confirmed in Chapter 8, where the poet is compelled to take his leave of the hero. In the last epigraph the description of the end of a poetic dream is summarized quite transparently by a citation from Byron: "Fare thee well! and if for ever,/ Still for ever, fare thee well."[14]

Having so established the thematic pertinence of each epigraph preceding the other seven chapters of *Evgenij Onegin*, it remains to be seen whether the two citations from Dante and Malfilâtre considered above can help one better understand the love dream of Tat'jana as described in the third chapter. Puškin's admiration for the *Divine Comedy* was the result of both his deep interest in Italian literature[15] and his participation in a general worship by Romantic culture throughout Europe of the main "poet-prophet" of Christianity.[16] His first selecting a quotation from the fifth canto of the *Inferno* and then replacing it with a line taken from a minor eighteenth-century French poem seem to indicate an internal evolution in the ideological planning of this chapter. To explain this evolution, one should move from an evaluation of the functional meaning of both models in the cultural context of Puškin's times.

Byron's translation of the episode of *Francesca of Rimini* (*Inferno* V, 97–133) can be considered one of the best proofs of the popularity of this Dantesque theme in the Romantic age. However, when the third chapter of *Evgenij Onegin* was written (1824), Puškin could not have been influenced by this translation, for it was not published until 1830. Francesca da Polenta's obscure love affair with her brother-in-law, Paolo Malatesta, in thirteenth-century Rimini had been the object of interpretations and discussions since 1815 because of Silvio Pellico's tragedy, *Francesca da Rimini*. Pellico's literary fame in those years was not yet so great as that which he would acquire in a later period with the publication of his *Le mie prigioni*. He was well known, in any case, to many eminent personalities of the contemporary literary world. Stendhal, Madame de Staël, and Byron visited Milan, where he lived, shortly after the great success of his tragedy. Lord Byron, during his stay in Milan in 1816, undertook the translation into English of Pellico's *Francesca da Rimini* in collaboration with his good friend Hobhouse.[17] This enterprise was never completed, but Byron's positive evaluation[18] certainly contributed to a greater popularity throughout Europe of both the tragedy by Pellico and its Dantesque motif. It is no wonder that in 1824 Puškin was still under the spell of Romantic discussions on whether Dante's Francesca had been guilty of adultery or whether she had been the victim of a base conspiracy.

Pellico's answer was that Francesca and Paolo had not committed adultery and that Francesca's only fault lay in confessing her love. This was an impossible love because Paolo was not her husband, as she had first been led to believe. As soon as Francesca realized that she had been misled, she refrained from further effusions, but this did not prevent her from becoming the innocent victim of her own sincerity.[19]

There is no evidence of a direct influence of Pellico's Francesca on Puškin's Tat'jana. At any rate, Puškin's originally choosing a citation from Dante's *Inferno* V to introduce his readers to Tat'jana's impossible love[20] for Onegin can be evaluated in the same literary atmosphere that had given rise to Pellico and Byron's interest in Dante's Francesca as a symbol of tragic love.

At what stage of his work on the third chapter did Puškin decide to omit the epigraph taken from Dante's *Inferno* and use only a line from Malfilâtre's *Narcisse*? Did he delete nothing but a three-line citation, or was his decision followed by the complete elimination of a motif which he had originally selected from the Divine Comedy? The analysis of the third chapter shows that Puškin actually used both Dante and Malfilâtre as literary sources for his countrified love story.

Tat'jana and Francesca are both victims of a dangerous type of fanciful literature founded on adventure and love. They both believe in what they read to such a point that they confuse the world of fiction with the reality of their own lives. Dante's sympathy with the sufferings of Francesca implies his moral condemnation of the type of literature represented by the tales of the knights of the Round Table and in particular by the story of Lancelot and Guinevere: "*Noi* leggevamo *un giorno per diletto/Di Lancialloto, come amor lo strinse:/. . . Per più fiate gli occhi ci sospinse/Quella* lettura *e scoloroc-ci il viso . . ./Quando* leggemmo *il disiato riso/esser baciato da cotanto amante . . ./Galeotto fu 'l* libro *e chi lo scrisse . . .*"[21]

(In Byron's translation: "*We* read *one day for pastime, seated nigh,/ of Lancelot, how love enchain'd him too* . . ./*But oft our eyes met, and our cheeks in hue/all o'er discoloured by that* reading *were/* . . ./ *When we* read *the long-sigh'd for smile of here,/To be thus kiss'd by such devoted lover* . . ./*Accursed was the* book *and he who* wrote!")[22] In Tat'jana and Puškin's time the same type of literature was represented by modern versions of romantic stories founded on adventure and love: "*Teper' s kakim ona vniman'em/*Čitaet *sladost-nyj roman/S kakim živym očarovan'em/*P'ët *obol'stitel'nyj* obman!/ . . . *Voobražajas' geroinej/svoix* vozljublennyx tvorcov,/*Klarisoj, Juliej, Del'finoj/Tat'jana v tišine lesov/Odna s* opasnoj knigoj *brodit.* . . ."[23]

Dante's influence on the spiritual image of Tat'jana can be traced thematically as well as textually. When Dante asks Francesca the reason for her perdition, he cannot refrain from shedding tears: "*Francesca, i tuoi martiri/A lagrimar mi fanno tristo e pio.* . . . (Byron: "*Francesca, thy sad destinies/Have made me sorrow till the tears arise.* . . ."). In turn, Puškin's words sound like a free translation or adaptation of precisely these lines: "*Tat'jana, milaja Tat'jana!/S toboj teper' ja slëzy l'ju.*"[24]

Up to this point there is a clear similarity between the two characters as readers of the same type of corrupting literature: on the one hand, the stories of Guinevere and Lancelot circulating in medieval society and on the other hand the daydreams of the British muse ("*Britanskoj muzy nebylicy*")[25] pervading Romantic Russia. But the story of Tat'jana was destined to develop in a different way. Whereas Francesca and Paolo are both victims of the same passion, Tat'jana's partner is incapable of loving. Evgenij is not a "modern Paolo"; that is to say, he is not capable of identifying himself with "Grandison" in the way Paolo identifies himself with Lancelot: "*No naš geroj, kto b ni byl on/Už verno byl ne Grandison.*"[26]

Francesca and Tat'jana share a rash faith in an abstract ideal of love. The same type of erotic excitement leads both girls to perdition. Dante: "*Amor condusse noi ad una morte/* . . . *Quanti* dolci pensier, *quanto* disio/*Menò costoro al* doloroso passo!" (Byron: "Love *to one* death *conducted us along* . . ./*How many* sweet thoughts, *what* strong ecstasies/ *Led these their* evil fortune *to fulfil!*"); Puškin: "Pogibneš, *milaja; no prežde/Ty v* oslepitel'noj nadežde/Blaženstvo tëmnoe *zovës,/Ty* negu žizni *uznaëš,/Ty* p'ëš volšebnyj jad želanij. . . . . .")[27] However, in spite of this common yielding to the

misleading spell of literary fashion, Francesca of Rimini and Tat'-
jana are victims of different circumstances. Puškin follows Dante up
to the moment when the pilgrim in the Second Circle expresses his
sympathy for Francesca (cf. the passages cited above: "*Francesca i
tuoi martiri*" and "*Tat'jana, milaja Tat'jana.* . . ."). Immediately
after this passage in *Inferno* V (118–120) are the lines that Puškin
selected as a motto for *Onegin III*: "*Ma dimmi: al tempo de' dolci
sospiri,/A che, e come concedette amore,/Che conosceste i dubbiosi
disiri?*" Francesca's answer to this question contains the story
of her dubious passion. Neither the question nor the answer
could apply to the situation that Puškin was about to create
in the third chapter, and thus the citation from Dante was omitted
in the final text. Dante's Francesca provided a model for defining
the nature of the Russian girl, Tat'jana, but this model could not
be used to tell her story.

After the turning point represented by Tat'jana's confession of
her erotic excitement ("*Ja . . . znaeš', njanja, . . . vljublena*")[28]
which marks the actual beginning of her love story, the Dantesque
sub-text affects Puškin's narrative only as far as the moral evaluation
of the heroine's behavior is concerned. Is Tat'jana guilty? Puškin
engages in a discussion on this matter without explaining why
Tat'jana should be condemned. His polemic question, "What is
Tat'jana's fault?" ("*Za čto ž vinovnee Tat'jana?*")[29] surprises the
reader who has not been given any concrete reason to think that
Tat'jana's behavior might be compared to that of those St. Petersburg coquettes on whose eyebrows Puškin would have stamped
Dante's words "*Lasciate ogni speranza*" ("*Ostav' nadeždu nav-
segda*").[30] As a matter of fact, Puškin's response to an imaginary
moral indictment of Tat'jana can be better understood against the
background of Romantic discussions concerning Francesca of
Rimini's sin of love. Tat'jana's "crimes" are the same ones that a
large part of Romantic literary criticism was willing to impute to
Francesca, namely credulity and frivolity, with all possible extenu-
ating circumstances: "*Uželi ne prostite ej/Vy legkomyslija stras-
tej?*"[31]

As mentioned above, the epigraph that appears in the final version
of Chapter 3, "*Elle était fille, elle était amoureuse,*" is taken from
the Second Chant of *Narcisse dans l'île de Vénus*, a poem by Jacques-
Charles-Louis Malfilâtre (1732–1767). Nowadays very few people
besides specialists in late eighteenth-century French literature read
this poem or know its author's name. It is not even mentioned in

most standard literary histories. In Puškin's time, however, it was well known. Some critics maintained in those years that Malfilâtre was the best representative of modern French poetry.[32] It is no wonder, therefore, that Puškin might have assumed that a reference to Malfilâtre's *Narcisse* was sufficiently transparent for his readers. Malfilâtre's *Complete Works* were readily available.[33] Gilbert's denunciation of an alleged literary conspiracy that would have condemned to oblivion the young poet of Caen in the 1860s ("*La faim mit au tombeau Malfilâtre ignoré*")[34] was often repeated in France as well as in the French-speaking literary circles of St. Petersburg. La Harpe had given a positive, though very superficial, evaluation of *Narcisse*.[35] All these circumstances indicate that Puškin's eventually selecting this line by Malfilâtre as the epigraph for Chapter III of *Evgenij Onegin* was intended as an invitation to his readers to interpret Tat'jana's love story as a symptom of the modern *maladie du siècle* rather than as a universal example patterned after the model of Dante's Francesca.

Malfilâtre's poem, *Narcisse dans l'île de Vénus*, belongs to the genre of late-classicist/early pre-Romantic didactic poetry. Its main thesis is that selfishness and insensibility, that is, love for oneself instead of for one's fellow creatures, are the main plagues of modern society. Toward the end of the poem these ideas are expressed in the form of a polemic "moral of the story":

> Vivre insensible est une mort cruelle
> Que chaque jour, chaque instant renouvelle.
> N'avoir du moins de sensibilité
> Que pour soi-même, et dédaigner les autres,
> N'aimer enfin la grâce, la beauté,
> Les agréments qu'autant qu'ils sont les nôtres,
> C'est être mort pour la société. . . .[36]

It is a pity that the meaning of *Narcisse* as an ideological source of the character of Evgenij Onegin has escaped the attention of too many critics. Puškin's hero is one of those modern men whose soul has been poisoned, in Malfilâtre's words, by "*et l'amour-propre et l'oubli de l'amour.*"[37] How and why has modern society fallen a prey to this spiritual disease? Malfilâtre's answer consists of a symbolic interpretation of the mythical story of Narcissus. Venus has created a happy island (a mixture of erotic Utopia, Rousseau's primitive purity, the Earthly Paradise, and so forth), where natural love was the supreme law. On that island old, blind Tiresias has taken shelter after losing his fitness for heterosexual love as a consequence of Juno's wrath. Tiresias takes care of Narcissus, who is also threatened by Juno with the same curse. Echo, a symbol of natural response to the call of love, becomes the object of Narcissus' desire and returns his love. Tiresias and Venus meet in secret and discuss how to prevent Narcissus from losing his fitness for natural love. They do not know that Echo is hiding behind a bush and listening to them. It is her passion for Narcissus that makes Echo commit this sin of inquisitive impertinence. But is this a real sin? Malfilâtre's opinion is to be found precisely in the passage that contains the line chosen by Puškin as the epigraph to the third chapter of *Evgenij Onegin*:

> Mais un buisson déroboit à ses yeux
> La jeune Écho, qui s'étoit, auprès d'eux,
> Dans le tillis glissé avec finesse.
> En surprenant ce qu'ils disoient tous deux,
> Echo vouloit pénétrer ce mystère
> Qui l'interesse et que l'on veut lui taire.
> Injustes dieux! pourriez-vous la punir
> D'avoir tenté de sauver ce qu'elle aime?
> Seroit-il vrai qu'elle eût fait elle-même
> Tout son malheur, voulant le prévenir?
> *Elle étoit fille; elle étoit amoureuse;*
> Elle trembloit pour l'objet des ses soins;
> C'étoit assez pour être curieuse,
> C'étoit assez; filles le sont pour moins;
> Mais je ne veux fronder ce sexe aimable,
> Et pour Écho sa faute est excusable.
> Si cette nymphe est coupable en ceci,
> Je lui pardonne, Amour la fit coupable.
> Puisse le sort lui pardonner aussi!...[38]

When Echo and Narcissus are ready to fulfill their natural desire, Narcissus looks at his own image which is mirrored by the water of a pond that Juno has managed to pollute with a subtle, antilove potion. This marks the beginning of the end of both Narcissus and the island of Venus. Narcissus forgets about Echo and is attracted by nothing but his own image. Attempting to grasp this image, he perishes in the mirroring water of Juno's pond. A flower, the narcissus, then grows in that place and in turn poisons the inhabitants of the island. Narcissus' *"amour-propre et l'oubli de l'amour"* spread throughout the earth. Modern society springs from Narcissus' error and Venus' defeat.

If we compare the terms of the Romantic discussions devoted to Francesca of Rimini's sin of love with Malfilâtre's defense of the sin committed by Echo for the sake of her beloved Narcissus, the combination of the two citations that Puškin originally selected for the third chapter of his *Evgenij Onegin* becomes less enigmatic. In the light of Malfilâtre's poem one can also better understand Puškin's comparison of pure Tat'jana with the self-loving coquettes of St. Petersburg (*"Koketka sudit xladnokrovno/Tat'jana ljubit ne šutja/I predaëtsja bezuslovno/Ljubvi, kak miloe ditja"*).[39] Malfilâtre's description of French society may have represented a direct source for Puškin's critical remarks on contemporary Russian high life:

> Ce même esprit, cet insipide goût
> Par qui chacun, devenu son idole,
> Et se compare et se prefère à tout,
> Régna depuis dans cette île frivole;
> Et c'est de là, si l'on croit nos aieux,
> Que nos François virent fondre chez eux
> Ce tourbillon de ridicules êtres
> Qu'on a nommés coquettes, petits-maîtres:
> Narcisses vains, pour eux seuls prévenus,
> Paons orgueilleux, qui se rendent hommage,
> Insolemment étalent leur plumage
> Et font la guerre aux oiseaux de Vénus.[40]

Tat'jana, too, is a victim of this type of social disease. She, too, *"était fille"*; she, too, *"était amoureuse."* The literary origin of her sin (i.e., her infatuation with fanciful stories) is similar to that of Dante's Francesca, but her love story resembles Malfilâtre's Echo. One may assume that Puškin needed this typological similarity mainly because of the parallel that he was about to draw between the objects of Tat'jana's and Echo's love. In fact, the allusion in the epigraph may be interpreted as a thematic clue regarding *Evgenij* as the counterpart to *Narcissus*. In the light of this indication one could infer that Tat'jana's erotic dream is frustrated by Onegin's *narcissism*. If this critical suggestion is worth the attention of Puškin scholars, further studies on the meaning of Malfilâtre's *Narcisse* as a literary source may be necessary.

NOTES

1. Cf. Puškin, *Polnoe sobranie sočinenij*, Tom VI (Izdatel'stvo Akademii Nauk SSSR), *Evgenij Onegin* (red: V. V. Tomaševskij), (Leningrad, 1937), 573.
2. Byron's translation of these lines is "*But tell me, in the season of sweet sighs,/By what and how thy love to passion rose,/So as his dim desires to recognise?*" I quote from *The Works of Lord Byron: with His Letters and Journals, and his Life,* by Thomas Moore, Esq., vol. XII (London 1833), 4–11. This translation is clearly inadequate, but it still represents an interesting document of Romantic response to Dante's poetry when Puškin was working on his *Onegin*.
3. The first edition of this poem appeared in 1768: *Narcisse dans l'île de Vénus*, poème en IV chants accompagné de l'ode intitulée: *le Soleil fixe au milieu des planètes* et d'une préface de MM. de Savine et Collet de Messine (Paris, Lejay pub., 1768).
4. P., 6, p. 51.
5. "*Tiré d'une lettre particulière,*" (6).
6. Ibid. In this as well as in the subsequent citations, the italics are mine.
7. P., 6, p. 543.
8. Stanza 58: ibid, p. 30.
9. Cf. in particular stanza 49 "... *obretut usta moi/Jazyk Petrarki i ljubvi.*" The critical cliché, according to which Petrarch was the highest example of love poetry as opposed to the more thoughtful poetry of Dante, was very much in fashion in those years, especially under the influence of Ugo Foscolo's critical essays published in English in the early 1820s. In his essay, *A Parallel Between Dante and Petrarch*, Foscolo maintained that "Petrarch attained the main object of erotic poetry; which is, to produce a constant musical flow in strains inspired by the sweetest of human passions." See U. Foscolo, *Saggi e discorsi critici*, edizione critica a cura di Cesare Foligno (Edizione nazionale delle opere di Ugo Foscolo, vol. 10; Florence, 1953), p. 113.
10. These words by Necker are taken from Madame de Staël's *Considérations sur la Révolution Française*, Part II, Chapter 20.
11. Žukovskij's warning perfectly applies to Tat'jana's inclination to play with mystery and blindly believe the words of Martin Zadek

(cf. stanza 22), the author of a popular book on the meaning of dreams (3rd Russian edition, 1821). This reference to superstitious literature represents a variant on the same theme of the influence of cheap romantic literature which Puškin had already developed in Chapter 3.

12. F. Petrarca, *Rerum vulgarium fragmenta*, XXVIII (*O aspectata in ciel beata et bella*), lines 49 and 51 with omission of line 50 ("nemica natural-mente di pace") in Puškin's quotation. The omission is obviously intentional.

13. "*Moskva, Rossii doč ljubima,/Gde ravnuju tebe syskat'?*" (Dmitriev). (Moscow, beloved daughter of Russia,/Where can we find another city equal to you?); "Kak ne ljubit' rodnoj Moskvy?" (Baratynskij) (How is it possible not to love our Moscow?); "Gonen'e na Moskvu! čto značit videt' svet! Gde ž lučše?/Gde nas net." (Griboedov).

14. This final "Fare thee well!" should be interpreted as a general poetic "envoy" rooted in romantic ambiguity rather than as the actual farewell song of both the poet and the main hero.

15. Puškin's knowledge of the Italian language was good. He probably wrote letters in Italian to Amalia Ristić, whom he had met in Odessa (I. N. Goleniščev-Kutuzov, *Tvorčestsvo Dante i mirovaja literatura* [Moscow, 1971], 457, note 23). See also J. Verxovskij, *Puškin i ital'janskij jazyk*, in *Puškin i ego sovremenniki*, XI, (Petersburg, 1909), 101–106. As to the general problem of Dante's influence on Puškin, cf. I. N. Goleniščev-Kutuzov, op. cit., pp. 456–460.

16. In the early 1820s a general critical reaction began in Europe against the widespread opinion according to which, to use Foscolo's words, "the conflict of opposite purposes *thrills in the heart* of Petrarch and *battles in the brain* of Dante" (U. Foscolo, op. cit., p. 112). Byron rejected Schlegel's statement that Dante's "chief defect" was "a want of gentle feelings" and maintained that the opposite was true: "Of gentle feelings! — and Francesca of Rimini — and the father's feelings in Ugolino — and Beatrice — and 'La Pia!' Why, there is a gentleness in Dante beyond all gentleness, when he is tender. . . . Who but Dante could have introduced any 'gentleness' at all into Hell? Is there any in Milton's? No — and Dante's Heaven is all love, and glory, and majesty" (Byron, op. cit., ed. cit., p. 3). In 1824, when Puškin was working on the third chapter of *Evgenij Onegin*, this opinion was shared by most of the leading men of letters in Europe.

17. J. C. Hobhouse, *Recollections of a Long Life* (London, 1909–1911), vol. 2, p. 52; G. Foà, *Lord Byron poeta e carbonaro* (Florence, 1935), 158.

18. Cf. Lord Byron's review of Pellico's tragedy in *Quarterly Review*, XXIV (1820), 47, 97–101.

19. G. Finocchiaro Chimirri, "Francesca da Rimini nella fruizione ottocentesca mediata dal Pellico," *Studi Danteschi,* L1 (1974): 229–232. See also: N. Kauchtschisvili, *Silvio Pellico e la Russia* (Milan, 1963).
20. As to the reasons why Tat'jana's love ought to be an impossible one, see the critical hypothesis submitted at the end of this paper.
21. *Inferno* V, 127–137.
22. Byron, op. cit.
23. Stanza 9; P., 6, p. 55.
24. Stanza 15: ibid., p. 57.
25. Stanza 12: ibid., p. 56.
26. Stanza 10: ibid., p. 55.
27. Stanza 15: ibid., p. 58.
28. Stanza 19: ibid., p. 60.
29. Stanza 24: ibid., p. 62.
30. Stanza 22: ibid., p. 61.
31. Stanza 24: ibid., p. 62.
32. See the introduction to *Poésies de Malfilâtre, Poèmes, odes et traductions.* Avec une note bio-bibliographique par L. Derome (Paris, 1884): "Dans l'intervalle du 18 brumaire à 1810, il s'était élevé au rang d'un astre. . . . Il ne falloit qu'un pas de plus, écrit Dussault—article inséré au *Journal des Débats* du 25 novembre 1810—pour que Malfilâtre se plaçait parmi les maîtres de la poésie françoise. Les Muses ont pleuré sa perte avec amertume; elles ont gémi sur son tombeau comme sur le tombeau de Camoëns ou du Tasse . . ." (pp. 29–30). ". . . La rivalité de Malfilâtre et de Delille, qui n'avait été qu'une escarmouche du vivant de Malfilâtre, fut une guerre civile. Delille était encore là; Malfilâtre ne faisait désormais envie à personne. Ce fut à lui qu'on adjugea la branche de lourier . . ." (27). Cf. also *Nouvelle Biographie générale,* Firmin Didot, sous la direction de M. le Dr. Hoefer, 33 (article on Malfilâtre by L. Louvet), pp. 46–47; *Dictionnaire des Lettres Françaises, XVIII siècle* (Paris, 1960) (article by G. Laisney), pp. 154–156.
33. *Oeuvres complètes de Malfilâtre,* précédées d'une notice historique et littéraire par Auger (Paris, Collin, 1805); *Id.,* 2nd ed. (Paris, Longchamps, 1812); *Narcisse dans l'île de Vénus* (Paris, Bertrand, 1813); Oeuvres de Malfilâtre (Merville, Paris, 1822); *Poésies de Malfilâtre* (Collin de Plancy, Paris, 1822); *Poésies de Malfilâtre* (Berquet, Paris, 1825); Oeuvres de Malfilâtre (Lemoine, Paris, 1826).
34. Cf. Berquet's edition (op. cit.) where this citation is used as a motto.
35. In his *Cours de littérature,* La Harpe wrote (as quoted in Berquet's introduction to *Poésies de Malfilâtre,* 1825): ". . . C'est le ton de la Fontaine pour la naiveté; et la peinture de la nymphe . . . est égale à

celle de l'amant de la *Fia netta* (Flammette) de l'Arioste (sic!),
quoique dans une situation différente. . . ." It is clear that La Harpe
got mixed up; he meant to say "Boccaccio," but he wrote "Arioste."

36. Quoted from Derome's edition (op. cit.), p. 100.
37. Ibid.
38. Ibid., p. 54.
39. Stanza 25: P., 6, p. 62.
40. Op. cit., p. 102.

FRENCH MEDIEVAL POETRY AS A SOURCE OF INSPIRATION FOR PUŠKIN

Elisabeth Stenbock-Fermor
Stanford University

We know so much about Puškin that it is rather presumptuous to look for new facts in his creative biography, and even more presumptuous to try and track down that elusive imponderable: the inspiration in the background of a definite poem. When we find in a poem similitudes with the poetry of another nation, have we always the right to say that they are connected? And how are we to prove it?

Researchers must deal with facts, and in many respects they are like investigators of a crime. They would like to catch the poet red-handed, or at least have good circumstantial evidence. Such is the case of Puškin's poem, usually referred to by its first line, *Žil na svete rycar' bednyj*, though Puškin spoke of it as a "ballad" and entitled the version he prepared for publication in 1830 (but did not publish) "A Legend" (*Legenda*). This title is already an indication that one should search for its origin in medieval literature. Following this clue N. F. Sumcov in 1900[1] suggested that the origin of Puškin's poem lies in two "Miracles of Our Lady" by Gautier de Coinci, a thirteenth-century abbot who composed a whole book of poems glorifying the Virgin Mary. The book was extremely popular; about eighty manuscript copies have come down to us. A few of his "Miracles" appeared in a nineteenth-century anthology, where Sumcov found two of them. Following up that information,

N. K. Gudzij[2] discovered in the same anthology a third "Miracle" that by its contents (except for the beginning) stood even closer to Puškin's "A Legend." But as there are no proofs that Puškin was acquainted with this particular anthology, and none of these "Miracles" were found in books owned by Puškin at the time of his death, Gudzij, being a conscientious researcher, stopped short of coming to a conclusion. It was a case of "lack of concrete evidence."

The study of Gautier's "Miracles" in a modern edition[3] prompted this paper, which deals not only with the subject matter of "A Legend" but also with the form of two other poems by Puškin. As I was searching through collections which were or might have been familiar to Puškin, I could not help noticing that at least two of Puškin's poems followed a medieval pattern and differed by their organization and choice of rhymes from Puškin's usual handling of such matters. They are *Pevec*, written in 1816 when he was still at school, and *Ja pomnju čudnoe mgnoven'e . . .* (1825). Therefore, after discussing the origin of "A Legend," I am going to speak about the form of these two poems.

The first question, of course, should be: how much did Puškin know about French medieval poetry? Let's start *ab ovo*, as Puškin said of Ezerskij's genealogy.

Though I shall have to mention other nations, we shall be dealing with French poetry: the national borders in the Middle Ages were no borders at all insofar as the romance dialects which later died out or developed into modern languages are concerned. Latin texts translated or versified in vernacular were the common patrimony of all nations. In England the poets around the Plantagenets used the same idiom as their French counterparts. One of the prolific poets of the thirteenth century, Count Thibault of Champagne, was king of Navarre, which at that time included part of northern Spain. The German emperor Frederic II of Hohenstaufen listened to Provençal troubadours in Sicily, and his father-in-law, then king of Jerusalem, composed French pastorals. Puškin had in his library several books on medieval literature. To one of them we should pay particular attention: it is a work by Simonde de Sismondi, *On the Literature of the South of Europe*, and is mainly about the literatures of Italy, Spain, and Portugal.[4] But most of the first volume is about the early poetry of southern and northern France with whole poems quoted in vernacular and translated in modern French. Sismondi considered that the poetry of other nations developed under Provençal and French influence. Puškin probably consulted this work in the 1830s when he put down his own thoughts on early French literature. He stopped reading in the middle of the third volume: the pages remained uncut.

I did not look for clues in old Russian literature. Gudzij quotes a short seventeenth-century text, a translation from Polish which in turn was a translation from the Latin "Speculum Magnum." Puškin might have known it, but it still takes us back to the Western Middle Ages, and also to Gautier de Coinci, who developed the same theme in the "Miracle" discovered by Gudzij. Gautier found the subject for most of his "Miracles" in Latin collections and did not make a secret of it: the Latin origin was for him a proof of authenticity, and he frequently starts his poems with the assertion: "I find."

One of the greatest authorities on Puškin, Boris Tomaševskij, wrote in his book, *Puškin i Francija*:

One can without exaggeration assert that French poetry before the classics of the seventeenth century was alien to Puškin.[5]

By "alien"—*čužda*—Tomaševskij probably meant that Puškin knew little about it and was neither interested nor appreciative. But immediately after that statement he adds that this negative attitude was not absolute, that Puškin owned a few books of and about medieval poetry, and that in the 1830s he even attempted to translate into contemporary French 162 verses from the fourteenth-century *Roman de Renart* (the *Tale of Renard the Fox*). He deliberately left untranslated many obsolete but still understandable words, just as he frequently introduced Church Slavic words in his Russian poems when he wanted to give a specifically religious, solemn, or old-fashioned flavor to the language. We find that method in his "Prophet," in "Boris Godunov," etc.

Tomaševskij simply dismisses the question, saying that

one may surmize that with this attempt [the translation of 162 lines] Puškin's studies of old French came to an end.

As a schoolboy Puškin already was familiar with the language of sixteenth- and seventeenth-century French poetry, and he was completely at home with contemporary French, but he was not well acquainted with the earlier idiom. He was unable to render certain passages correctly. It was not only a problem of vocabulary: the syntax of a language that has lost its flections and has not yet systematically replaced them by prepositions, new pronouns, and articles can be baffling. We shall see later that even "specialists" in Puškin's time and later were unable to understand some of Gautier's verses. The woman who helped N. K. Gudzij to translate the "Miracles" (he mentions her in a footnote) misinterpreted certain important lines. Tomaševskij renders the title of a collection of medieval tales in Puškin's library, Les contes du gay Sçavoir, as meaning "The Tales of a Merry Savoyard," while it means "The Tales of Merry Science"; the last two words embraced in the Middle Ages the whole repertory of jugglers and troubadours. The term is clearly defined by La Harpe in his history of literature (sixteen volumes), the accepted textbook for literary studies in Puškin's school years.[6] La Harpe did not devote many pages to French medieval literature: he believed that there was not much worth discussing between antiquity and the classics of the seventeenth century.

Besides three different editions of the Tale of Renard the Fox one of them by a certain Méon, who was working at the French Imperial Library in the section of manuscripts, Puškin also had in his library the medieval epic about Queen Bertha and the Fabliaux ou contes in five volumes, edited and expurgated by P. Le Grand d'Aussy. They appeared in the eighteenth century, were republished in the nineteenth, and became extremely popular both in France and in England, where they underwent new editing and translating.

There existed at that time another anthology published in 1808 by the above-mentioned Méon, who was evidently a tireless researcher.[7] In his four volumes Méon included a collection already published in 1756 by Barbazan and added to it many unexpurgated texts. Sismondi in his first volume commends this edition and quotes from it, warning the readers that Méon had reproduced ancient texts in their "primitive coarseness," a quality that would certainly appeal to Puškin, who despised bowdlerized versions. He certainly knew about that anthology, having read Sismondi's first volume. This is the book mentioned by Sumcov and Gudzij, and it contains the three "Miracles" of Gautier believed to have inspired Puškin's "A Legend." But we have no proof that Puškin ever read it, and this consideration, as I said earlier, this lack of evidence stopped Gudzij when he tried to find a connection between Puškin's "A Legend" and French ones.

Now there exists another piece of evidence. The St. Petersburg

Hermitage Library owned since 1805 one of the best preserved and beautifully illustrated manuscripts of Gautier's works.[8] It contained, besides 58 "Miracles," about 30 poems (depending on the way one counts them) glorifying the Virgin Mary or praying to her. Many of them are of elaborate sophisticated versification. This book is mentioned by no less a personality than Deržavin, who saw it when it still belonged to its former owner, Petr Dubrovskij, a member of the Russian embassy in Paris. Dubrovskij collected manuscripts and autographs, and when the Russian Government acquired the collection, it was described in the *Vestnik Evropy.*

Gautier's manuscript was surrounded by a legend: executed in the thirteenth century for a great lady, it had belonged to French kings, had been taken away by the English when they occupied Paris during the Hundred Years' War, and was brought to the Tower of London. Later it fell into the hands of Mary, Queen of Scots, who enjoyed reading these poems about the Virgin's intercession during her long captivity. These details, and many more, are given by Grégoire Lozinski in his *Glanures Bibliographiques* in the *Neuphilologische Mitteilungen* in 1937. He discovered Deržavin's interest in Gautier's poems, but though we have an article by Lozinski on "French Literature and Puškin" written in the same year, there is no mention in it of any connection between the "Miracles" and Puškin's poem.

In his old age Deržavin had prepared a "Dissertation on Lyric Poetry or Ode" to be delivered at the meetings of the *Beseda ljubitelej russkogo slova.* It was published in the *Čtenija* of this society in 1811, 1812, and 1815. In the second part he speaks of medieval Western (Provençal and French) poetry, discusses the appearance of the rhyme, calls Gautier de Coinci a troubadour, and offers to his readers the original of one of Gautier's introductory poems and its Russian translation. This translation demonstrates how difficult it was even for people who knew contemporary French well — Dubrovskij was an official interpreter — to understand the old idiom. The first lines enumerate various forms of lyrics: rotruenge, pastoral, song, sonnet, etc., but not knowing that "rotruenge" was a song with a refrain, the translators understood that a "shepherdess named Rotruenge composed sonnets"![9]

It seems impossible that Puškin would have been unaware of Deržavin's "Dissertation." He was only thirteen at that time, but he would certainly be obliged to read it later. Any publication of

Deržavin must have been discussed at the Lyceum for the benefit of the students. The *Čtenija* were probably in the Lyceum library. The acquisition of Dubrovskij's collection was mentioned in foreign newspapers, and the manuscript had been the topic of foreign dissertations. Were there many opportunities for scholars and privileged persons to examine it? Even if Puškin had access to the manuscript, he would not have been able to read and study it without help, but it is quite possible that a summary of its contents and of the contents of some "Miracles" was made during the first decades of the century. The archives of the Russian Academy, where some of the Deržavin's papers still remain unpublished, may have an answer to these questions. But before research is started in this direction, we should ascertain whether it is worthwhile. Is there indeed any obvious connection between the "Miracles" and Puškin's "A Legend," and, also, was Puškin truly interested in medieval literature?

There is no doubt that there was a time when Puškin was interested in medieval literature. Otherwise he would not have written in 1834 in an unfinished draft:

Having examined innumerable short poems, ballads, rondeaus, virelays, sonnets, allegorical and satirical poems, romances of chivalry, tales, fabliaux, mysteries, which flooded France at the beginning of the seventeenth century, one cannot but confess to the sterile worthlessness of this imaginary plenty. A difficulty conquered by artistry, a happily matched repetition, a lightness of touch in phrasing, a naive joke or a sincere adage—seldom reward the weary researcher.[10]

Should we accept this as a simple elaboration on his teachers' (mainly La Harpe and Boileau) condemnation of French medieval poetry—this is Tomaševskij's opinion—or should we suspect that Puškin, for a time at least, was that kind of weary researcher? The words "having examined innumerable" and the long enumeration of genres, many of which he had already mentioned in his writings in 1825, seem to prove that he knew through personal perusal what he was talking about. As early as 1825 in a reply to Bestužev and an essay on romantic (meaning preclassic) and classic poetry, he speaks of the historical development of medieval genres and credits the troubadours with the creation of many new forms that became possible when poets started experimenting with that important innovation particular to the romance poetical language—the rhyme.

Puškin believed that after the southern troubadours had made their great innovations, they transmitted their art of versification to the northern French trouvères who developed it so far that poetry was forced into the wrong path of complicated rhyming and elaborate stanzas, and got lost in meaningless, pretentious word- and sound-play to the detriment of genuine feeling and original ideas. The consequence was endless repetition with variations of the same devices. This lasted for two centuries, and when printing became easy, writers flooded sixteenth-century France with publications that were nothing but imitations and vulgarizations of older poems. Therefore we can say that Puškin was well acquainted with certain aspects of Romance and French medieval poetry (he does not insist on the epics) but appreciated it with great reservations.

It was impossible to live in the first half of the nineteenth century and remain immune to the infatuation of the reading public with a romanticized Middle Ages, its myths, its faith, its ironclad knights, its mystic and courtly love. Be they ballads translated and imitated by Russian poets, French and English poems, novels, or plays, Puškin read them in translation or in the original, was inspired by them, even made fun of them. Puškin's poems connected with the Middle Ages are mostly translations or adaptations of ballads by Southey and other Western poets, even of fakes like Macpherson's *Ossian*. We also meet in his poetry with *Faust, Joan of Arc, The Divine Comedy*. These poems are the result of something we could call secondhand or indirect inspiration. There are also works in which the medieval element is just a borrowed setting for the artistic expression of a contemporary idea. Under that kind of inspiration a plot could be moved from Scotland to Germany, Spain, Italy, or France by the introduction of appropriate material details, names, and epithets, or images evocative of a certain period and country. Puškin's play in verse, *The Covetous Knight* is an excellent example of this process.

If we admit that Puškin was acquainted, even superficially, with Gautier's poems, we could single out the "Miracle" entitled "Of a Rich Man and a Widow." It describes the death of an important and respected man who has made a fortune through usury and must go to hell for it, while his family waits for the inheritance. But *The Covetous Knight* could also have been written without any inspiration from the "Miracles." In order to create a tragic conflict, all that Puškin needed was the contrast of the conventional ideal of knighthood and unknightly avariciousness. We know that the events take place in France and in the Middle Ages because of the French names, the mention of tournaments, swords, Jewish moneylenders, etc. But in the Middle Ages a nobleman who hoarded money by sheer brutality or extortion was not unusual. A son whose father denied him support was no exception either in medieval reality or in poetical legend.[11] A medieval knight was entitled to the armor and steed of his defeated opponents, even to a ransom in money, and the self-conscious reaction to poverty of the young man in the play is that of some character in an eighteenth- or nineteenth-century novel, dressed up as a medieval knight. Puškin knew it, and put things right in the dialogue of the "Scenes from the Age of Chivalry," his next attempt to use the medieval setting for his artistic visions. Here a knight is not ashamed of being poor.

The dramatic scenes are in prose. There exists in the drafts an attempt to rewrite them in blank verse. The main subject—the love of a man from the middle class for a highborn lady, and his dream to become a knight—was a popular subject in nineteenth-century romantic literature. The events had to take place in Germany because the outcome of the plot depended on the invention of gunpowder by Berthold Schwartz, who is one of the characters. We also know that Faust, said to be the inventor of printing, was to be brought in by Mephistopheles at the end of the play. Gunpowder, which destroyed the power of the ironclad knights, and printing, that forerunner of enlightenment, were to sound the toll of the Middle Ages.

N. Demidov in 1900 insisted on the similitudes in Puškin's "Scenes" with passages in "The Jaquerie" of Prosper Mérimée, author of "The Guzla," which had furnished Puškin with the material for his "Songs of the Western Slavs."[12] Gudzij denied that they were borrowings; Blagoj and Bondi admitted them. There are certainly many similitudes, which cannot all have occurred just because both authors were describing a similar situation in the same historical setting of peasants' revolts. The difference is that "La Jaquerie" took place in northern France and Puškin's "Scenes" in Western Germany, but some of the names in the "Scenes" are French, and he wrote the plan in French. Of course, some passages that we find in both Puškin and Mérimée could have been borrowed by both from Froissart's "Chronicles."

One thing is certain: to be able to creat a dialogue that would render with verisimilitude the medieval vocabulary and way of thinking, Puškin, besides reading history books, had to resort either to the few available medieval documents, like Froissart's descriptions, or to secondhand information from fiction by authors who had the reputation of realistically reproducing the speech and customs of the past. It is quite possible that he hoped to find that in Mérimée, who had won that reputation.

In "The Jaquerie" the young man in love improvises a tale—a parody of romances of chivalry—and thus betrays his feelings. He also offers to read a fabliau. In Puškin's "Scenes" the hero sings two songs. Both are of medieval inspiration; both are connected with the plot, a device already used by Puškin when he introduced folk songs in a narrative. In *Evgenij Onegin* the song of the peasants (a song composed by Puškin for the occasion) predicts the disturbance created by the intrusion of a man in the carefree life of young girls. In "The Captain's Daughter" the song of the robbers (an authentic one) predicts Pugačev's fate. In "Scenes" one of the songs is an adaptation of a Scotch ballad. It tells of a miller who discovers that his wife's lover wears spurs, which means that he is a knight, and the knights who listen to the song are delighted; while the opposite situation, a lady in love with a man from the middle class would be shocking. The other song is an abridged version of "A Legend." The complete poem written between 1828 and 1830 had fourteen stanzas. The version prepared for publication was shorter (there could have been censorship requirements to keep in mind). Now, for the play, Puškin eliminated stanzas 3, 6, 7, and the three last ones, and made a few changes in 10 and 11. Thus the Virgin is not named, only designated by initials, and the knight dies insane from unrequited love for an unknown woman. The song moves the lady in the "Scenes" to beg for the singer's life, even though the mere idea of being loved by a commoner was insulting.

Demidov believed that a reference of Mérimée to a fabliau "about a robber who enters paradise by the intercession of the Virgin Mary, who was the only one to whom he prayed" inspired Puškin's stanzas 6 and 14. If Puškin wrote "A Legend" after "The Jaquerie" was published, it could be the case, but this is not certain. On the other hand, we find that there are at least three "Miracles" in Gautier's manuscript about sinners admitted to paradise, though their allegiance was exclusively to the Virgin. In one "Miracle" Gautier describes a wicked knight as "so contradictory that he hated God and loved his Mother" (cf. stanza 6). The knight died unshriven, and the devil claimed his soul. There ensued an argument between the devil, the angels, and God, and the intercession of the Virgin saved him (cf. the last four stanzas).

Of the two "Miracles" that in Sumcov's view influenced "A Legend," one tells about a knight who missed a tournament because he chose to stay in church during special offices in honor of the Virgin. The Virgin took his place at the tournament, and defeated all his challengers for him.[13] There does not seem to be any similitude between this "Miracle" and "A Legend," except special devotion to the Mother of God. The other "Miracle" is about a youngster who put his engagement ring on the finger of the Virgin's statue. Years later during his wedding night he had a dream in which the Virgin angrily reproached him and claimed his fidelity as a jealous mistress would, threatening him with eternal damnation. The young man abandons his bride and renounces the world. Again, I don't believe that in this case we can speak of a similitude with "A Legend," except that in both cases there is a vision that changes the man's life.

Gudzij pointed to a third "Miracle" found in the Barbazan-Méon anthology.[14] There a knight in utter desperation and almost insane from love for a lady who rejected him is advized by a priest to recite one hundred and fifty *Ave Marias* daily for a whole year. Then the Virgin will grant him his heart's desire. The knight becomes a recluse in his castle and prays as he was told. On the last day of the year he goes hunting and gets lost in a forest, finds a dilapidated chapel with a small old image of the Virgin and falls on his knees, praying. Suddenly the Virgin appears to him as a woman of such awesome beauty and splendor that he almost loses his senses (cf. stanzas 2 and 3). The apparition challenges him to choose between her and his first love. He chooses the Virgin in terms that would be more appropriate to violent human passion (cf. stanza 13). He renounces women and the world, cuts his hair in a way that would disfigure him and becomes a monk until the Virgin comes to claim him as her bridegroom forever.

This "Miracle" is the closest to "A Legend." Even the first line in Gautier's text: "There was, I find, a knight," resembles Puškin's first line in an early version: "*Byl na svete rycar'.*" But from there on the characterization of the knight is absolutely different. Puškin does not even mention the knight's love for a lady. The description of the last years of his life in "A Legend" corresponds to the description of his life as a recluse before the vision in the "Miracle." In "A Legend" he becomes a heroic fighter. In the "Miracle" the Virgin forbids her knight to fight anymore. But there exists another "Miracle" in Gautier's manuscript where the Virgin resurrects a knight and sends him to fight the infidels.[15] There is a striking resemblance between the description of this fight and stanzas 9 and 10 in one of the variants of "A Legend." Latin exclamations (cf. stanza 10) are very frequent in Gautier's other poems.

All this, I believe, authorizes us to assume that Puškin was acquainted with the whole book of "Miracles." He may have had a superficial understanding of Gautier's colloquialisms and lyrical outbursts, but enough to be impressed by the image of the Virgin's knight, the *Marienritter*, as he is called in German, for the Latin tales on that subject had also made their way into Germany. There exists a tradition that the tale about the knight who had a vision originated in medieval England. Puškin told the story in the simplest possible, objective manner, as legends about saints were told in the oldest Russian and Latin tradition, and used the trochee meter as the most appropriate for rendering folk tales. Fourteen stanzas (but he soon discarded stanza 3 as unnecessary) created a new legend by means of blending several elements picked from various poems. Later, from that new naive legend of his own making, he eliminated several stanzas, changed a few words, and obtained a rational picture of a pathological case in the modern sense. This he fitted in the dramatic "Scenes."

Puškin discarded Gautier's mysticism and personal, highly emotional attitude toward the Virgin. The cult of the Virgin expressed in the same terms as passionate longing for a woman was something unknown and even shocking both to freethinkers and people reared in the Russian orthodox tradition, and Puškin must have recalled his *Gavriliada* when he wrote stanza 13.

Like the French critics of his time Puškin probably had only scorn for Gautier's poetical devices of which such phrases as "to marry Mary" can give only a faint idea. Gautier enjoyed creating puns (mostly untranslatable) for the sake of rhyming and stringing up rhymes derived from the same root with different prefixes and suffixes. Puškin's "A Legend" is rhymed in the simplest possible manner. We can even suspect that in stanza 3 the word *Ženevu* was introduced only for the sake of rhyming with *Devu*.

Research for circumstantial evidence can be very productive, but speculations should be confronted, whenever possible, with hard facts, and this is fraught with danger. In 1830 Puškin wrote a sonnet, "Madonna," in which he tells his fiancée how her appearance in his life fulfilled his longing for a perfect image of the Virgin with Child to watch over him in his home. D. Blagoj finds a connection between this sonnet and "A Legend" written sometime earlier. [16] He sees in the sonnet a development of the theme of "A Legend" finally culminating in a reversal: now terrestrial love is stronger than the cult of the Virgin.

But there exists a letter of July 30, 1830, in which Puškin writes in French to Natal'ja Gončarova that he spends hours in contemplation of a Madonna with Child exhibited in Moscow, because the Madonna is a perfect likeness of Natal'ja, and that he would have bought the painting if it did not cost 40,000 rubles. Should we accept the sonnet simply as a poetical transmutation of a real situation, or decide that Puškin, besides the real situation, was also inspired by the cult of the Virgin recently treated by him in "A Legend"? In any case, in the sonnet he refers to the Virgin as *Prečistaja*, her usual epithet in Russian litanies, and in the closing lines addressing his fiancée, he tells her that it is she who is now his "Madonna, *čistejšej prelesti čistejšij obrazec.*" Gautier de Coinci would have approved of such repetition of word roots at the end of a poem. Only he would multiply them until all possibilities were exhausted.

It is possible that "having examined innumerable" creations of French medieval poets and their sixteenth- and seventeenth-century imitators, Puškin was struck by the challenging difficulties their poetical tradition had faced and the manner in which they surmounted them. And just as he accepted the sonnet and experimented with the tercino (not only when he imitated Dante), he tried his hand on other medieval forms.

In view of the later development of Russian poetry, one likes to recall Puškin's remark on the penury of perfectly rhyming words in the Russian language and hence the necessity to search for new poetical devices. If we judge by statements in his poems, for him "rhyming" was synonymous with "writing poetry," and difficulty in finding rhymes was equivalent to lack of poetic inspiration. In one of his poems he expresses regrets that the rhyme was unknown in ancient Greece and imagined that she was the daughter of Apollo and Mnemosyne (Memory). In another poem, written in classic hexameters, Rhyme is the daughter of Apollo and Echo, and Mnemosyne is acting as midwife. Rhyme is also his "strange servant," and he is her "tormented lover." He knew that the important passages in "Boris Godunov" would be strongly enhanced by sudden rhyming. He stressed the importance of the appearance of rhyme in southern France, and though he deplored, as we saw, the exaggerated role of the rhyme in the poetry of the troubadours and trouvères, he could not help admiring their virtuosity if it was accompanied by genuine feeling, and did not degenerate in preciosity.

One of the requirements for certain medieval genres was to use no more than two or three rhymes per poem. In 1830 Puškin wrote a song (imitated from Barry Cornwall), : *P'ju za zdravie Meri*, in which 15 lines are built around two rhymes and the name *Meri* appears six times in rhyming position. This is very much in Gautier de Coinci's manner.

Was Puškin ever tempted to emulate the virtuosity of French poets on themes of his own and in situations corresponding to contemporary emotions? I believe that he did once as a very young man, still at the Lyceum when some poetry of preclassic romanticism, as he called it, may have been the object of reading and study. It is the *Pevec* of 1816. It treats the typically elegiac theme of a melancholy young man suffering from some vague, hopeless sorrow. The hero and the setting are those of Žukovskij's poems. But the construction is that of a *rondeau*, though it could be also called a *virelai*, the two genres being unstable and very much alike. The poem is built around three rhymes. The second line is identical in each stanza. The first three words of each stanza, repeated in the refrain, are of identical syntactic construction throughout. These are typically medieval devices. There is a caesura after the first four syllables of each line. The poem follows the usual progression of courtship according to the rules of the age of chivalry. There is a singer, and his songs are the Sweet Words of the allegorical poems on the subject of courtly love. The next step is the meeting, the exchange of Sweet Glance. And, finally there is the Sigh of the lady, the birth of reciprocated feeling.

The other poem is addressed to Anna Kern: *Ja pomnju čudnoe mgnoven'e*. Its content fits well with the medieval tradition of glorifying the lady of one's dream as a paragon of all virtues and as an inspiration. But the vocabulary Puškin uses is that of the nineteenth century and a typically romantic one. The medieval inspiration is apparent in the economy of rhymes, in the repetition of lines and phrases. There is even a deliberate challenge to the demanding public in the choice of words for rhymes: they had been used so often for rhyming that they had become almost stale. There are two different feminine rhymes, and they all have the sound *n* before the last syllable. The masculine rhymes end in *y* and *i*, and only in the last stanza when the mood changes, there is a truly different rhyme: *vnov'—ljubov'*. Three lines of the first and fifth stanzas are identical; phrases and words of the second stanza are repeated in the third one; the two last lines of the fourth and last stanzas consist of the same words with sound changes required by grammatical cases. This transformation of a negative statement (genitive case ending) into a positive one (nominative case) creates in the last stanza a triumphal note. This sudden change from despair to triumph is not medieval or romantic, but exclusively Puškin's dynamic style.

There is one medieval genre I did not mention: it is the so-called Noëls written by Puškin when he was a very young man. Like the sonnet, the rondeau, and the virelay, the Noëls were not stabilized as a form in the Middle Ages and underwent changes during the next centuries. The Noëls Puškin wrote followed the very complicated eighteenth-century pattern and were political satires as their models had been, while the medieval Noëls were drinking songs for various occasions, sung not only at Christmas time, because "Noël!" was an exclamation of joy for various occasions. They consisted of rather simple stanzas and were punctuated by Latin words. They were frequently improvised during a festivity and later forgotten; very few Noëls of that kind came down to us. Puškin did not include Noëls in his enumeration of medieval genres.

NOTES

1. N. F. Sumcov, *Puškin* (Xar'kov, 1900).
2. N. K. Gudzij, "*K istorii sjužeta romansa Puškina o bednom rycare*" in *Puškin, sbornik statej* (*Puškinskaja komissija Obščestva ljubitelej russkoj slovesnosti*. Moscow, 1930).
3. Gautier de Coinci, *Les Miracles de Nostre-Dame*, publiés par V. Frédéric Koenig (Geneva, 1955–1970), 4 vols.
4. J. C. L. Simonde de Sismondi, *De la littérature du Midi de l'Europe* (Paris, 1829), vol. 1.

5. B. V. Tomaševskij, *Puškin i Francija* (Leningrad, 1960) pp. 98ff.
6. J. F. de La Harpe, *Lycée ou Cours de littérature ancienne et moderne* (Paris, 1821). Part II, Book One.
7. *Fabliaux et contes des poètes François*... publiés par Barbazan. Nouvelle édition augmentée... par M. Méon (Paris, 1808), vol. 1, pp. 82, 347; vol. 2, p. 420.
8. This manuscript of the *Miracles de Nostre-Dame* by Gautier de Coinci is now in Leningrad in the Saltykov-Ščedrin Public Library. Catalogue Number: FR. f. v. XIV 9. In studies on Gautier it is usually designated as *R*. The "Miracles" mentioned in this paper are, according to F. Koenig's classification: I Mir 15; I Mir 19; I Mir 21; I Mir 28; I Mir 30; I Mir 41; II Mir 11. According to Mme Ducrot-Granderyo, who was the first to describe the manuscript, in *Annales Academiae Scientiarum Fennicae*, B. XXV, 2 (Helsinki, 1932), it would be: 17, 21, 23, 30, 32, 43, 62.
9. G. R. Deržavin, *"Rassuždenie o liričeskoj poèzii"*... in the one-volume 1845 edition by D. P. Štukin, or in the 1864 edition by Grot (vol. 7).
10. Those and other Puškin thoughts on the subject are expressed in: '*O francuzskoj slovesnosti"*; *"O pričinax, zamedlivšix xod našej slovesnosti"*; *"O stat'e A. Bestuževa"*; *"O poèzii klassičeskoj i romantičeskoj"*; *"O ničtožestve literatury russkoj."*
11. Cf. *Three Old French Chronicles of the Crusades*, trans. E. N. Stone (Seattle, 1939). Chapter 16 of the "Chronicle of Reims," p. 287, tells the story of John of Brienne, King of Jerusalem, who started life as a penniless knight.
12. N. Demidov, *"O scenax iz rycarskix vremen' A. S. Puškina."* (*Izvestija otdela russkogo jazyka i slovesnosti A. N.*, 1900), pp. 631–640. Prosper Mérimée, *La Jaquerie* (sometimes spelled *Jacquerie*) (Paris, 1928). First published in 1828.
13. The "Miracle" about the Virgin going to a tournament is not in the Koenig edition but is ascribed to Gautier de Coinci in the Barbazan-Méon anthology (vol. 1, pp. ix and 82). It is allegedly from a Sorbonne manuscript now lost.
14. Barbazan-Méon, vol. 1, pp. 347–356; I Mir 41 according to Koenig's classification. Translated into English in *The Tumbler of Our Lady and Other Miracles* (London, The Medieval Library, Chatto and Windus Publshers, 1908).
15. In the "Miracle" entitled "Saint Basile"; II Mir 11 (in vol. 4 of Koenig's edition).
16. D. D. Blagoj, *Tvorčeskij put' Puškina* (Moscow, 1967), p. 446.

"ARION": AN EXAMPLE OF POST-DECEMBRIST SEMANTICS

Walter Vickery
University of North Carolina at Chapel Hill

The aim of this study is to establish the presence in Puškin's "Arion" of connections with or "reminiscences" *(reminiscencii)* from Horace's ode to Pyrrha (I, 5).

"Arion" was dated by Puškin July 16, 1827 — three days after the first anniversary of the hanging of five of the Decembrists. It is normally viewed as an expression of Puškin's solidarity with the Decembrists, a veiled "message to Siberia." In this connection attention has been called to the extreme caution displayed in the manner of publishing "Arion." Puškin waited, just as he waited with "Ančar," for a considerable time — three years — before publishing. Also, as G. S. Glebov points out in his informative study of "Arion," the draft variants of the poem indicate that before publishing Puškin made unavailing efforts to switch the narrative from the first to the third person — presumably in order to minimize the dangers posed by a suspicious censorship ("*Ix* bylo mnogo na čelne"; "A *on* — bespečnoj very poln — "; "Liš' *on* — tainstvennyj pevec — "). The poem was published twice in Puškin's lifetime — in 1830 and 1831[1] — but on neither occasion did it carry Puškin's signature, again presumably to avoid harassment from the censorship. Moreover, Puškin excluded "Arion" from his collected works. Thus, he never publicly admitted to authorship. The need for caution was paramount.[2]

71

We therefore approach "Arion" on three different but not mutually exclusive levels:

1. We can take the poem at face value, without political overtones or undertones, as it was presumably taken by the censor.

2. We can see it as a veiled "message to Siberia," i.e., as an expression of Puškin's closeness to his Decembrist friends.

3. In view of the caution attending its publication, we can legitimately raise the question as to whether there are not other elements in the poem which escaped the notice of both the censor and of those who were able to recognize the parallels between the narrative of the poem and Puškin's relationship to the Decembrists. One such element is, in our opinion, brought to light by a comparison of Puškin's "Arion" (with variants) and Horace's ode to Pyrrha.

The main thrust of the Puškin scholarship devoted to "Arion" and its place in the literary tradition has been to emphasize the basic difference between the Puškin poem and the Greek legend of Arion. In the legend Arion is treated with great hostility by the sailors, who threaten his life; whereas in Puškin's poem, on the contrary, the singer is joined by friendship with the other members of the crew, who represent the Decembrists. Thus, for example, "our clever helmsman" ("naš kormščik umnyj") is seen as a reference to Ryleev or — more probably correct — to Pestel'. At the same time, one possible point of agreement between poem and legend — a point which cannot be read out of the poem itself and is not strictly relevant to the task of literary interpretation, belonging rather in the realm of background speculations — has been noted by scholars: the likelihood that Puškin thought of his singer, like Arion in the legend, as being saved from destruction by his art, both the Greek and the Russian thus being saved by the beauty and power of their singing.[3] The attention directed by scholars to the differences and similarities between legend and poem appears to have led to the overlooking of a somewhat different link between "Arion" and the tradition of antiquity, the link between "Arion" and the ode to Pyrrha mentioned above. Nowhere in critical literature have we been able to discover a statement to the effect that Horace's ode is a factor to be reckoned with in studying "Arion."[4] And if some statement has been made, it has certainly not received adequate attention. We here attempt to point out the significant parallels between "Arion" and the Horatian ode — parallels which are, in our view, an integral part of the creative process which produced "Arion."

Below we reproduce the two poems in question. Those words and phrases are italicized which are particularly relevant to a comparison:

Quis multa gracilis te puer in rosa
Perfusus liquidis urget odoribus,
Grato, Pyrrha, sub antro?
Cui flavam religas comam,
Simplex munditiis? Heu quoties *fidem*
Mutatosque deos flebit et *aspera*
Nigris aequora ventis
Emirabitur insolens,
Qui nunc te fruitur credulus aurea;
Qui semper vacuam, semper amabilem
Sperat *nescius aurae*
Fallacis. Miseri, quibus
Intentata nites! *Me* tabula sacer
Votiva paries *indicat uvida*
Suspendisse potenti
Vestimenta maris deo.[5]

Nas bylo mnogo na čelne;
Inye parus naprjagali,
Drugie družno upirali
V glub' moščny vesla. *V tišine*
Na rul' sklonjas', naš kormščik umnyj
V molčan'e pravil gruznyj čeln;
A ja—*bespečnoj very poln,*—
Plovcam ja pel . . . *Vdrug lono voln*
Izmjal s naletu vixor' šumnyj . . .
Pogib i kormščik i plovec!—
Liš' ja, tainstvennyj pevec,
Na bereg vybrošen grozoju,
Ja gimny prežnie poju
I rizu vlažnuju moju
Sušu na solnce pod skaloju.

We note the following differences and similarities between the two poems:
1. In both poems sea and wind play a decisive role.

2. In Horace the basic action is located ashore—somewhere in the vicinity of the attractive but faithless Pyrrha—whereas in Puškin the entire narrative is played out on the background of the sea.

3. In other words, in Horace sea and wind are a metaphor, whereas in Puškin they are taken at face value; they are simultaneously background and agent for the action described in the poem.

4. However, the metaphor in Horace of sea and wind, launched in the sixth line, is sustained throughout the remainder of the ode, acquiring by virtue of its durability and the frequent repetitions of the image—*aspera nigris aequora ventis, credulus aurea, nescius aurae fallacis, potenti . . . maris deo*—an autonomy of its own.

5. At the end of both poems the first-person narrator has suffered shipwreck, but is now safe on shore—by contrast with the "other" person or persons who either will suffer shipwreck or have perished by shipwreck.

6. In both poems the first-person narrator's wet garments (*uvida . . . vestimenta* and *rizu vlažnuju moju*) testify to shipwreck and escape.

7. The first six Puškin lines describe calm weather, and purposeful activity on the part of the crew, while the first four and a half lines of the Horatian ode (*mutatis mutandis*, since here the theme is love) also describe constructive activity. In both poems the activity belongs to someone other than the narrator—in Horace to the graceful young man, in Puškin to the remainder of the boat's crew, i.e., in both cases to those people who by the poem's end will suffer shipwreck or have perished by shipwreck.

8. Horace's opening lines are in the form of a question, whereas Puškin's opening lines are in the form of a statement. However, the question in Horace is limited in scope. The constructive and pleasurable activity is taken for granted, and is the equivalent of a statement; the question relates only to the identity of the youth who engages with Pyrrha in this activity and for whom Pyrrha binds her yellow hair.

9. In Puškin *v tišine* indicates the initially calm sea; when the sea is next introduced (*vdrug lono voln. . . .*), the storm has been unleashed. In Horace the sea is introduced only *after* it has become rough (*aspera/Nigris aequora ventis*); however, the initial calm is indicated by the whole tenor of the ode, more specifically by the

phrases: "Emirabitur insolens"; "credulus aurea"; "nescius aurae/Fallacis."

10. In both poems there is naiveté and lack of foresight as to the possiblity of calm changing to storm. In Horace we have already noted the phrases: "Emirabitur insolens"; "credulus aurea"; "nescius aurae/Fallacis." The relevant phrase in the Puškin poem is: "bespečnoj very poln." Lack of foresight in Horace is thus attributed to the unknown graceful youth who has taken the place of the narrator in Pyrrha's affections, whereas in Puškin it is the first-person narrator who lacks foresight. However, two assumptions are inevitable: first, the narrator's lack of foresight in Puškin is shared by the remaining members of the crew; second, not only the graceful youth lacks foresight in Horace, but also the first-person narrator clearly at one time lacked foresight, since he describes himself at the end of the ode as having earlier suffered shipwreck and as having now hung up his wet garments as an offering to Neptune. In fact, it may be safely assumed that any activities in present or future time, ascribed in Horace to the graceful youth are recapitulations of the experiences of the first-person narrator.

11. In Puškin, there is *one* shipwreck, with the crew perishing and the singer-narrator surviving. In Horace there are by implication two shipwrecks (and possibly more — "Miseri, quibus/Intentata nites!"); each and every one of Pyrrha's lovers will experience the joys experienced by the narrator only to suffer the shipwreck experienced by the narrator. Thus, in Horace the reader is not told that the narrator's successors in love will perish irretrievably. They may indeed survive, as the narrator has survived. However, the whole ode rests on the distinction drawn between the narrator and, on the other hand, the graceful youth and any other successors: the narrator *has*, though presumably bruised, survived, whereas his successors have their ordeal ahead, and the emphasis is not on their survival but on the catastrophe awaiting them.

12. Clearly the most basic difference between the ode to Pyrrha and "Arion" has to do with the theme. Horace's theme is love. Puškin's theme, taking the poem at face value, is shipwreck. Or, to inject a political content into "Arion," Puškin's theme is the Decembrist disaster. However (and we have already discussed the extended metaphor of the sea in Horace), this basic thematic difference is more than offset by the similarities noted and — more importantly — is resolved when we look at the two poems, as it

were, from a more elevated vantage point and recognize, as we must, that a thematic common denominator does exist: namely, the unforeseen change of fickle Fate, worked out in images of the sea changing from calm to gale, with both narrators escaping while the "other" person or other "persons" will suffer shipwreck or have perished by shipwreck.

Our comparison of the two poems leads us, therefore, to the conclusion that Horace's ode to Pyrrha is a presence and a factor in "Arion."

The intrusion of Horace into "Arion" should be no cause for surprise. D. P. Jakubovič has pointed out that "among all the poets of antiquity Horace, through Puškin's entire life span, takes first place in terms of the number of references made to him. He is even ahead of Ovid, although the latter had for Puškin a greater significance." Jakubovič further points out that Puškin's references are primarily to the first book of odes (which includes the ode to Pyrrha) (five times), to the second book (three times), and to the third (twice). [6]

It is, moreover, entirely appropriate that the ode to Pyrrha, dredged up perhaps from Puškin's lycée days, should have come to mind at this particular period when Puškin, and others, were so preoccupied by the still recent Decembrist catastrophe and when images of the sea, storms, disasters at sea had become for Puškin, as for others, almost synonymous with that catastrophe.

For Puškin images of sea, storm, disaster, and salvation were closely connected with his own predicament. As Glebov points out in the above-mentioned article, these images occur in his correspondence and poetry of this period. Thus, in a letter dated June 12, 1826, while Puškin was still in exile in Mixajlovskoe, his friend and fellow poet, P. A. Vjazemskij, had written him: "In your place I would write to the czar a sincere and convincing letter: I would confess to the pranks of both your tongue and your pen, pointing out at the same time that your words were never backed up by deeds, for you remained *safe and sound* in the midst of the *general storm* [italics added]; I would promise for the future to keep both tongue and pen on a leash, devoting my entire time only to *activities which could be openly avowed* (and most of all, I'd keep my word), and I would request permission to go for treatment to Petersburg, Moscow or abroad. This is my advice." Puškin did, of course, write the czar somewhere between May 11 and the first half of June. Vjazemskij apparently saw this letter in Petersburg, as he tells Puškin in a letter dated July 31, 1826. But he found Puškin's letter "dry, cold, and insufficiently convincing" and repeated the advice given in his earlier letter: "In your place I would write another letter and send it to Moscow. You undoubtedly have the right to consideration, for *you were not involved in the general storm* [italics added], but at the same time you must also, for the future, too, give a guarantee as to the legality of your conduct, i.e., a promise that you will *write only for publication* and, of course, having given your word of honor, never in any way violate your promise. For you there is *no other salvation.*" In two successive letters, then, Vjazemskij uses the storm (*burja*) as a metaphor for the Decembrist calamity. He twice singles out Puškin from the Decembrists as not involved. And he twice warns Puškin that his salvation depends on his writing only for publication or devoting himself "only to activities which could be openly avowed"—a condition which Puškin was failing to observe in writing and later publishing "Arion."[7]

Vjazemskij's second (July 31) letter is prefixed by a poem entitled "More." The sea in Vjazemskij's poem, as in Byron's famous passage in *Childe Harold* (Canto IV, 179ff.), is contrasted with the land. It remains unsubservient to man, and takes its revenge on man's arrogance, thus providing both solace to the poet and a symbol of independence:

> Sjuda poèzii žrecy!
> Sjuda, suščestvennosti žertvy!
> Ešče zdes' svetit plamen' mertvyj,
> Ešče zdes' živy mertvecy.

Puškin's poem in response, in a letter dated August 14, 1826, pessimistically lumps sea and land together: "So the sea, the ancient killer of men, is inflaming your genius? With golden lyre you glorify the trident of awesome Neptune. Do not glorify him. In our vile age Gray Neptune is the ally of Land. In all elements man is tyrant, traitor, or prisoner."

> Tak more, drevnij dušegubec,
> Vosplamenjaet genij tvoj?
> Ty slaviš' liroj zolotoj
> Neptuna groznogo trezubec.

> Ne slav' ego. V naš gnusnyj vek
> Sedoj Neptun Zemli sojuznik.
> Na vsex stixijax čelovek —
> Tiran, predatel' ili uznik.

We note in Puškin's poem "Neptuna groznogo" and in Horace's ode "potenti . . . maris deo."

This Vjazemskij-Puškin exchange preceded Puškin's return from exile. But in the period following his return, as the poet surveys the political scene and his own precarious position, the same image recurs in a poem which, as is now generally agreed, is thematically connected to "Arion." We refer to Puškin's "Akafist Ekaterine Nikolaevne Karamzinoj":

> *Zemli dostignuv nakonec,*
> *Ot bur' spasennyj providen'em,*
> Svjatoj vladyčice plovec
> *Svoj dar neset s blagogoven'em.*
> Tak posvjaščaju s umilen'em
> Prostoj, *uvjadšij moj venec*
> Tebe, vysokoe svetilo
> V efirnoj tišine nebes
> Tebe, sijajuščej tak milo
> Dlja našix nabožnyx očes.

The poem was dated July 31, 1827, two weeks away from "Arion," and the connection is obvious. True, as early as 1821, in an earlier crisis, Puškin had written:

> Pod *burjami* sud'by žestokoj
> *Uvjal* cvetuščij *moj venec* . . .

Both *burja* and *venec* were poetic words much used by Puškin. But in 1827 the context was specific and the reference was to the Decembrist affair.[8]

It is not necessary and probably quite impossible to establish in what version Horace's ode to Pyrrha came to Puškin — consciously or not — at the time he wrote "Arion." The original Latin was almost certainly familiar to him from his lyceum days. And there was no lack of Russian and French translations.[9] Meanwhile, there is one translation which is of special interest. We refer to the translation by Puškin's uncle, V. L. Puškin. This translation Puškin certainly knew. Its main claim on our attention lies in the fact, kindly pointed out to me by M. L. Gasparov, that the same word — *riza* — is used by the uncle to translate "vestimenta" and by the nephew in his "Arion." V. L. Puškin's version concludes:

> Ot gibeli spasennyj,
> Bogam kovarnyx voln
> Ja rizu omočennu
> V vostorge posvjatil.

A more substantive question arises. To what extent does our acceptance of Horatian "interference" affect our interpretation of "Arion"? Most important, in our view, is the confirmation it provides to the thesis that "Arion" required extremely cautious handling from Puškin and others. Noted above in this connection are the delay in publication, the omission of Puškin's signature, and Puškin's attempt to switch his narrative from the first to the third person. Extreme caution on the part of the first-person narrator is precisely the tone of Horace's ode, in particular his conclusion:

> Me tabula sacer
> Votiva paries indicat uvida
> Suspendisse potenti
> Vestimenta maris deo.

Indeed, one English translation of the ode ends with the warning:

> Once bitten is twice shy.[10]

Puškin, on the contrary, concludes with the assertion that he will continue to sing his former songs:

> Ja gimny prežnie poju.

However, we note, as others have noted before, that the draft variants of this line tell a different tale:

> 1. Gimn izbavlenija poju . . .
> 2. Ja pesni prežnie poju . . .
> 3. Spasen Del'finom ja poju . . .
> 4. Spasen Del'finom   poju . . .[11]

Clearly, a hymn describing and presumably giving thanks for the singer's escape is far removed from the final version. But it is close to Horace's mood. It is also close to the mood and title of Puškin's "Akafist Ekaterine Nikolaevne Karamzinoj," written so close in time to "Arion." In addition to the matter of thanksgiving and gift-bearing ("plovec/*Svoj dar neset s blagogoven'em*") which is present in Horace's ode, "Akafist" contributes a further point to our general understanding of Puškin's thinking at that time. The poet-singer offers to the addressee, Karamzina, his faded wreath or crown ("uvjadšij moj venec"). This surely amounts to recognition by Puškin both that his muse *has* been roughly handled and, by implication, that he will be forced (we recall the advice given by Vjazemskij) to put a rein on his muse, i.e., he will not be able to express himself with complete freedom. Admittedly, the thanksgiving, the gift-bearing, and the need for caution are completely absent from the final version of "Arion." But they are there as a relevant fact of literary history. They are present in the "Akafist," so similar in theme and imagery. They are present in the ode to Pyrrha. And there is no reason why they should be puristically eliminated from any consideration of the different factors which went into the making of "Arion." An understanding of the different strands of Puškin's thought makes all the more emphatic and impressive the proud and humane assertion in the final version:

> Ja gimny prežnie poju. . . .

The conditions under which sympathizers with the Decembrists worked to communicate with them and to bring them back into print were truly amazing. Even Benkendorf, Head of the Third Department, was "guilty" of one such act. Vjazemskij, Puškin, Del'vig, and others, and members of the civil service took incredible risks to reincorporate the Decembrist writers in the mainstream of Russian culture, to have them published, and to let them know that they were not forgotten. The conditions of extreme repression and the acts of extreme courage have been nowhere better documented nor more movingly described than in *Skvoz' "umstvennye plotiny"* by V. E. Vacuro and M. I. Gillel'son.[12] Under such repressive conditions complete frankness would have been impossible, self-defeating, suicidal. Under such conditions the publication of "Arion" was truly an act of courage—on the part of Puškin and others who were aware of the political message the poem contained.

NOTES

1. *Literaturnaja gazeta*, No. 43, July 30, 1830; and *Venera, ili Sobranie stixotvorenij raznyx avtorov* (Moscow, 1831).
2. See G. S. Glebov, "Ob Arione," *Puškin: Vremennik puškinskoj komissii* (Moscow-Leningrad, 1936–1941), VI, 296–305. For the draft variants of the poem noted here, see P., 3, I, pp. 593–594.
3. Glebov, op. cit. See Puškin's 1828 lyric "Druz'jam" ("Net, ja ne l'stec . . .").
4. Glebov's article, which is probably the most thorough study of "Arion" refers in a footnote to V. V. Vinogradov's *Jazyk Puškina* (Moscow-Leningrad, 1935), p. 197. The passage quoted from Vinogradov reads as follows: "Characteristic of Puškin's language are the freedom and boldness of his choice of Church Slavonic expressions, which undergo transformation, losing their 'ecclesiastic' (cerkovnobytovoj) or religious character." And Vinogradov gives the last four lines of "Arion," with the word *rizu* italicized as an example of this characteristic. Glebov's footnote then continues: "Cf. in Horace's ode 'Quis multa gracilis . . .' (I,5) the image 'uvida vestimenta'," i.e., wet garments. This is, of course, the ode in question. But Glebov carried his comparison no further. Nor does Wolfgang Busch's very useful *Horaz in Russland* (Munich, 1964) make any connection between the ode to Pyrrha and Puškin's "Arion." In discussing Puškin's own political position after his return from exile, D. P. Jakubovič ponders as follows: "Whether he [Puškin] was formulating his own position as that of Arion who had escaped, when he wrote the bitter words: 'And I dry my wet garment in the sun, beneath the cliff,' or whether he was mentally likening himself to Horace who flung away his shield and was happily carried from the battle field by Hermes, he [Puškin] must have felt keenly a spiritual dichotomy that was innate in his position as a writer." See "Kapitanskaja dočka i romany V. Skotta," *Puškin: Vremennik puškinskoj komissii*, IV–V, 185. But Jakubovič makes no connection with the ode to Pyrrha.

5. The ode to Pyrrha has been translated many times in many languages. It is notoriously difficult to translate. Well known in English is John Milton's frequently criticized but reliable version:

> What slender youth, bedew'd with liquid odours,
> Courts thee on roses in some pleasant cave,
>   Pyrrha? For whom bind'st thou
>   In wreaths thy golden hair,
> Plain in thy neatness? O, how oft shall he
> On faith and changed gods complain, and seas
>   Rough with black winds, and storms
>   Unwonted shall admire!
> Who now enjoys thee credulous, all gold,
> Who always vacant, always amiable
>   Hopes thee, of flattering gales
>   Unmindful. Hapless they,
> To whom thou untried seem'st fair! Me, in my vow'd
> Picture, the sacred wall declares to have hung
>   My dank and dropping weeds
>   To the stern God of sea.

6. D. P. Jakubovič, "Antičnost' v tvorčestve Puškina," *Puškin: Vremennik puškinskoj komissii* (Moscow-Leningrad, 1936–1941), VI, 110.

7. The two letters are in the 21-volume Academy edition, XIII, 284–285 and 286–290. The translations are from Joseph T. Shaw, *The Letters of Alexander Pushkin* (Bloomington, Indiana, and Philadelphia, 1963).

8. V. F. Xodasevič notes the recurrence in Puškin's work of such words as *burja, groza, tuča* and *grom* which tend to make their appearance at moments of personal and political crisis. See "Buri," *O Puškine* (Berlin, 1937), pp. 150–159. Puškin himself has indicated a link between "Akvilon" and "Arion" by jotting down the following two lines together:

[Začem ty burn ⟨yj Akvilon⟩]
[Nas bylo mnogo ⟨na čelne⟩]

See *Rukoju Puškina* (Moscow, 1935), p. 279. No less a scholar than P. E. Ščegolev at one time denied the link between the "Akafist" and "Arion." For his polemics with N. O. Lerner, see *Puškin i ego sovremenniki* (St. Petersburg/Leningrad, 1903–1930), XV, 27–33, 171–174, 175–178. On one point Lerner was certainly right: the connection exists.

9. The V. L. Puškin version appeared in *Vestnik Evropy*, 1808, č. 38, and was reprinted in the 1895 St. Petersburg edition of his works, edited by

V.I. Saitov, p. 66. Two pre-1827 French translations available to me are in *Les poésies d'Horace, traduites en françois par le R.P. Sanadon de la Compagnie de Jésus* (Amsterdam and Leipzig, 1756), II, 67, and *Oeuvres d'Horace, traduites en vers par Pierre Daru* (Paris, 1804), p. 59. An 1816 edition of the latter work is listed as item no. 1001 in Puškin's library. (See "Biblioteka A. S. Puškina," *Puškin i ego sovremenniki*, ix–x, 252). The pages were uncut. Neither of these translations does justice to the original. Not only that: in place of the "wet garments" it is the remains of the wrecked vessel which are consecrated to Neptune:

1. Je n'en ai que trop fait l'expérience; et ce tableau de mes infortunes que j'ai attaché au Temple de la Divinité qui préside à cette mer orageuse est une preuve publique que je lui ai consacré les tristes débris de mon naufrage, pour n'en plus courir le danger;

2. J'en fis moi-meme, hélas! l'épreuve trop cruelle.
   Mais par mes voeux enfin les cieux furent fléchis,
   Et j'ai de mon vaisseau consacré les débris
   Au Dieu de cette onde infidèle.

The wreckage, of course, fulfills the same function as the "wet garments," since, according to tradition, the shipwrecked sailor was supposed to paint a picture of his shipwreck ("ce tableau de mes infortunes," in Horace "tabula votiva") and dedicate it to Neptune. Thus, battered ship or wet garments: both in picture tell the same story. But obviously Puškin could not have used either of these translations—alone. He would have had to combine them with the original Latin or with a translation closer to Horace. Such a translation, in Russian, with "wet garments," is provided in the V. L. Puškin version or in Kapnist's 1819 translation which ends:

> O mne ž, — vselenna v xram svjaščennyj
> Obetna na stene doska
> Svidetel', čto ot zlostradan'ja
> Sred' burnyx izbežav zybej,
> Odeždy mokry, v dar priznan'ja,
> Ja posvjatil carju morej.

Deržavin also translated the ode to Pyrrha (1808); see *Sočinenija Deržavina*, ed. Ja. Grot (St. Petersburg, 1864), vol. 2, pp. 515–517. But in Deržavin, as in the French translations, there are no wet garments; in Deržavin we have a lowered flag:

No dnes', v znak moego spasen'ja,
Visit uže spuščen moj flag.

Horace would presumably have been surprised by some of his translators. For example, A. F. Merzljakov, V. Orlov, and V. L. Puškin all have Pyrrha's yellow hair coming down loose—in two cases over the bosom—instead of bound, presumably up or back, while Deržavin has her hair coming down over her eyes in strands, in obedience to a fashion in Russia around 1808, the date of writing, as may be seen from a surviving portrait of Deržavin's second wife; see Deržavin, op. cit. vol. 2, p. 516, for this information, and see vol. 2, p. 517 for a moving picture of Deržavin's boat with flag lowered. For reference to Merzljakov and Orlov, and to other translators, see Wolfgang Busch, *Horaz in Russland* (Munich, 1964).

10. Maurice Baring, *Have You Anything to Declare* (London, 1936), pp. 67–68.
11. P., 3, pp. 593–594.
12. V. E. Vacuro, M. I. Gillel'son, *Skvoz' "umstvennye plotiny"* (Moscow, 1972).

PART TWO
Puškin's Prose

"THE QUEEN OF SPADES" IN THE CONTEXT OF THE FAUST LEGEND

Andrej Kodjak
New York University

Puškin has traditionally been considered one of the founders of Russian realism who displayed some romantic characteristics mainly during his early period. Geršenzon's opening question in his article on "The Queen of Spades" included in Vengerov's edition of Puškin's works,

> Зачем понадобилось Пушкину рассказать такой странный, маловероятный анекдот?[1]

underscores the improbability of Puškin's inventing such an unrealistic plot. In the same article Geršenzon characterizes Puškin as a man

> с трезвым умом, с любовью к простому и реальному.[2]

After such a postulate about the author of "The Queen of Spades," Geršenzon's interpretation had to conform to Puškin's presumed intellectual bent. Whether the story sustained this interpretation was not the critic's main concern; rather his major preoccupation was Puškin himself. This fallacious presumption of Puškin's affection for realism has resulted in the consideration of only a few

87

signs in "The Queen of Spades" and, consequently, an inadequate reading of the story.

Two interpretations of "The Queen of Spades" are generally recognized. The most obvious and naive is the construe of the story as merely a ghost thriller. As Russian critics found this reading unacceptable, the search for another interpretation was on. Thus the first inductive attempts were made to uncover a sign system supporting the preconceived notion that "The Queen of Spades" could not be merely a ghost thriller and must be a psychological story. To support this interpretation, Puškin has included in the text a sufficient number of interrelated signs that are well known by this time.

The psychological interpretation of the story is based on two observations: (1) Germann's emotional state on the night of the Countess' posthumous visit and (2) the recurrence of certain numbers in both the card games and Germann's mind. Germann's feelings after the Countess' death support the first observation:

Не чувствуя раскаяния, он не мог однако совершенно заглушить голос совести, твердивший ему: ты убийца старухи![3]

The protagonist's mental state provides sufficient explanation for his nervous tension in the church at the moment when he is about to kiss the dead Countess' forehead and his first alleged hallucination occurs:

В эту минуту показалось ему, что мертвая насмешливо взглянула на него, прищуривая одним глазом.[4]

Those critics who have sought psychological overtones in the story are on solid ground here. Puškin had to add only the detail of Germann's lonely meal consumed with an inordinate amount of wine after the funeral, and the psychological background for Germann's second alleged hallucination—the appearance of the Countess in his bedroom—is well established. Germann's third hallucination at his last gambling session is easily ascribable to nervous shock due to the disastrous outcome of his card game.

A serious difficulty arises, however, when one tries to explain psychologically Germann's three correctly punted bets on the cards that the ghost of the Countess revealed to him either in his hallucination or in actuality. At this point the second set of observations, namely the numbers that pop into Germann's mind, is usually cited. Two numbers crop up in Germann's internal monologue long before the Countess' posthumous visit:

Нет! расчет, умеренность и трудолюбие: вот мои три верные карты, вот что утроит, усемерит мой капитал и доставит мне покой и независимость !⁵

The magic cards are the three, the seven, and the ace. Thus it appears that Germann has subconsciously determined two of the cards that the Countess would reveal to him. Here, however, the psychological theory breaks down; the third winning card — the ace — remains inexplicable. Furthermore, as to Germann's correctly punted bets this interpretation offers no better explanation than coincidence. Such a reading of "The Queen of Spades," which is one of the most tightly constructed of Puškin's stories, is strikingly unconvincing. It is also difficult to explain psychologically why Germann makes a fatal mistake on the third night and confuses an ace with a queen, as the designs of these two cards are not at all similar. In order to explain all these events, one must reserve some role to supernatural, evil powers; therefore, a fresh reading of the story is necessary.

In the course of analyzing "The Queen of Spades," one discovers several clusters of signs, each forming a system interrelated with other systems. For the sake of clarity these sign systems are classified as follows:

The first cluster the reader encounters are the number signs. They are not limited to gambling and Germann's thoughts and aspirations but embody rather the entire texture of life, thus establishing an equation between gambling and life in general.

The second sign system establishes the role of the narrator as an eyewitness who reveals certain knowledge not normally available to mortals, information that could not be extracted from the story without his inconspicuous assistance. For convenience this will be called the narrator sign system.

The third system — the ghost signs — establishes the supernatural aspect of the story and is concerned mainly with the appearance of the Countess' ghost in Germann's quarters.

The fourth and last system consists of the Faust legend signs which require the support of the ghost and narrator signs.

These four sign systems interact creating a complex story. Like most classifications, however, this one has its faults. To assume that every sign has only one function would be wrong; some signs belong to more than one system. The task of the critic is to discover the major role that each sign plays without, however, ignoring its secondary functions and thus simplifying the entire system.

I.   THE GAMBLING SIGN SYSTEM

1. One of the basic observations made in the psychological analysis of this story remains useful and can even be augmented in the attempt to reevaluate "The Queen of Spades." The numbers three and seven do recur with unusual frequency indeed. In addition to the emphasized association of the numbers three and seven with gambling, they are repeated in many other instances. Time is most often counted by periods of three days or a week, as for example:

> Однажды,—это случилось два дня после вечера, описанного в начале этой повести, и за неделю до той сцены, на которой мы остановились. . . .[6]

In this passage the numbers three and seven are disguised by other expressions of time, but the reader knows that Germann has seen Lizaveta Ivanovna on the third day after Tomskij's account of his grandmother's adventure in Paris, and one week is seven days. Three days later a shop girl delivers Germann's first letter to Lizaveta Ivanovna, who in the next chapter counts the period of her relationship with Germann again in terms of three and seven:

> Не прошло и трех недель с той поры, как она в первый раз увидела в окошко молодого человека. . . .[7]

The narrator implies that Germann appears in the Countess' bedroom at 3:00 A.M. Before the Countess returns from the ball, the clocks in the house strike two. She undresses and sits motionless in an armchair for a short while. One may thus assume that Germann enters her room and that her death occurs around three o'clock in the morning. Germann attends the Countess' funeral three days after his attempt to force the secret out of her. Finally it is easy to conclude that the Countess' ghost visits Germann at about 3:00 A.M. on the third night after her death and approximately three weeks after Germann has learned about her secret:

Он проснулся уже ночью: луна озаряла его комнату. Он взглянул на часы: было без четверти три. Сон у него прошел; он сел на кровать, и думал о похоронах старой графини.[8]

If Germann thinks about the funeral for fifteen minutes, the ghost appears at exactly 3:00 A.M. Thus Germann's and the Countess' reciprocal visits are arranged symmetrically—at the same time of day and with the number three implied in each case.

The gambling numbers, three and seven, do not occur exclusively in relation to time; they also appear in most of the settings of the story. In the first chapter three men react to Tomskij's story:

Случай!—сказал один из гостей.
Сказка!—заметил Германн.
Может статься, порошковые карты?—подхватил третий.[9]

Several times minor characters appear in groups of three. In the second chapter three young servants help the Countess dress, and in the third chapter three old servants help her undress after the ball. Three ladies interrupt Lizaveta Ivanovna's dance with Tomskij. Finally in the conclusion she is mentioned along with two other persons—her husband and her young ward.

The number seven also appears throughout the story in the most seemingly insignificant ways. The story is divided into seven parts: six chapters and the conclusion. In the conclusion seven persons are mentioned, and in the second chapter while Germann is standing under Lizaveta Ivanova's window, four servants (three of them women), the Countess, and Lizaveta Ivanovna assemble in the Countess' study—again a total of seven characters.

2. The list of trivial recurrences of the numbers three and seven in settings seemingly detached from gambling and magic secrets could be expanded, but the above examples suffice to demonstrate that the narrator persistently incorporates a meaningful system of numbers into the story and that they are not limited to the gambling table or Germann's mind. Thus it is impossible to perceive the numerical signs in "The Queen of Spades" merely as reflections of

Germann's psychological processes. The occurrence of the numbers and their interrelationships do not depend upon Germann. In the conclusion, for example, Germann is placed in a mental institution in room number seventeen. The number of Germann's room is not essential to the development of the plot; yet the narrator, so economical in his account, insists upon specifying this number. If "The Queen of Spades" is a psychological story, and if all the numerical coincidences originate in Germann's imagination, then no explanation for his room number can be found. Germann neither imagines the number seventeen, nor does he consciously choose that room in the madhouse. Rather the number is imposed upon him.

The number seventeen represents the total value of the three cards laid on the table during Germann's last and fatal game. On the bankers' right is a queen (numerical value: three); on his left, an ace (numerical value: eleven), but Germann to his astonishment finds the queen of spades under his heap of money. Thus the numerical value of the three cards appearing in the last game is three plus eleven plus three, or seventeen.

In the madhouse Germann mutters continuously:

Тройка, семерка, туз! Тройка, семерка, дама![10]

The number of Germann's room and the words he mutters, which are mentioned in the same sentence, summarize his three games with Čekalinskij. The first night both drew a three; the second night a seven. The third night Čekalinskij drew an ace while Germann ended up with a queen. Thus the first set of cards that Germann names is the one that the Countess' ghost revealed to him, but the second set represents his actual cards. Germann's muttering thus reflects the vertical sequence of the crucial cards in his three games while his room number reflects the horizontal sequence of the cards in the last and crucial game.[11]

3. Gambling is associated with a monotonous movement from right to left and from left to right reflecting the motion of the banker described in the sixth chapter of the story. The player's right, like the banker's, is his winning side while the left for each signifies loss. The swinging from right to left and back and the constant change of fortune are not limited in the story to the gambling table, however. This motion also plays a part in Germann's relationship with Lizaveta Ivanovna and with the Countess. Lizaveta Ivanovna in

her last letter to Germann writes:

В спальне за ширмами увидите две маленькие двери: справа
в кабинет, куда графиня никогда не входит: слева в коридор,
и тут же узенькая витая лестница: она ведет в мою комнату.[12]

In giving Germann directions, Lizaveta Ivanovna naturally assumes
his orientation and indicates the door leading to her room as the
one on his left, but if approached from the room in which she sits
writing the letter, this door would be the one on the right. This
difference in direction reflects the disparity in Germann's and
Lizaveta Ivanovna's aspirations. Germann's only intention is to
meet the old Countess; thus to him the door on his right means
success. Lizaveta Ivanovna, however, only wants to meet Germann,
with whom she has fallen in love, and, consequently, the door on her
right leading to her room signifies the fulfillment of her desires
and thus the win.

When Germann arrives at the Countess' house, the same pendu-
lumlike movement is repeated. Germann opens the door on his
left leading to Lizaveta Ivanovna's room but does not proceed,
turns back, and enters the door on his right leading into the Countess' study. Germann and Lizaveta Ivanovna's interests and the
significance of their respective right and left sides are diametrically
opposed as are the interests and positions of the banker and the
punter at the gambling table.

4. Certain of the gambling signs introduced in Germann's dealings
with Lisaveta Ivanovna are also implied in his brief encounter with
the old Countess. Germann enters her study after having chosen
between the doors to his left and right. This swinging motion is
repeated in several objects in the Countess' study: clocks made by
the famous Leroy with pendulums swinging back and forth, fans
which when in use display a similar motion, and roulettes, a prototype of the contemporary yo-yo, which bob repetitively up and down
like the fortune of a gambler whose card may fall to the right or to
the left.[13] Finally the Countess herself duplicates this monotonous
swinging—actual or potential—of objects in her study:

Графиня сидела вся желтая, шевеля отвислыми губами,
качаясь направо и налево.[14]

The concentration of gambling signs in this scene is explicit and indicates one of the themes of the story—the equation of life in general with gambling.

5. In gambling a sealed deck is indispensable. Before the third and fatal game between Germann and Čekalinskij, each unseals a new deck. It may appear that Puškin added this detail to increase the significance of the moment, to build suspense, and to render realistically the gambling custom protecting the players against cheating. One of Narumov's guests suggests such a possibility in Chapter 1:

Может статься, порошковые карты?—подхватил третий.[15]

Among gamblers a seal is synonymous with reliability; a deck without a seal may be marked.

The narrator introduces this same significant sign in Germann's dealings with Lizaveta Ivanovna. When she receives her first letter from Germann which is

нежно, почтительно и слово в слово взято из немецкого ро-мана,[16]

it is mentioned that this false declaration of love is unsealed:

Возвратясь домой, она побежала в свою комнату, вынула из-за перчатки письмо: оно было незапечатано.[17]

By contrast, however, Lizaveta Ivanovna's sincere response which she composes with great care is sealed. She throws her letter to Germann through a window:

Германн подбежал, поднял его, и вошел в кондитерскую лавку. Сорвав печать, он нашел свое письмо, и ответ Лизаветы Ивановны.[18]

Thus Germann's letter appears twice: once unsealed and the second time enclosed in Lizaveta Ivanovna's sealed envelope which reflects her trust.

II. THE NARRATOR SIGN SYSTEM

1. The narrator's personality, perhaps one of the most significant components of Puškin's story, is revealed even in the seven epigraphs to the various chapters. The sources of these epigraphs are unusual; most originate in private correspondence or conversations. Only two of the seven epigraphs are taken from published sources: one from a book on fortune-telling and one attributed to the Swedish mystic, Emmanuel Swedenborg, although this quotation has never been found in his writings and may be Puškin's own invention. Thus the narrator distinguishes himself by displaying his extraordinary access to private conversations and correspondence unrelated to the lives of the characters and, secondly, by his interest in literature dealing with extrasensory perception and supernatural phenomena.

Puškin has seemingly inconsistently endowed his narrator with several viewpoints. At the very beginning of the story the narrator is an eyewitness physically present.[19] In the first half of the second chapter he acquires some intimate knowledge of the former and present life styles of the old Countess and further demonstrates his omniscience by penetrating the characters' minds. With Germann's entrance into the Countess' house the narrator resumes the role of eyewitness while maintaining his omniscience. In the last two chapters and in the conclusion he becomes in addition a commentator disclosing his narrative strategy and revealing not only his viewpoint but also his knowledge of certain aspects of the universe concealed from mortals.

The narrator's role of commentator on his own strategy is the most important for the present study. The first instance in which the narrator appears in this role occurs early in the story and indicates that he does not include in his account all the information that is available to him but rather carefully selects certain facts. It also becomes clear that he makes his selections with a certain objective so that the facts he records are meaningful and purposeful. This is already clear when he characterizes Germann:

Он имел сильные страсти и огненное воображение, но твердость спасла его от обыкновенных заблуждений молодости. Так, например, будучи в душе игрок, никогда не брал он карты в руки. . . .[20]

Germann's strong character has doubtless saved him from many temptations, but the narrator selects only one that is relevant to the story and lays his device bare with the phrase:

Так, например, будучи в душе игрок, . . .

indicating to the reader that other aspects of Germann's past are omitted.

2. Another striking instance in which the narrator reveals his strategy occurs in the first paragraph of the sixth chapter:

Тройка, семерка, туз—скоро заслонили в воображении Германна образ мервой старухи. Тройка, семерка, туз—не выходили из его головы и шевелились на его губах. Увидев молодую девушку, он говорил:—Как она стройна! . . . Настоящая тройка червонная—У него спрашивали:—который час,—он отвечал:—без пяти минут семерка.—Всякий пузатый мужчина напоминал ему туза. Тройка, семерка, туз—преследовали его во сне, принимая все возможные виды: тройка цвела перед ним в образе пышного грандифлора, семерка представлялась готическими воротами, туз огромным пауком.[21]

The initial indication that the narrator is again making a purposeful selection from continual recurrences of the images suggesting the three cards is

Тройка, семерка, туз—не выходили из его головы и шевелились на его губах.

This introductory statement establishes the fact that these three cards are constantly on Germann's mind. The following text relating his daily perceptions to the three cards indicates that the narrator takes care in his selection of the random images bombarding Germann to preserve the sequence established by the Countess. Clearly the reader is not merely privy to Germann's thoughts and dreams but has the benefit of the narrator's editing which establishes two sets of images reflecting, emphasizing, and supplementing one another.

The first consists of a young girl, time, and an older man. The concepts are so basic that together they create a symbolic sequence suggesting the universal model of youth, passing time, and old age. The second tripartite set consists of a flower, a gothic gate, and a spider. The latter triptych elevates the first set to a higher level, adding to it an absolute sense suggesting fertility, historical time or successive generations, and finally destruction or death.

These two sets of images selected by the narrator from Germann's associations complement each other vertically as well. The young girl is linked with the flower; time, with the gothic gate; and the old man, with the spider. Finally the flower is associated with youth and potential motherhood; daily time becomes historic time; and the old man becomes a symbol of death—the spider. The two sets of images also complement each other in terms of the natural daily cycle. The first set represents Germann's conscious responses; the second, his subconscious associations. The first set occurs while Germann is awake; the second, while asleep. Thus the images embrace the diurnal-nocturnal cycle to include the totality of human awareness. The narrator apparently is presenting a hyperbolic reflection of Germann's mania, for he virtually equates the universe with the three magic cards that symbolize the controlling or ruling power of the gambling table.[22]

The second bit of information introduced by the narrator is less obvious than the first but equally important. The narrator implies that the metonymical associations of a half-insane gambler are not coincidences that may be dismissed but an important message from the narrator himself whose perceptions far exceed those of ordinary mortals and approximate those of supernatural beings.

3. The same purposeful selection of certain information can be seen in the description of the Countess' funeral in Chapter 5.

Молодой архиерей произнес надгробное слово. В простых и трогательных выражениях представил он мирное успение праведницы, которой долгие годы были тихим, умилительным приготовлением к христианской кончине. «Ангел смерти обрел ее,—сказал оратор,—бодрствующую в помышлениях благих и в ожидании жениха полунощного.»[23]

The contrast between the bishop's pious rhetoric and reality is already well established in the indirect rendering of his remarks. *Mirnoe uspenie* contrasts with *podnjala ruku, kak by zaslonjajas' ot vystrela. . . . Potom pokatilas' navznič'. . . .* The righteous woman,

pravednica, contrasts with her treatment of Lizaveta Ivanovna as
the Countess' long years of preparation for Christian death contrast
with her secret of the three cards and her relationship with the young
Čaplickij. The ironic effect is already well realized, and yet the
narrator selects one sentence from the bishop's lengthy speech to
quote directly. It turns out, however, that the images that the bishop
uses in this passage do not refer to the Countess so much as to Germann. It is he who may be associated with *angel smerti* and *ženix
polunoščnyj*.

Seen in this light, the evangelic imagery carries a blasphemous
and sinister flavor which seemingly plays no part in the development of the story and merely explicitly expresses the narrator's
viewpoint. A chain reaction which begins with the quotation from
the bishop's sermon and then develops independently emphasizes
the narrator's strategy in this scene. The morbid implications of the
bishop's imagery are lost upon Germann, who, eager to ask the
Countess' forgiveness, approaches the corpse. However, the sinister
irony of the bishop's remarks purposefully quoted by the narrator
is reflected in the reaction of the corpse:

В эту минуту показалось ему, что мертвая насмешливо взглянула на него, прищуривая одним глазом.[24]

The most important sign in this passage is the modifier, *nasmešlivo*,
which may be construed as the Countess' reaction to the bishop's
speech. Germann falls down, causing Lizaveta Ivanovna to faint
and to be carried out of the church, simultaneously provoking a
young relative of the Countess to invent the story that Germann is
the Countess' illegitimate son. This story whispered to an English-
man in the church ends with the anticlimactic response, "Oh?"

Thus the events in the church are perceived on three levels: (1)
the full awareness of the sinister implications unwittingly introduced
by the young bishop (to which the narrator and the dead countess
relate); (2) full knowledge of the actual cause of the Countess' death
(known also to Germann and Lizaveta Ivanovna); and (3) total
unawareness of all the implications (represented by the bishop, the
young relative of the Countess with his English friend, and the general public). Only two persons possess the highest level of understanding — the dead Countess and the narrator who shares
with her knowledge inaccessible to ordinary mortals.

4. Germann, the Countess, and Count Saint-Germain blend mysteriously into one group formally linked by the sound of their names and titles. In Russian the uniting phonemes are the "g," "r," and "n" and the consonantal clusters "rm" and "gr": *Germann, grafinja, graf Sen–Žermen*. The spelling of "Germain" in French is almost identical to the spelling of Germann's name in Russian, which underscores even more definitely some meaningful relationship between these two characters. The narrator includes the Countess in this group of characters by carefully omitting her last name and disassociates her grandson by changing his title. The last name of the Countess must be the same as that of her grandson, for Paul Tomskij is the offspring of her son, Alexander. Thus the Countess must be Grafinja Tomskaja. Furthermore, as we learn from Prince Tomskij in the first chapter, his maternal uncle, Ivan Il'ič, is a count:

> Но вот, что мне рассказывал дядя, граф Иван Ильич, и в чем он меня уверял честью.[25]

It remains unclear how the Countess' son, Alexander Il'ič, Tomskij's father, acquired the title of prince. This detail is important, for it disassociates by sound *knjaz'* Paul Tomskij from his grandmother, *grafinja*, and the other characters with dominating "g," "r," and "n" sounds in their names and titles.[26]

5. The narrator has constructed a complex sign system linking the three characters directly connected with the secret of the three magic cards. All of them know the secret at some point. Count Saint-Germain revealed it to the Countess, and posthumously she discloses it to Germann. Tomskij uses the same epithet twice when talking about Count Saint-Germain and Germann. In the first chapter he says:

> С нею коротко был знаком человек очень замечательный. Вы слышали о графе Сен-Жермене, ...[27]

and later he uses the same phrase in reference to Germann when speaking with Lizaveta Ivanovna:

> От приятеля известной вам особы, ... человека очень замечательного.[28]

Both Count Saint-Germain and Germann are of German origin. As Tomskij recalls, Casanova claims in his memoirs that Saint-Germain was a spy, i.e., a man seeking secret information. Germann also acts like a spy in trying to discover the Countess' secret.

The narrator thus incorporates into his narrative a very carefully constructed system grouping certain characters and selecting certain details. He acts like a man with some secret knowledge and also a certain concealed objective. The role of the narrator develops more fully in the second half of the story and in the conclusion further reveals his peculiar nature by seemingly unnecessarily introducing the number seventeen. Thus three details (the two triptychs, the bishop's remarks, and the number of Germann's room) reveal the narrator's supernatural insight into human destiny and the universe.

III.   THE GHOST SIGN SYSTEM

1. The question whether the Countess actually visits Germann and reveals to him the secret of the cards is, of course, crucial for determining whether the story should be interpreted in a psychological or supernatural key. In the former interpretation the Countess' visit must be construed as Germann's hallucination; in the latter, as an actual event. The critics advancing the psychological interpretation always consider Germann's intoxication from a large amount of wine consumed at dinner the main, if not the only, evidence. A closer examination of the text, however, proves the contrary.

One of the most important details generally overlooked is that of time. The narrator offers all the information necessary for determining how Germann spends his time between the funeral of the Countess and her appearance in his room:

Целый день Германн был чрезвычайно расстроен. Обедая в уедоненном трактире, он, против обыкновения своего, пил очень много, в надежде заглушить внутреннее волнение. Но вино еще более горячило его воображение. Возвратясь домой, он бросился, не раздеваясь, на кровать, и крепко заснул.[29]

The next paragraph states that Germann awoke at a quarter to three. Thus there is a span of time between his meal accompanied by heavy drinking and his wakening. The narrator calls the meal *obed* which in Puškin's time meant the midday meal as opposed to *užin*, or supper. On the other hand, the narrator says that Germann was extremely upset the *whole* day; thus Germann's lunch must have been a late one and yet not so late as to be called supper. One may, therefore, assume that Germann dined at the latest by six o'clock, returned home no later than eight o'clock, and immediately fell into a deep sleep. This time scheme allows one to determine with sufficient precision that Germann slept approximately seven hours, which is normally sufficient for alcoholic intoxication to wear off. At a quarter to three, as Germann's behavior clearly indicates, he awakened sober:

> Он проснулся уже ночью: луна озаряла его комнату. Он взглянул на часы: было без четверти три. Сон у него прошел; он сел на кровать, и думал о похоронах старой графини.[30]

Germann is evidently totally awake. He demonstrates perfectly normal vision by noting the time on his clock in a room lit only by the moon. Sitting up in bed for some time, thus also indicating complete sobriety, he is perfectly capable of concentrating on a single, definite event — the Countess' funeral. The narrator rapidly enumerates all these symptoms of sobriety, so that the reader's attention is not attracted. A contrast to Germann's behavior, however, serving as a supplementary sign in this highly important passage, is provided by his orderly:

> Германн долго не мог опомниться. Он вышел в другую комнату. Деньщик его спал на полу; Германн насилу его добудился. Деньщик был пьян по обыкновению: от него нельзя было добиться никакого толку.[31]

Thus the narrator first introduces the misleading signs of Germann's intoxication and then erases them by veiled symptoms of sobriety after he awakes and by an implied comparison between Germann's behavior and that of his drunk orderly.

2. The narrator, however, is aware of the insufficiency of his strategy in establishing the reality of the ghost's appearance. Germann's proven sobriety must not necessarily convince a skeptical reader that the appearance of the Countess is real rather than imaginary. The narrator, therefore, introduces a second set of

signs. The appearance of the ghost is framed by two seemingly unnecessary details — the mysterious glances of an unknown person through the window into Germann's room. The second instance when someone glances into Germann's room is described as follows:

> Германн слышал, как хлопнула дверь в сенях, и увидел, что кто-то опять поглядел к нему в окошко.[32]

The adverb, *opjat'*, refers to the first instance, the most important one, which is introduced inconspicuously:

> В это время кто-то с улицы взглянул к нему в окошко,—и тотчас отошел. Германн не обратил на то никакого внимания. Через минуту услышал он, что отпирали дверь в передней комнате.[33]

While all the appearances of the ghost may be perceived from Germann's point of view, the first glance into his room is presented exclusively from the narrator's viewpoint, for

> Германн не обратил на то никакого внимания.

This fact is reinforced by the phrase:

> и тотчас отошел.

If Germann did not pay attention to the sudden appearance of someone's face at his window, he certainly would not notice a stranger on the street quickly step away from the window.[34] All these signs indicate quite clearly that the omniscient narrator who merely records events and the characters' thoughts from their subjective viewpoint has resumed the role of eyewitness and, consequently, has become a source of objective information.

In this passage the narrator achieves two important effects. First he extends the ghost scene with two symmetrically placed glances into Germann's window that may well be ascribed to either the Countess' ghost itself or someone who has escorted her to Germann's quarters. Secondly Germann has noticed only part of this scene, not the first glance into his window that is described from the viewpoint of the narrator as an eyewitness. The presentation of the apparition from two different viewpoints establishes a reliable, objective account of the incident. The ghost is neither the hallucination of a drunk man nor his imagination. Germann has a witness, although he is not aware of him.

3. After Germann's sobriety has been established and his witness, the narrator, has implicitly testified to the reality of the Countess' posthumous visit, only the reliability of Germann's memory of the Countess' message remains questionable. The narrator removes this last possible objection by having Germann record the events of the night:

Германн возвратился в свою комнату, засветил свечку, и записал свое видение.[35]

IV. THE FAUST LEGEND SIGN SYSTEM

1. The acoustic and graphic signs uniting one group of characters that have already been discussed acquire special importance in the analysis of the Countess' funeral. The passage from the preacher's sermon chosen by the narrator introduces two images:

Ангел смерти обрел ее,—сказал оратор,—бодрствующую в помышлениях благих и в ожидании жениха полунощного.[36]

Both the angel of death and the midnight groom are directly associated with Germann. The two images are not identical, however; the angel is merely an instrument, a messenger of death, whereas the midnight groom is the lord, the possessor who arrives to claim what belongs to him. Thus Germann's role in the Countess' bedroom broadens, incorporating simultaneously the instrumental and imperative functions, servile as well as authoritative.

In this light the similarity of Germann's and Saint-Germain's names becomes important. Two pairs of interacting signs are crucial in this respect. One pair consists of two names—Germann and Saint-Germain; the second is the midnight groom and the angel of death. The latter pair referring to Germann also relates to Saint-Germain through the association of their names. Thus it is not only Germann who is in the Countess' bedroom at night but mysteriously also Saint-Germain in the guise of Germann. The Countess in that scene acts ambiguously, as is shown later, for she is apparently not relating to Germann exclusively.

2. Germann's complex personality is gradually introduced in the story beginning with the first chapter. At Narumov's quarters Germann displays his dual nature. On the one hand, he behaves like a calculating German; on the other, like a passionate gambler spending entire nights observing card games. Germann's complexity acquires further mystery in the fourth chapter when Narumov says:

у него профиль Наполеона, а душа Мефистофеля.[37]

This double image, which contains the first direct reference in the story to the Faust legend, recurs in Lizaveta Ivanovna's mind when Germann talks to her in her room. First she calls him *čudovišče*, echoing Narumov's reference to Mephistopheles, and then it strikes her that Germann resembles Napoleon. The narrator in his quotation from the bishop's speech also implicitly emphasizes Germann's dual nature.

3. Incorporating the Faust legend—the main elements of which are the revelation of some occult knowledge after the signing of a contract with Mephistopheles and finally the devil's collection of his due in the form of a human soul—Puškin has created a complex story with characters with interchangeable roles. It is the contract between the Countess and Count Saint-Germain that triggers the sequence of events leading to Germann's appearance in the Countess' bedroom in a triple role as the midnight groom, i.e., Saint-Germain himself; the angel of death who moves the plot along; and finally the seeker of occult knowledge—the role of Doctor Faustus. In the latter role Germann begins to bargain with the Countess and sets his own very high price for the secret of the three cards:

Может быть [ваша тайна] сопряжена с ужасным грехом, с пагубою вечного блаженства, с дьявольским договором. . . . Подумайте; вы стары; жить вам уже не долго,—я готов взять грех ваш на свою душу.[38]

At this point Germann as the midnight groom changes roles with the Countess, for from now on she assumes the authority.

Only one of Germann's roles remains unplayed—that of the angel of death. When he points his unloaded pistol at the Countess, she raises her hand and nods. Her gestures may be interpreted in two ways: (1) self-protection and consent to disclose her secret or

(2) acceptance of Germann's price and a bidding of farewell. The entire text suggests rather the second interpretation. From now on the Countess assumes the role of Mephistopheles and becomes the holder of the contract with Germann. After revealing her secret to him, she also assumes the role of the angel of death, or destruction, and appears at Germann's last game as the queen of spades.

4. The more complex a sign system, the more times must the reader return and reevaluate the whole. In light of this analysis certain details that formerly appeared insignificant begin to take on meaning.

A few quotations may serve to shed light on the relationship between the Countess and Count Saint-Germain. Tomskij describes his grandmother's attitude toward the Count:

> Бабушка до сих пор любит его без памяти, и сердится, если говорят об нем с неуважением.[39]

Demanding respect for a dead man with a dubious reputation is unusual, especially when such veneration is expressed by one as authoritative and independent as the old Countess. This detail is important for a correct evaluation of the scene in her bedroom with Germann. The behavior of the Countess is ambiguous throughout this scene. When Germann enters, her blank face changes radically:

> Вдруг это мертвое лицо изменилось неизъяснимо. Губы перестали шевелиться, глаза оживились: перед графинею стоял незнакомый мужчина.[40]

This observation of the Countess' excitement is made not by Germann, who says:

> Не пугайтесь, ради Бога, не пугайтесь,[41]

but rather by the narrator who does not help the reader to understand why the eighty-seven-year-old Countess is so excited to see a stranger in her bedroom. Only the following events, carefully considered, reveal that she perceives the stranger as her master, Saint-Germain, whom she recognizes in the guise of the *neznakomyj mužčina*.

The entire conversation between Germann and the Countess is

devoid of real communication. Each listens to his own thoughts rather than the response of his opponent. Neither responds to the other directly. The Countess' behavior in chapters two and three contrasts sharply with her conduct on the night of her death. Initially she appears as an old but forceful and masterful woman, loud and authoritative. The verbs describing her speech and behavior are *zakričala* and *načala zvonit' izo vsej moči*. She uses emphatically imperative and humiliating expressions, such as:

Громче! . . . Что с тобою, мать моя? с голосу спала, что ли? Погоди: подвинь мне скамеечку, ближе . . . ну!—[42]

At night in her bedroom her behavior is totally different as the following phrases indicate:

молча смотрела, . . . казалось, не слыхала, . . . молчала по-прежнему, . . . казалось, искала слов для своего ответа, . . . видимо смутилась.[43]

She does not ring the bell as in the second chapter, although it must have been placed within her reach. She does not behave authoritatively with Germann but rather as a subordinate to her master. After his introductory statement she says:

Это была шутка, клянусь вам! это была шутка![44]—

There is absolutely nothing in Germann's statement to which the demonstrative pronoun *èto* could refer. It could indicate an adventure she had, perhaps in Paris with Saint-Germain, but since Germann does not mention it now, there is no direct connection between his request and the Countess' reply. Germann's reaction indicates even more clearly a misunderstanding between him and the Countess:

Этим нечего шутить. Вспомните Чаплицкого, которому помогли вы отыграться.[45]

The pronoun *èto* as used by the Countess and Germann has different connotations, and each character misses the other's point.
    An important detail in the Countess' response is her use of the

polite form, *vy*, and the rather humble phrase, *kljanus' vam*. Germann's reply is rude; the phrase, *ètim nečego šutit'*, indicates authority. The Countess' reaction is again enigmatic: *grafinja vidimo smutilas'* can hardly be expected from a spoiled and authoritative, old countess under normal circumstances.

This strange exchange of statements and reactions seemingly indicates nothing more than a misunderstanding caused by the Countess. What she means by her statement and why she is embarrassed by Germann's rude remark remain unknown and may be meant to pose an insoluble problem; yet this enigmatic exchange becomes significant at the very end of this scene. The Countess does not say another word before her death. Only Germann speaks and makes a fatal commitment to take her sins on his own soul. Finally he pulls his pistol and thus causes the Countess' death:

Потом покатилась навзничь . . . и осталась недвижима.[46]

The phrase *pokatilas' navznič'* indicates there is a space between the Countess' body and the back of the armchair in which she has been sitting all this time. This means that in the last moment of her life she was not leaning back in her armchair but rather was bent forward toward Germann, who stood in front of her with the pistol in his hand.[47] The Countess' precise position is important for evaluating her previous gestures:

При виде пистолета графиня во второй раз оказала сильное чувство, Она закивала головою, и подняла руку, как бы заслоняясь от выстрела. . . .[48]

The Countess raises her hand, according to the narrator, as if fearfully protecting herself. The following text, *potom pokatilas' navznič*, however, indicates that the Countess, while raising her hand, was leaning forward *toward* the pistol, a position unassociable with fear. Seen in this light, the narrator's comment, *kak by zaslonjajas' ot vystrela*, is purely descriptive rather than interpretative.

The Countess' nodding might indicate her agreement firstly to honor Germann's request for the secret of the three cards and secondly to accept his offer to assume her sins. The Countess has already reacted ambiguously and evasively to Germann's request. Now facing his pistol, she could change her mind, but his threat evidently does not impress her, since she evinces no fear. Thus one must interpret the Countess' nodding as her acceptance of Germann's offer.

The indispensable event common to the Faust legend — the sealing of a contract — is thus introduced twice: implicitly the first time in Paris and directly the second time in St. Petersburg, where a covenant is reached according to which Germann's soul is condemned in exchange for occult knowledge. The initial seeming misunderstanding between Germann and the Countess appears to result from her knowledge of some circumstance of which he is ignorant. The Countess seems to expect a night visitor possibly in fulfillment of a covenant she made with Count Saint-Germain sixty years earlier. This may explain her lack of fear both when Germann enters her room and when he pulls his pistol. The Countess apparently mistakes Germann for someone else to whom she does not speak in her usual authoritative way, whose questions she answers apologetically, and whose accusations may cause her extreme embarrassment. This interpretation is fully consonant with the implications of both the bishop's remarks and the Countess' ghost.

5. In Germann's bedroom the Countess speaks to him for the second time but in contrast to her first meeting with him now dispenses with the polite form, *vy*, and addresses him with the authoritative *ty*. At the same time she does not claim the highest authority for herself, for she emphasizes that she is reluctantly carrying out another's command:

Я пришла к тебе против своей воли,—сказала она твердым голосом,—но мне велено исполнить твою просьбу.[49]

The complete change in the Countess' personality serves as an additional sign of the reality of the ghost. Indeed Germann saw the Countess up close only once in his life and never heard her speak before they met in her bedroom. As the description of the Countess in the second and third chapters is inaccessible to Germann, it is extremely unlikely that he would imagine her behavior to be different from that which he witnessed. Apparently the ghost is not a figment of Germann's imagination. Secondly, the ghost refers to some other authority unknown to Germann — the Countess' master, whom, according to Tomskij, she loved beyond measure — Count Saint-Germain.

6. The Countess' change of tone during her ghostly appearance is emphasized by the epigraph to this chapter, allegedly a quotation from the mystic, Swedenborg, but apparently invented by Puškin himself. It reads:

В эту ночь явилась ко мне покойница баронесса Фон-В***. Она была вся в белом и сказала мне: «Здравствуйте, господин советник!»[50]

The point is the form of address. The baroness in the epigraph uses the polite form, *vy*, whereas the Countess uses the authoritative *ty* with Germann. The placement of this epigraph in the same chapter with the ghost scene clearly demonstrates that the speech of ghosts addressing mortals does not conform to a particular pattern.

7. In light of the Faust legend one seemingly unimportant and persistently overlooked detail in the story becomes meaningful. The narrator in the first paragraph of the sixth chapter says about Germann:

Все мысли его слились в одну,—воспользоваться тайной, которая дорого ему стоила.[51]

The high price that Germann has paid for occult knowledge cannot be traced in the traditional interpretations of this story. On the surface it appears that up to now Germann has paid no price at all. His murder of the Countess remains a secret from the law; his conscience does not trouble him; and the loss of Lizaveta Ivanovna's love does not disturb him. Thus the high cost in the narrator's phrase presumably refers to the covenant between him and the Countess. In this case the price is extremely high indeed.

8. One small detail becomes especially meaningful in light of the bishop's sermon. The midnight groom is a term taken from the parable about the maiden with the oil lamps (Matt. 25:1–13). It is not coincidental that the Countess' bedroom on the fatal night of Germann's visit is lit by an oil lamp and is the only room in the entire story that is so illuminated. Upon the visit of the Countess' ghost to Germann his bedroom is lit by the moon, and during his visit to Lizaveta Ivanovna's room only a candle is burning although it would have been quite natural for her also to have an oil lamp in front of her icon. Thus even this detail reinforces the scriptural metaphor of the lord appearing to his subject.

9. Finally the scene describing Germann's fatal game takes on a sinister cast. At this time he is surrounded by the guests and gamblers at Čekalinskij's establishment. Throughout the story the narrator has carefully segregated these two groups and adheres to that practice here:

Все его ожидали. Генералы и тайные советники оставили свой вист, чтоб видеть игру столь необыкновенную. Молодые офицеры соскочили с диванов; все официанты собрались в гостиной. Все обступили Германна.[52]

The last phrase, *Vse obstupili Germanna*, concludes the enumeration of observers whose only interest is seeing an unusual game and separates them from the actual gamblers:

Прочие игроки не поставили своих карт, с нетерпением ожидая чем он кончит.[53]

The contrast between these two groups is emphasized by their different interests. The laymen are curious about the game itself; the gamblers, on the other hand, want to see *čem on končit*. This expression carries exclusively negative connotations in Russian. The narrator ascribes this attitude to the experts, the gamblers comprising Čekalinskij's entourage.

Finally the same hierarchy of visitors in Čekalinskij's gambling house is apparent in the last scene when Germann discovers the queen of spades in place of his ace:

Германн стоял неподвижно. Когда отошел он от стола, поднялся шумный говор.—Славно спонтировал! говорили игроки.[54]

The public merely creates noise when discussing the event while the comment of the gamblers is precisely conveyed to the reader. Their last remark is highly controversial. Whom did they have in mind when they exclaimed '*Slavno spontiroval!*'? There was only one punter, Germann, who lost and whose punting thus could not possibly provoke praise. One may argue that the gamblers' remark is ironic. Two grammatical factors, however, mitigate against this explanation. Irony does not tolerate repetition; it can be used only once; after that it loses its sting. Yet it is precisely a repeated remark that the narrator emphasizes by using the imperfective verb, *govorili*, and the plural subject, *igroki*. Thus the players are expressing an expert opinion rather than making a single ironic remark. Their evaluation of the tragic outcome of Germann's last game remains ambiguous at this point.

The circle of gamblers over whom Čekalinskij presides may also be controlled by Saint-Germain. After all, Čekalinskij moves to St. Petersburg just at the time when Germann is ready to test his occult knowledge. In light of Čekalinskij's mysterious relationship to supernatural, evil powers, his entourage—the gamblers—must also have some arcane knowledge and understanding of the events they witness. The only possible explanation that I have for their comment, *slavno spontiroval*, is that the subject of this elliptical phrase is not Germann but rather someone else. As the similarity of names and the various functional links suggest, the gamblers apparently mean Count Saint-Germain. Thus there are two punters confronting Čekalinskij—Germann and his double, Saint-Germain. Germann punts the first two times, and Saint-Germain punts famously the last time and also summons his devoted subject, the old Countess, disguised as the queen of spades who winks at Germann for the last time.

10. After having analyzed the formerly concealed Faust legend signs, one may find it interesting to see which of the signs Puškin laid bare. There are two: Germann is associated with Mephistopheles, and in his conversation with the Countess he alludes to a covenant with the devil. The two signs are usually ignored, for without the support of the additional sign systems in the story, the overt Faust legend signs do not carry any weight.

* * *

"The Queen of Spades" is one of the links in the chain of Faustian images found in Puškin and his only completed work reflecting the Faust legend. Other significant fragments based on the Faust theme are "*Scena iz Fausta*," published in 1828; "*Nabroski k zamyslu o Fauste*," also known as "*Adskaja poèma*," written in 1825; a plan for a dramatic work, "*Papessa Ioanna*," dated 1834–1835; and "*Sceny iz rycarskix vremen*," written in 1835.[55] In two of these Faustian fragments certain parallels with "Queen of Spades" can be found. In "*Scena iz Fausta*," Mephistopheles emphasizes Faust's ambivalent feelings about Gretchen. A similar duality can be observed in Germann's relationship with Lizaveta Ivanovna. One may find a closer link between "Nabroski k zamyslu o Fauste" and "The Queen of Spades." While in the former, Mephistopheles says to Faust, *"Prisvistni, pozvoni, i migom/Javljus'*,*"*[56] in "The Queen of Spades," Tomskij says about his grandmother:

> Бабушка знала, что Сен-Жермен мог располагать большими деньгами. Она решилась к нему прибегнуть. Написала ему записку, и просила немедленно к ней приехать.
> Старый чудак явился тотчас, . . .[57]

In Tomskij's narration appears the verb *pribegnut'*, which when applied to a person usually occurs in a religious context or emphasizes a difference in power, authority, or position. The introduction of this verb implies Saint-Germain's supernatural authority, which makes his prompt arrival described in an almost identical manner by Mephistopheles appear even more striking.

Dishonest card games seem to be characteristic of Puškin's "diabolic cycle." In *"Nabroski k zamyslu o Fauste"* death plays cards and cheats her partner, and a queen and an ace appear on the table as in the last scene of "The Queen of Spades" in which a kind of cheating also occurs. "The Queen of Spades" is even more closely related to Puškin's orally narrated story, *"Uedinennyj domik na Vasil'evskom,"* in which a card game also takes place, and some kind of covenant with the devil is either negotiated or sealed. A prose fragment, *"Naden'ka,"* also contains a gambling scene in which there appears a dishonest banker of Polish origin reminiscent of Čekalinskij in "The Queen of Spades." In the remaining two fragments, *"Papessa Ioanna"* and *"Sceny iz rycarskix vremen,"* the development of the Faust theme apparently took a totally different direction from that in "The Queen of Spades."

There is, however, a definite connection between "Queen of Spades" and another group of Puškin's works which were linked in a most original manner by Roman Jakobson in his article, "The Statue in Puškin's Poetic Mythology."[58] Puškin's works that Jakobson focuses on are "The Stone Guest," "The Bronze Horseman," and "The Tale of the Golden Cockerel." The title of each of these works indicates the protagonist—a moving statue—and the material of which it is made.[59] It is essential that all these statues are models of living beings, and all of them begin to move at the denouement and destroy the character who has previously offended them. This set of observations applies almost literally to "The Queen of Spades" as well. A playing card is not a statue, of course, but it is not merely a picture either. It possesses a statuelike quality, suggesting, for example, a chess piece. The card lends itself to interpretation as a statue, especially when in the jargon of the gamblers the verb "to stand" is used in connection with the queen:

Германн вздрогнул: в самом деле, вместо туза у него стояла пиковая дама.[60]

The queen of spades acts like a statue that comes alive and also serves as the title of the story. The title contains an equivalent of the epithets in the other titles of Puškin's works studied by Jakobson — *mednyi, kamennyi, zolotoj*. The epithet, *pikovaja*, of course, does not indicate a material but distinguishes the card in the only way possible — by suit — and thus parallels the materials used as adjectives to describe the other statues.

As the bronze horseman, the statue of the commander, and the golden cockerel are controlled by a mysterious, extrinsic power and act in accordance with its will, so does the queen of spades serve her master, Saint-Germain, and, as the other statues destroy their offender, she destroys Germann. The victims insult and/or kill the human beings associated with or represented by the statues. Eugene insults Peter; Don Juan offends and kills the commander; and Czar Dadon insults and kills the eunuch. The plot of "The Queen of Spades" echoes this pattern: Germann calls the old Countess "*staraja ved'ma*" and pulls his pistol.

Even more important, however, is the almost exact parallel between the plots of Puškin's three works studied by Jakobson and that of "The Queen of Spades." Jakobson's scheme is threefold: (1) A weary man desires a woman; (2) a statue, or more exactly, a being identified with a statue, has a mysterious, unfathomable power over the woman; (3) after a vain struggle the man is destroyed by the statue, and the woman disappears.[61] With only slight modifications these points are applicable to "The Queen of Spades." Impatient to attain financial independence and social status, Germann seeks a change of fortune through a woman, the old Countess, and indirectly through Lizaveta Ivanovna. It is interesting that both these women are controlled by extrinsic powers: Lizaveta Ivanovna by the Countess, who later becomes the queen of spades, and the Countess by Count Saint-Germain. Presumably he forbids the Countess to reveal her secret to anyone, including Germann (whose mention of Čaplickij embarrasses her), then he sends the Countess' ghost to reveal the secret to Germann, and finally destroys him through a moving, statuelike figure — the winking queen of spades.

The scheme in Puškin's three works as established by Jakobson grows more complex in "The Queen of Spades" but remains basically the same. The roles of the individual characters representing, for example, Faust and Mephistopheles, become interchangeable. As the moving statue the Old Countess has a complex function. When Germann enters her room, she appears almost like a lifeless object, or statue, set in motion by some galvanic mechanism. Though living, she appears almost dead while in her coffin she acts as if she is alive when she winks at Germann. Then another transformation occurs, and she appears as a ghost openly declaring her subordination to a mysterious authority. Finally she appears as a playing card, a statue "standing" at the table in front of Germann, winking at him for the second time, and driving him mad.

As Jakobson points out, static and dynamic states overlap in Puškin's works as do life and death. "The Queen of Spades" adds another contrasting pair of concepts which are constantly overpowering, interchanging with, and replacing each other. They are destruction and its victim, victory and defeat, sanity and madness.

As this analysis has demonstrated, there are several possible interpretations of "The Queen of Spades," all of them mutually supportive. It is interesting that the various readings do not conflict with nor invalidate one another. The only shortcoming of the earlier readings is that they are far from definitive because they do not take into account all the signs in the text. One cannot say that the most elementary reading of the story as a ghost thriller is wrong. Such a reading simply fails to address itself to certain problems that must lead one to conclude that some of the mysterious events are foreshadowed in Germann's mind.

On the next level of interpretation in which Germann's psychological state is considered the key to the entire story, some of the ghost and gambling signs are ignored while the ghost itself is construed as Germann's hallucination. As soon as Germann's intoxication undergoes examination and his three bets (two winning and one correctly punted but, nevertheless, losing) with Čekalinskij are accepted as a sign demanding explanation, the reader must again interpret the story in a supernatural key. This reading in turn leads to the discovery of the ghost sign system which does not annul any previous observation but rather shifts the functions and interrelationships of the signs. Germann's psychological state, for example, becomes an instance of evil inflicted upon human beings by transcendental powers.

The ghost sign system leads the reader to an examination of the narrator's role. From now on the Faust legend sign system which, interacting with the narrator sign system, broadens the scope of the story, adds important events, and thus changes the reader's perception of the plot and the content of the story without, however, voiding any of the preceding interpretations. Now Germann again assumes the central role not on account of his madness, however, but rather because of his covenant with the Countess.

The Faust legend sign system creates a new context for "Queen of Spades" and places it in direct conflict with Christian metaphysics positing the polarities of good and evil in a world dominated by God. In this broadened context a very basic characteristic of the story becomes apparent, namely, its creation of a one-sided, godless model of the universe. Thus the story lends itself to a theological interpretation and poses the question of the very existence of God or at least His role in this world which seems to be controlled entirely by Mephistopheles.

At this point one has reached the top of the spiral. After having made several turns, one finds oneself back at the starting point—the elementary, ghost-thriller reading—only several spirals higher. "Queen of Spades" is not a thriller anymore but rather a story that concerns itself with a theological vision of the world. The consequences of this change are far-reaching. Germann seems deprived of free will; he cannot alter the course of his actions through repentance as Goethe's Faust can. Germann, like the Countess, is entirely in the power of the Prince of Darkness. Furthermore, by subtly interchanging the functions of the characters and dispersing gambling signs throughout everyday life, Puškin creates a picture of pervasive evil.

When "The Queen of Spades" is viewed in the context of the Faust legend, features common to this story and the three works discussed by Jakobson in his article on the moving statue become more obvious. In these works the statues invariably represent a certain basic authority: the bronze horseman symbolizes imperial power; the commander acts in accordance with canon law; and the golden cockerel serves his master, the astrologer-magician who represents the power of knowledge. To this trio of images—state, church, and knowledge—may be added a fourth—the old Countess—the queen of spades—serving Count Saint-Germain, or Mephistopheles, who employs one of his most reliable agents—the power of gold.

NOTES

1. M. Geršenzon, "Pikovaja Dama," *Puškin, pod redakciej S. A. Vengerova,* (St. Petersburg, Brokhaus and Efron, 1910), p. 328.
2. Ibid.
3. P., 8, p. 246.
4. Ibid., p. 247.
5. Ibid., p. 235.
6. Ibid., p. 234.
7. Ibid., p. 243.
8. Ibid., p. 247.
9. Ibid., p. 229.
10. Ibid., p. 252.
11. J. B. Shaw interprets the number seventeen differently in his article, "The 'Conclusion' of Puškin's 'The Queen of Spades'," *Studies in Russian and Polish Literature* (The Hague, 1962), p. 120.
12. P., 8, p. 239.
13. M. P. Alekseev interprets the details in the Countess' study as a special device indicating the idiosyncrasies of Germann's perception. For example, being an engineer, he could recognize a clock by Leroy. Rather it seems that Puškin was much less preoccupied with Germann's psychology in this scene than with gambling signs which persist throughout his adventure at the Countess' palace. See M. P. Alekseev, "Puškin i nauka ego vremeni," *Puškin, issledovanija i materialy* (Moscow, 1956), vol. 1, pp. 76–88.
14. P., 8, p. 240.
15. Ibid., p. 229.
16. Ibid., p. 237.
17. Ibid.,
18. Ibid., p. 238.
19. This very interesting observation was made by V. V. Vinogradov on the basis of the closing sentence of the first chapter: *V samom dele,*

uže rassvetalo: molodye ljudi dopili svoi rjumki, i raz'exalis'. The first phrase in this sentence indicates the surprise of one of the listeners—the narrator. See V. V. Vinogradov, "Stil' 'Pikovoj damy'," *Vremennik puškinskoj komissii* (Moscow, 1936), II, pp. 107–108.

20. P., 8, p. 235.
21. Ibid., p. 249.
22. In H. B. Weber's article, "'Pikovaja dama': A Case for Freemasonry in Russian Literature," *The Slavic and East European Journal*, 4 (1968), p. 442, this passage was analyzed for the first time. However, it seems that the images used by Puškin are not of masonic origin but rather are found in basic folklore or superstitions.
23. P., 8, p. 246.
24. Ibid., p. 247.
25. Ibid., p. 229.
26. Another group of characters consists of Prince Paul and Princess Paulina, whose marriage is mentioned in the conclusion and who are additionally united by the obvious phonemes common to their names. A really puzzling group of characters united not only by the phonemes in their names but also by nationality are Čaplickij and Čekalinskij. Both are gamblers, and the three secret cards play a role in both their lives.
27. P., 8, p. 228.
28. Ibid., p. 243.
29. Ibid., p. 247.
30. Ibid.
31. Ibid., p. 248.
32. Ibid.
33. Ibid., p. 247.
34. The verbs in this passage are highly significant. *Posmotrel* and *otošel* refer to some unknown subject. Then follow two verbs referring to Germann, *ne obratil* and *uslyšal*. Finally, *otpirali* is a plural impersonal verb. The negative verb *ne obratil* separates Germann from the subjects of the first two verbs. The second verb referring to Germann, *uslyšal*, is affirmative and definitely indicates his perception of the following action. The verbs in the sentences at the beginning and the end of this passage lack a definite subject: the first two refer to an indefinite pronoun, *kto-to*, and the last has no subject. Thus the only person on whom this passage focuses is Germann, and his awareness of various events is the most important message in this scene.
35. P., 8, p. 248.
36. Ibid., p. 246.
37. Ibid., p. 244.
38. Ibid., p. 241.

39. Ibid., p. 228.
40. Ibid., p. 241.
41. Ibid.
42. Ibid., p. 233.
43. Ibid., p. 241.
44. Ibid.
45. Ibid.
46. Ibid.
47. Alexander Benua, one of the best and most thoughtful illustrators of Puškin, has obviously analyzed this passage and must have come to the same conclusion. His illustration shows the countess not only leaning forward but even standing in front of her armchair stretching both hands toward Germann. In Benua's nor in my interpretation of this scene there is no indication of the Countess's fear. See: *Pikovaja Dama A. S. Puškina* (Petrograd, 1917), p. 31.
48. P., 8, p. 242.
49. Ibid., p. 247.
50. Ibid., p. 246.
51. Ibid., p. 249.
52. Ibid., p. 251.
53. Ibid.
54. Ibid., p. 252.
55. See. V. Žirmunskij, *Gete v russkoj literature* (Leningrad, 1937), pp. 136–139.
56. P., 2, p. 380.
57. P., 8, p. 229.
58. See Roman Jakobson, "The Statue in Puškin's Poetic Mythology," *Puškin and His Sculptural Myth* (The Hague, Mouton, 1975).
59. Ibid., p. 4.
60. P., 8, p. 251.
61. Jakobson, op. cit., pp. 4–6.

NOTE

This article was already in print when an interesting study on "The Queen of Spades" was published which in many instances takes an approach identical to that of this article. See: Nathan Rosen, "The Magic Cards in *The Queen of Spades*," *Slavic and Eastern European Journal*, 19 (1975), pp. 255–275.

STRUCTURAL PECULIARITIES IN "PUTEŠESTVIE V ARZRUM"

Krystyna Pomorska
M.I.T.

Already Puškin's contemporaries had perceived the text of "Putešestvie v Arzrum" as something peculiar, as "non-literature." Our contemporary called it "an artistic puzzle" where "elements of form are hidden."[1] Such opinions are caused by the fact that Puškin's travelogue offers something opposite to the reader's expectation. First of all described facts do not seem to be selected according to any hierarchy of importance; moreover, there are no *events*, that is, the author speaks only of what *he saw*, and not of what *happened to him*. In a travelogue of the time one also strongly expected a specific type of reflections, according to the reigning pattern of a "sentimental journey," especially when the sensitivity of a traveler was stimulated by an exotic country. But Puškin's text neither does bring about such reflections, if any at all, nor is his Caucasus presented as "exotic." The hierarchy of facts is obliterated: death stands next to comments on "bad roads" or by a light anecdote about a Persian prince. Everything is equally important. Above all there is one peculiarity about this journey: no movement is felt; the text has a quality of a static description.

To explain all these qualities, so far intuitively observed, the question must be asked: what is the aim of the traveler? The answer is: to join the army of the general Paskevič in order to observe the battle. So the hero is not traveling in order to observe the area and to study it sympathetically, as was the case of the "sentimental traveler"; his endeavor is to reach one particular point of destination. Thus his observations stand as something of a by-product and not the major point of his journey. That is why they are purposefully presented as mixed, unsystematic, and dispersed, but this seeming "disorganization" (or rather the *expected* principle of organization) is compensated by other structural factors.

ORGANIZATION OF THE TEXT

The diversity of subjects observed and their purposeful mixture divides the text into disintegrated *episodes*. However, the integrating factor is their organization into very strictly marked paragraphs.[2] Indeed, each episode coincides with a paragraph, and there is no transition between one subject to another across paragraphs. According to the contemporary "stylometric" studies, a paragraph is "a repetition of similar semantic elements in contiguous phrases."[3] Or, in terms of another scholar, it contains a description that refers to "one and the same object."[4] Thus, Puškin's episode makes an ideal paragraph. Furthermore, the beginning and the end of each paragraph carries strong stylistic signals. Most often such a signal is a repetition of words which display semantic affinity, referring at the same time to the main object of description, eg.: "My ezdili v nemeckuju koloniju i tam *obedali.* . . ." "Čert poberi tiflisskogo *gastronoma.*" Sometimes such a role is carried by synonyms and antonyms, e.g.: 'Žiteli p'jut kurskuju *vodu* . . ." "Vpročem *vino* zdes' . . . v obščem upotreblenii . . . ," or "*Žizn'* Griboedova byla zatemnena nekotorymi oblakami . . ." "Samaja *smert'* . . . byla mgnovenna i prekrasna."

Without trying to classify all types of stylistic signals pertaining to the boundaries of a paragraph, we show only typical samples of such a signal. It can be thus stated that an episode in Puškin's travelogue constitutes a discrete unit of the text segmentation semantically, stylistically, and graphically.

So far two opposite factors running through the text can be discerned: referential diversity ("mixed" subject matters) and formal uniformity (similarity in the organization of the paragraph). Still closer examination should reveal the inner differentiation of a paragraph on the thematic level. Each episode contains some kind of a *paradox*, explicit or implicit. Be it a frustrated expectation of the traveler who confronts the real Caucasus with its legend; be it the meeting with Ermolov, whose abilities, temperament, and even his appearance ("golova tigra na gerkulesovom torse") create a sharp contrast with his being forced into passivity, instantly evoking an image of an encaged, ferocious animal. Or take an amusing anecdote about a Persian prince who considered a carriage as not a shelter but a trap! Or an account about the conflicting nature of Griboedov and his paradoxical life and death; or else — the traveler's mistaken assessment of the habits of the natives. All this can be reduced to the principle of a contrast verging on a paradox. Such an organization of the episodes introduces still another opposition against the similar organization of all the episodes, and so counterbalances the "monotony" of the whole.

There is one more function that the paradoxes carry in the text. They can be treated as a compensation for "sentimental reflections" that Puškin's travelogue is devoid of. The puzzle of a paradox stands for a traveler's "lesson" rather than "preaching" — the last being the feature of a sentimental journey. Furthermore, by connecting the message organically with an episode, Puškin avoided a digressive type of discourse (again a "sentimental journey" type), and thus endowed his episodes with an extreme coherence and compactness.

COMBINATION PRINCIPLE

We have already noted the tendency toward a discontinuity of the text. Episodes constitute a panorama of curiosities rather than a coherent system. They are strung together like an ornament — since the *organization* of each paragraph displays strict similarity; but the *diversity*, due to some other principles, makes the attention jump from one episode to another, as if at a display at the ethnographic museum.

The contiguity axis is thus very much weakened, and it is due to several factors. First of all, there is no causal relation between episodes because there is no need for it: the traveler passing by the large area does not regard the sequence of episodes as cause-effect stages if they do not create any chain of events involving himself as a real protagonist. The episodes are related to each other on purely *spatial* principle. But, curiously enough, although all that is being observed pertains to one area, yet there is no impression of the wholeness or even one-directedness. Therefore the episodes sometimes lend themselves to reversability, and the text's consistency is based primarily on the reader's knowledge of geography. Rarely the stages of some systematic changes are admitted: e.g., a transition from one climatic area to the other.

The organization of space is intimately connected with a *time factor*. The very beginning of the text, where one expects the starting point of the voyage to be mentioned, is very indicative in this respect: "... Iz Moskvy poexal ja na Kalugu, Belev i Orel, i takim obrazom sdelal *200 verst lišnix.*"[5] First of all, no time indication is to be noted: as to the space one does not know whether Moscow was a starting point or only a consequential stage of some former itinerary. One feels so even more because this *initial* phrase of the text is preceded by ellipsis points and thus can be read as a text formerly interrupted and continued—"*res porro tractatur.*" The important *space indicator* is the phrase: "no sdelal 200 verst lišnix"—it marks the space as an obstacle that bars the traveler's way to his point of destination. The text further develops exactly along these lines. The episodes have either no time indication at all, even in cases when it is strongly expected, e.g., the following samples of beginnings of the episodes: "Ždali persidskogo princa"; "V Gergerax vstretil ja Buturlina"; or time indicators are purely abstract: "*Na dnjax* posetil ja kalmyckuju kibitku"; "Mne *slučalos' v sutki* proexat' ne bolee pjatidesjati verst"; "*Na drugoj den'* my otpravilis' dalee'—with no indication of the former day in any concrete terms.

As can be derived from the quoted samples, there is no coherent *system of time*, the episodes constitute basically a timeless chain, and *that* makes their reversability possible. The final episode which falls under the same principle forms thus an unmarked ending, the absense of time factor being here the most important, next to other features mentioned above and valid for all the episodes.

The time factor, however, does manifest itself in Puškin's text very specifically: not as a time flow but as the extreme impatience of a traveler to reach his destination place.[6] The motif of such impatience is displayed in two basic instances: once, when the traveler strives to get into the deep Caucasus as quickly as possible and then to his final destination; the second time when he declines Paskevič's invitation to follow him further, and impatiently wishes to get back to Russia.

The first instance is described in the following way: Chapter I: "Neterpenie doexat' do Tiflisa isključitel'no ovladelo mnoju"; "Ja rešilsja otpravit' moju tjaželuju peterburgskuju koljasku . . . i exat' verxom do Tiflisa"; "Ja pošel peškom, ne doždavšis' lošadej"; "Mne skazali, čto do goroda Dušeta ostalos' ne bolee kak desjat' verst, i ja opjat' otpravilsja peškom." Then the traveler's desire to reach army headquarters as quickly as possible and the fear that he may miss it grips him. *Chapter II*: "Ja s neterpeniem ožidal razrešenija svoej učasti . . . ja vyexal na drugoj že den'"; "No demon neterpenija opjat' mnoju ovladel. . . . ja otpravilsja odin, daže bez provodnika"; "Ja sledoval [za turkom], mučajas' bespokojstvom; učast' moja dolžna byla rešit'sja v Karse. Zdes' dolžen ja byl uznat' . . . budet li ešče mne vozmožnost' dognat' armiju." The second instance (Chapter V), the impatience to get back to Russia, is marked by the repeated phrase: "No ja spešil v Rossiju."

Thus neither does the time factor create a coherent, sequential system, nor is it connected with space in an integrated way. It is indicated as a *set of leaps*, strictly personally perceived by the traveler as a "demon of impatience" ("demon neterpenija") — that is, as time passing too slowly. In this way, the space is emphatically treated as an *obstacle to be conquered in a minimum amount of time,* and *not* as an area to be systematically observed, investigated, and commented on, as a geographic wholeness. Consequently, separated comments on an area express *surprise* and *aversion* rather than delight, and thus, contrary to tradition, the Caucasus is stripped of glory and mainly of *exoticism.*

On the still higher level of interpretation the opposition between the static character of the episodes and the inner *impetus* of the traveler models a Sisyphean labor to conquer the stagnation of existence. The idea is further supported by a number of explicit statements pertaining to the futile efforts of the traveler: either the maneuver was poorly calculated (e.g., the way on horseback turns out to be longer than by carriage) or else the game was not worth the candle even though the aim had been achieved.

Since the contiguity axis in the text organization is weakened, the compensation is to be found on the axis of similarity. Reading the text along this axis brings about the most important message expressed in a set of striking parallelisms. We have chosen the leading images only, and there are two pairs of such parallels: (1) the meeting with Ermolov and the meeting with the Terek river (Chapter I), and (2) Griboedov (Chapter II) and the first contact with the war (Chapter III). The first pair is cemented by the image of a prisoner striving to get back to freedom. The exterior similarity is striking, and it was noted by Bicilli in a quoted article: Ermolov's main characteristic is "golova tigra na gerkulesovom torse"; the characteristics of Terek are close to a ferocious animal. Neither the man nor the river is satisfied with his *cage*; especially Terek is dangerous when imprisoned by cliffs and artificial weirs. All this, in turn, pertains to the situation of the author himself, who is striving in vain "to go abroad."

The second pair—Griboedov and the battle—display the following similarities. Having met the coffin with Griboedov's body being just carried from Persia to Russia, Puškin reflects a while on the life of his fellow poet. "Smert' ego byla mgnovenna i prekrasna," and yet *"Obezobražennyj trup ego,* byvšij tri dnja igrališčem tegeranskoj černi, uznan byl tol'ko *po ruke,* nekogda prosterelennoj pistoletnoju puleju." In the description of the first battle, in the following chapter, we read: "turki ... isčezli, ostavja na gore *golyj trup kazaka, obezglavlennyj i obrublennyj.* Turki otsečennye golovy otsylajut v Konstantinopol', a *kisti ruk,* obmaknuv v krovi, otpečatlevajut na svoix znamenax."[7]

Both pairs—first carrying the *theme of a prisoner,* second, the *theme of death*—destroy the legend of the Caucasus and the Near East as well as symbols of freedom, extolled so eagerly by the romantics, including Puškin himself in his young years. Having come to the legendary Caucasus, the poet not only becomes disillusioned as to its exotic and unique beauty, but, above all, he meets here enslavement and death inflicted in the most cruel forms. "The theater of war" turns out to be not a beautiful and captivating spectacle—as in the romantic poems, again—but a cruel and senseless episode of life. "Obezobražennyj trup kazaka" brings to mind the corpse of a fellow poet, treated in the same way, and that turns Puškin's thoughts to his own fate; it sounds like an ominous prophecy about his own end that has already been expressed at the same period in *Evgenij Onegin.*

Now, after all this, the poet's refusal to accompany Paskevič further becomes understandable. The reason for the refusal, though it is never expressed explicitly, is implicitly present in the symbolic imagery generated from the parallelism. That is also the reason for the strange haste to go back to Russia ("No ja *spešil* v Rossiju"). It is an escape from death and enslavement.

NOTES

1. "Xudožestvennaja zagadka," v kotoroj "elementy formy skryty," in P. Bicilli, "Putešestvie v Arzrum," *Belgradskij Puškinskij sbornik* (Belgrad, 1937).
2. This was noted by P. Bicilli, who saw in it an analogy to a strophe organization.
3. ". . . povtorenie v smežnyx frazax odinakovyx semantičeskix èlementov." See E. Padučeva, "O strukture abzaca," *Trudy po znakovym sistemam*, 2 (Tartu, 1965).
4. M. R. Mayenowa, "Spójność tekstu a postawa odbiorcy," *O spójności tekstu* (Ossollineum, 1971).
5. Ellipsis points at the beginning of the phrase are Puškin's; italics mine.
6. Cf. about it the quoted article by P. Bicilli.
7. Interesting that in the poem "Delibaš," written after the Arzrum experiences, Puškin comes forth with the same image of a beheaded man. The last lines relating the result of a "perestrelka" read as follows:

Delibaš uže na pike,
A kazak bez golovy.

СТРУКТУРНАЯ ТЕМА «ЕГИПЕТСКИХ НОЧЕЙ» А. ПУШКИНА

Л. **Ржевский**
New York University

Критическая литература о «Египетских ночах», этом сравнительно небольшом и незаконченном произведении Пушкина, весьма обширна. Очередному исследователю тут, кажется, если процитировать Твардовского, «ни убавить, ни прибавить». Ну, убавить, вероятно, возможно, потому что среди написанного встречаются и пустяки, но сказать что-то новое не так легко!

Многообразие написанного о «Египетских ночах» связано с особенностями их творческой истории и с гаданиями относительно предполагаемых продлений этого неосуществленного полностью пушкинского замысла.

В немногих словах—чтобы лишь вкратце напомнить—творческая история «Египетских ночей» такова:

К теме о Клеопатре, которая продавала ночь своей любви за жизнь своих обожателей, Пушкин впервые обращается в 1824 году, когда пишет стихотворение (историческую элегию) «Клеопатра». Через четыре года он это стихотворение перерабатывает, и оно в этом виде включается в текст «Египетских ночей», каким он печатается ныне. В 1835 году Пушкин задумывает прозаическую повесть, фрагмент которой представлен в отрывке «Мы проводили вечер на даче». В этой пове-

сти тема о Клеопатре как бы проектируется на жизнь петербург-
ского светского общества. Как пишет М. Гофман: «. . . . главной частью повести должна была явиться параллель: Клеопатра и современность».[1] Но эту повесть Пушкин оставил и
несколько позже, в том же, вероятно, году, начал новый вариант, где стихотворные строки о Клеопатре вложены в уста
импровизатора, которому собственно и посвящены все три
дошедших до нас главы.

В свете такой творческой истории структура «Египетских
ночей» представляется исследователю некой агглютинацией,
«склеенностью» написанного—и задуманного, структурного
фокуса Клеопатры—и структурного фокуса Импровизатора.

Многообразие критических работ о «Египетских ночах» и
объясняется такой склеенностью: одних исследователей инте-
ресовал мотив Клеопатры, его генезис, его продление; других—мотив импровизатора и предыстория этого мотива.
Такое раздвоение отразилось и в собственно творческих
откликах на эту пушкинскую повесть: сюжетно незавершенную
импровизацию о Клеопатре пытался закончить Валерий
Брюсов, а едва намеченную пушкинскую историю о Клеопатре
петербургской продлил сочинительски Модест Гофман.

Отвлекаясь от генезиса или гадательных продлений «Египетских ночей», следует вспомнить еще один аспект критиче-
ского их рассмотрения: утверждение, что эта незавершенная
повесть является «самым полным, самым законченным произ-
ведением нашей поэзии.»[2]

Слова эти принадлежат Достоевскому. Правда, еще раньше
Достоевского утверждал то же самое П. Анненков,[3] но мотиви-
ровал это утверждение глубоко и страстно именно Достоевский.

Достоевский нашел в «Египетских ночах» в теме Клеопатры
как бы предсказание и пример духовного разложения современной цивилизации, «погрязшей», как он выразился, «в неправде
и грехах». Причем, по мнению Достоевского, Пушкину удалось
творчески выразить все это в одном лишь моменте, эстети-
чески законченном и совершенном. Катков назвал как-то
«Египетские ночи» фрагментом. «. . . Неужели вы не понимаете,
—возражал ему Достоевский,—что развивать и дополнять
этот фрагмент в художественном отношении более чем невозможно» . . . И дальше: «Пушкину именно было задачей . . .

представить момент римской жизни и только один момент, но так, чтобы произвести им наиполнейшее художественное впечатление ... Так, чтобы по этому моменту, по этому уголку, предугадывалась бы и становилась понятною вся картина. И Пушкин достиг этого в такой художественной полноте, которая является нам как чудо поэтического искусства».

Такова аргументация утверждения насчет «законченности» «Египетских ночей».

Должен признаться, что до меня эта сопоставительная трактовка Достоевского—мир Клеопатры и мир современный —как-то не доходит, не кажется сколько-нибудь убедительной. Но вот утверждение о творческой завершенности и совершенстве «Египетских ночей» очень подкупает, и я напомнил здесь концепцию Достоевского, чтобы перенести ее с композиционного фокуса Клеопатры на композиционный фокус Импровизатора,—фактически ведь именно тема Импровизатора нам печатно и исчерпывающе дана, именно она оказывается творческой темой этой пушкинской вещи, то есть определяет ее построение и ее творческую плоть. «Поэт, как носитель высокого вдохновения, и общество»—такова конкретизация этой темы в плане авторского творческого самовыражения.

Утверждение это не ново, но и не повторение чего-то уже вполне установленного: образ-тема Импровизатора все еще предмет критических разнотолков. Так, например, в интересной работе Виктора Вейнтрауба «The Problem of Improvisation in Romantic Literature»[4] образ импровизатора противопоставляется облику поэта, что весьма спорно, а заключительное представление, будто повесть Пушкина «отказывает дару импровизации в какой-либо духовной значительности» (denies the gift of improvisation any spiritual significance) ставит, как мне кажется, пушкинский замысел на голову.

*

Тему «Поэт, как носитель высокого вдохновения, и общество» Пушкин развертывает, я бы сказал, в двух контрастах: прямом и интроверсированном. Оба контраста, как и сама тема, творчески исключительно для него органичны, гомогенны. Первый, который я назвал «прямым», находит идентичный заголовок в стихотворении 1828 года «Поэт и толпа»; мотив повторяется в сонете «Поэту» (Поэт, не дорожи любовию народной») 1830 года и в—того же года—«Ответе анониму» («Холодная толпа взирает на поэта Как на заезжего фигляра . . .»). Контраст второй, «интроверсированный»,—контраст двух ипостасей духовного облика поэта: обыденности и озаренности вдохновением; этот контраст, как известно, представлен в стихотворении 1827 года «Поэт» («Пока не требует поэта/К священной жертве Аполлон»), где состояние безвдохновенности определено вполне уничижительно: «И меж детей ничтожных мира/Быть может, всех ничтожней он».

Контраст первый представлен в «Египетских ночах» уже в эпиграфе к 1-ой главе. Вспомним его—в переводе на русский: «Кто этот человек?»—«О, это огромный талант; он делает из своего голоса всё, что захочет».—«Ему бы нужно было, сударыня, сделать из него штаны» . . . (s'en faire une culotte).

Контраст этот продлит затем в повести Чарский, сам одаренный поэт,—продлит в автобиографического характера рассуждениях о жизни поэта в «свете», которыми повесть и открывается. В этих рассуждениях—неприкрытая ирония по поводу светского небрежения талантом: «Публика смотрит на него (поэта. Л.Р.) как на свою собственность; по ее мнению, он рожден для ее пользы и удовольствия . . . Задумается ли он о расстроенных делах своих, о болезни милого ему человека, тотчас пошлая улыбка сопровождает пошлое восклицание: верно, что-нибудь сочиняете?» И так далее. Ирония эта—сквозная, меняется только предмет, но сохраняется тональность: «. . . если у вас никто не понимает итальянского языка,—спрашивает Чарского импровизатор,—кто же поедет меня слушать?»—«Поедут, не опасайтесь: иные из любопытства, другие, чтобы провести вечер как-нибудь, третьи, чтоб показать, что понимают итальянский язык»,—отвечает Чарский. В черновиках—еще беспощаднее:«. . . третьи притворятся, что понимают вас и итальянский язык.»[5]

Интересно, может быть, отметить ведущую в смысле поэтической экспрессии лексику этого мотива. Здесь прежде всего выделяется гнездовое слово толпа; оно командовало в относящихся к этому же мотиву стихотворениях, которые я уже упоминал,—«Поэт и толпа», «Поэту»—, обрастало в первом из них такими выразительными параллелями, как чернь тупая, бессмысленный народ, рабы безумные и прочее. В тексте «Египетских ночей» слово толпа встречается дважды, но я назвал его «гнездовым», потому что оно окружено здесь синонимическими родичами: так, дважды же встречается «свет» и 10 раз слово публика, причем не только в нейтральном значении «аудитория», но и в обобщенном, как в уже приведенном мною примере: «публика смотрит на него как на свою собственность». К этому же гнезду относится сочетание первый встречный («первый встречный спрашивает его: «Не привезли ли вы нам чего-нибудь новенького?»). сюда же из первой импровизации итальянца принадлежит слово прохожий, имевшее в черновике другой интересный эквивалент. Об этом стоит сказать . . .

Первая импровизация итальянца начинается так: «Поэт идет—открыты вежды,/Но он не видит никого;/А между тем за край одежды/Прохожий дергает его . . .». В черновике символ «прохожий» множится: поэта «дергают»; «Он верно дремлет,/Толкуют эти господа»—стоит в черновике, и вариант «эти господа» вместо «прохожий» очень знаменателен.

Противная сторона контраста лексически представлена так: слово поэт повторяется в повести 17 раз, художник дважды, талант—четыре раза; сюда же относится сочетание человек, одаренный талантом и душою. Но перейдем ко второму контрасту, где также и лексические наблюдения не менее интересны,—к контрасту двух ипостасей внутреннего облика поэта: его озаренности и его обыденности, может быть—ничтожности. Надо подчеркнуть еще раз звучность этого контраста в творчестве Пушкина. Представлен он отнюдь не только в стихотворении 1827 года «Пока не требует поэта» . . . , но в сущности и в метаморфозе «Пророка»: «И он к устам моим приник/И вырвал грешный мой язык,/И празднословный, и лукавый . . . ». Празднословие и лукавство и принадлежали одному из «детей ничтожных мира» до его перевоплощения. Тоже ведь и в словах Сальери, жалующегося на то, что «Гений . . . озаряет голову безумца,/Гуляки праздного», сквозит та же антитеза.

В повести «Египетские ночи» эта антитеза двух состояний поэта дана в эпиграфе ко второй главе, взятом из оды Державина «Бог» и отнесенном к Импровизатору: «Я царь, я раб, я червь, я Бог»; развернута же она в противопоставлении внешнего облика Импровизатора его таланту. Весьма необыч-

но для пушкинской прозы находим дважды в повести темпо-
ральный, т.е. преходящий портрет Импровизатора—его лицо,
вся его стать меняется, когда озаряет его вдохновение. Эту
перемену дважды же подчеркивает одежда—странная вначале,
во второй главе—он в ней походит на разбойника, полити-
ческого заговорщика или шарлатана; а в третьей—безвкусная
и бутафорская; противопоставление тут же и сформулирова-
но по-пушкински лапидарно: «Чарскому . . . неприятно было
видеть поэта в одежде заезжего фигляра».

Еще одна фаза контраста представлена в заключении 2-ой
главы: после первой своей вдохновенной импровизации итальн-
нец вдруг переходит к материальной стороне своего высту-
пления и обнаруживает—читаем мы— «. . . такую дикую
жадность, такую простодушную любовь к прибыли, что он
опротивел Чарскому . . .»

Нейтральна стилистически лексика портрета итальянца до
озаренности вдохновением: побелевший уже по швам
фрак, панталоны летние, шершавая шляпа, жалкий
вид и пр. Она сменяется романтической экспрессией словоотбо-
ра: «глаза итальянца засверкали»; в другом месте: «глаза
его засверкали чудным огнем»; «он затрепетал как
в лихорадке» и т.п.

Непременно нужно подчеркнуть, что в «Египетских ночах»
Пушкин стремился передать состояние творческого озарения,
которое называют «вдохновением»; в черновых набросках
повести есть у него замечательное выражение: «механика
вдохновения». Запись такова: «. . . захотят/публика.Л.Р./ви-
деть самое действие, механику вдохновения»[6]. И он тщатель-
но ищет самые точные для передачи слова. Вот строчки
из текста, описывающего импровизацию: «. . . он . . . гор-
до поднял голову, и пылкие строфы, выражение мгновенного чувства, стройно излетели из уст его». А вот авторские
поиски нужного эпитета—вычеркнутые варианты, как они
следуют в черновике: «. . . и пылкие строфы . . . и звуч-
ным голосом, и стройные оды, и звучная, легкая ода, и гар-
монические строфы, выражение мгновенного чувства, мгно-
венное изъяснение чувства стройно излетели, легко излетели,
легко и стройно излетели . . .»

«Механика вдохновения» в какой-то степени передавалась
Пушкиным и в его отрывке «Осень» (1833 год). Вот строфа

оттуда:

> И мысли в голове волнуются в отваге,
> И рифмы лёгкие навстречу им бегут,
> И пальцы просятся к перу, перо к бумаге,
> Минута—и стихи свободно потекут . . .

«И рифмы лёгкие навстречу им бегут . . .»—строка эта почти полностью войдет в описание того состояния вдохновения, которое в «Египетских ночах» испытывает Чарский: он «чувствовал то благодатное расположение духа, когда мечтания явственно рисуются перед вами, и вы обретаете живые, неожиданные слова для воплощения видений ваших, когда стихи легко ложатся под перо ваше и звучные рифмы бегут навстречу стройной мысли».

Но вернемся к импровизатору. Вершину контраста между обыденностью и озаренностью его облика составляет, конечно же, его импровизация, которая сама по себе утверждает его высокий дар. Импровизация первая—прежде всего, по ее мастерству, по непосредственной отнесенности к главной теме, по ее знаменательности в смысле авторского самораскрытия; в самом деле: Чарский, этот отчасти автобиографический персонаж повести, предлагает собственно импровизатору не тему, но заветный творческий тезис самого Пушкина: «Поэт сам избирает предметы для своих песен; толпа не имеет права управлять его вдохновением»,—и тот складывает 18 чудесных строк в ответ на критический из толпы вопрос «зачем?». Отметим, что в образно-лексической сфере этих восемнадцати строк лидирует, символически и многозначно, слово орёл; Пушкин в черновиках начинал вторую строфу этого ответа пять раз—и в каждом варианте слово орёл было непременно. Вспомним эти восемнадцать строк—как наиболее убедительную иллюстрацию внутренней законченности произведения и, кстати сказать, самую яркую в русской литературе апологию независимости поэтического творчества:

> Зачем крутится ветр в овраге,
> Подъемлет лист и пыль несет,
> Когда корабль в недвижной влаге
> Его дыханья жадно ждет?

Зачем от гор и мимо башен
Летит орел, тяжел и страшен,
На чахлый пень? Спроси его
Зачем арапа своего
Младая любит Дездемона,
Как месяц любит ночи мглу?
Затем, что ветру и орлу
И сердцу девы нет закона.
Таков поэт: как Аквилон,
Что хочет, то и носит он—
Орлу подобно он летает
И, не спросясь ни у кого,
Как Дездемона, избирает
Кумир для сердца своего.

*

В заключение—вопрос, который представляет собой заголовок одной ценной статьи проф. В. Ледницкого: «Почему Пушкин не окончил «Египетские ночи».[7] Проф. Ледницкий имеет в виду тему о Клеопатре и современности; он сопоставляет пушкинский набросок «Мы проводили вечер на даче» с романом «Барнав» (1831) Жюля Жанена, в последних главах которого содержатся сюжетные аналогии, и с рассказом Жанена «Портрет», где эти аналогии с пушкинским замыслом особенно очевидны, и делает вывод: «Пушкин не окончил своих произведений, связанных с этой темой (Клеопатры. Л.Р.) —это сделал за него Жанен».

Но, всё-таки, если считать, как считает и сам В. Ледницкий, что главная тема «Египетских ночей»—это тема «поэтической импровизации и судьбы поэта в обществе», то что же помешало продлению дошедших до нас трех глав?

Можно предполагать, что помешала этому именно внутренняя их завершенность, при которой начатая во второй импровизации тема Клеопатры оказывалась дополнительным и замыкающим, но не новым композиционным моментом. Б. Томашевский отмечал, что эта импровизация заключена в узкий сюжет вызова Клеопатры ее поклонникам. «Нельзя предположить, писал он,—чтобы Пушкин задумывал «продолжение» (например, описание ночей, казни и т.д.)»[8] К законченности как признаку этих трех глав нужно добавить художественное их совершенство. Тургенев, например, говорил о прозаической части «Египетских ночей», что она «представляет лучший образец русской речи», который он «когда-либо читал»...[9]

Таким образом продолжение этих глав в направлении фокуса «Клеопатры» могло бы явиться им композиционно чужеродным: известный закон физики о том, что в пространстве, занятом каким-либо одним телом, другое тело свободно помещаться не может, действителен и в эстетике, где он выражается в чувстве меры и гармонии. Мне кажется, что у Пушкина такой конфликт между продлением замысла и его уже осуществленною частью встречается не однажды. Отчетлив такой конфликт, например, в «Дубровском»—романе совершенной законченности, несмотря на намеченный автором план второй части. То же, как кажется мне, случается и в «Русалке»: последние слова князя: «Откуда ты, прекрасное дитя», обращенные к маленькой русалочке, вполне гармонически заканчивают целое, не начиная «нового», которое творчески, может быть, оказывалось предшествующему структурно и стилистически чужеродно. Но это, конечно, уже другая тема...

NOTES

1. М. Гофман, «Клеопатра» и «Египетские ночи» (неосуществленный замысел Пушкина). *Современные записки*, (т. XVII Париж, 1922).
2. Ф. Достоевский. Полн. собр. соч., т. 13. Ленинград, 1926-30, стр. 214.
3. См. под его ред. Соч. Пушкина, т. 1. (Петербург, 1855).
4. *Comparative Literature*, Vol. XVI, No. 2.
5. П., 8, II, стр. 846.
6. Там же.
7. *Новый журнал* № 90, Нью-Йорк, стр 244-255.
8. Б. Томашевский, *Пушкин*, кн. 2-ая. Москва-Ленинград, 1961.
9. А. Луконина, «Мое знакомство с Тургеневым.» *Северный вестник*, (№ 2, 1887).

ЗАМЕТКИ ОБ ЭПИСТОЛЯРНОМ СТИЛЕ ПУШКИНА

Светлана Умрихина
State University of New York at New Paltz

Стиль писем Пушкина почти еще не подвергался подробному изучению. Исследователи стиля пушкинской прозы обычно едва касались писем или только намечали пути будущих исследований. Один из таких путей был намечен Г. О. Винокуром,[1] усмотревшим в письмах зародыши различных прозаических жанров и указавшим на взаимосвязь эпистолярного и художественного творчества Пушкина.

Изучением этого вопроса занялись другие исследователи.[2] Назвав письма, вслед за Винокуром, «лабораторией прозаических стилей Пушкина», они, не пытаясь оспаривать этот тезис, классифицировали письма согласно их жанровым признакам—и сопоставили их стиль со стилем соответствующих им жанров художественной прозы Пушкина.

Однако, их интересные и ценные выводы относятся фактически только к нескольким письмам, которые, действительно, можно целиком отнести к какому-нибудь жанру. Стиль же всех остальных писем Пушкина остался вне поля их зрения.

Между тем, результаты более углубленного анализа довольно определенно указывают на то, что письма Пушкина представляют собой самостоятельный литературный жанр с собственной стилевой системой, значительно отличающейся от стилевой системы остальной прозы.

135

А поскольку по своей экспрессивности, по силе воздействия на читателя, по совершенству отделки многие письма ни в чем не уступают другим прозаическим произведениям Пушкина, то их можно смело назвать не «лабораторией прозы» а блестящей ее разновидностью.

В сущности, мы имеем дело с дяумя типами эпистолярного стиля: стиль писем, относящихся к официальной деловой переписке и стиль личных писем, адресованных друзьям и жене.

Даже деловые письма Пушкина, написанные в основном в традиции современной ему официальной коммуникации,—это материал литературный. Среди них можно найти немалое количество писем, содержащих художественную задачу, осуществляемую с помощью различных средств литературной стилизации.

На основании анализа сохранившихся черновиков можно заключить, что и тяжелое канцелярское косноязычие одних, и тонкий сарказм других, и утрированная орнаментальность третьих или архаический стиль четвертых могли являться конечной творческой задачей Пушкина.

С другой стороны, в личных письмах Пушкина обнаруживаются резкие отступления от формальных эпистолярных шаблонов. Их стилистические средства воспроизводят живые разговорные интонации—явление совсем не типичное для остальной прозы Пушкина.

Однако, анализ черновиков личных писем указывает на то, что их непринужденная разговорная «небрежность» и «необработанность» тоже могли быть продуктом литературной стилизации.

Возможно, что одним из факторов, стимулировавших литературную стилизацию личных писем, было то обстоятельство, что Пушкин предназначал многие из них для прочтения вслух. Можно предположить, что это также побуждало его абстрагировать личные темы, чувства и переживания, вследствие чего далеко не все высказывания Пушкина, выражения его чувств, отзывы о людях и оценочные обобщения следует считать биографическими информациями.

Надо заметить, что изучение стиля писем могло бы помочь биографам Пушкина разобраться, какие информации можно принимать всерьез, а какие считать просто вставками для «красного словца». Например, Иван Новиков в своем биографическом романе «Пушкин в изгнании», характеризуя отношения Пушкина с Алексеем Вульфом, говорит о том, что Пушкин, после попыток быть на «ты», «вынужден был отодвинуться в сферу обычных светских условностей»[2] и перейти на «Вы», основывая, очевидно, свое заключение на семи сохранившихся письмах Пушкина Вульфу, где, действительно, только в первом он обращается к нему на «ты». Но Новиков не учел, что три следующих письма написаны намеренно деловым стилем и содержат в себе зашифрованные распоряжения о предполагаемом бегстве за границу, а остальные четыре—в шутливо-высокопарном стиле, к которому совсем бы не подошло «ты».

В этой статье затрагивается только один аспект стиля писем Пушкина—проявление в них живых разговорных интонаций, и так как объектом моего внимания являются те средства и приемы речи, которые воспроизводят интонацию, и, отчасти, ритм устной речи, то здесь я не буду касаться стиля официальных писем, где такие элементы отсутствуют. Для удобства я условно называю письма, содержащие разговорные интонации, интонированными или фоническими письмами, а письма сухого канцелярского стиля—афоническими.

Даже при поверхностном чтении фонических писем читатель улавливает в них особый тон. Их яркая интимная выразительность, непринужденная смена мыслей и разговорная живость речевых оборотов напоминают скорей устную речь; и читателю начинает казаться, что он не читает, а, скорее, слушает произносимый вслух отрывок какого-то непрерывного мысленного монолога. Это впечатление усиливается еще и тем обстоятельством, что громадное большинство фонических писем даже и не выглядят как письма: очень часто в них нет ни начального обращения, ни заключительных фраз, ни подписи.

Вот как может начинаться и кончаться такое письмо:

начало: «*Сам съешь*! заметил ли ты, что наши журнальные антикритики основаны на *сам съешь*.»
конец: «ты вбил ему в голову, что я объедаюсь гонением. Ох,

душа моя—меня тошнит, но предлагаемое да едят,» (№ 214—
П. А. Вяземскому)[3]
начало: «накупался ли ты в море, и куда из Ревеля думаешь
отправиться?»
конец: «что вам больше нравится? запах розы или резеды?—
Запах селедки.» (№ 200—П. А. Вяземскому)

Таких примеров можно привести множество. Фактически,
только 15% фонических писем содержат обращение, заклю-
чительную фразу и подпись.

Естественно, что разговорный стиль писем опирается прежде
всего на их лексику и фразеологию. Простой статистический
подсчет показывает наличие большого количества разговорных лексико-фразеологических элементов, разговорных иди-
ом, просторечных слов, вульгаризмов, междометий и т.д.
Объем этой статьи не разрешает остановиться на этом аспекте
стиля подробно. Достаточно привести для иллюстрации
разговорные элементы только *одного* письма (№ 951—жене):

«удрать к тебе»
«сестры баламутят»
«какая ты безалаберная»
«сладить свадьбу»
«с женою в три обхвата»
«славная баба»
«уши выдрать»
«ты ведь махнешь»
«у него хандра»
«тетеха»
«нашла за что браниться»
«я сам по себе»
«пропадет даром»
«останутся на подножном
   корму»
«а им и горя мало»
«с кем тебе знаться»
«черт с ними»
«ехать к ней на поклон»
«ух, кабы мне удрать»
«того и гляди»

«упаду как снег на голову»
«в нем толку мало»
«это дело другое»
«не заманили и московским
   калачем»
«Боже мой»
«свинский Петербург»
«скверные толки»
«салопница»
«подале от двора»
«на тетку нельзя вам всем
   навалиться»
«бабы»
«меня же будут цыганить»
«не он виноват в свинстве его
   окружающем»
«живя в нужнике привыкнешь
   к ———»
«и вонь его тебе не будет
   противна»

(На разговорную природу писем косвенно указывает и наличие в них иноязычных [гл. обр. французских] вставок. В большинстве случаев они не несут никакой стилистической нагрузки а просто, как в устной речи, «срываются с языка». Это особенно значительно, если принять во внимание, что в афонических письмах Пушкин никогда не смешивал языков: писал или по-русски, или по-французски).

Здесь будут кратко освещены только два аспекта разговорного стиля—синтаксическая структура предложений и пунктуация.

В отличие от упорядоченного строя письменного языка разговорная речь очень часто содержит такие конструкций, построение которых отражает спонтанное формирование мысли, не позволяющее заранее предусмотреть все элементы синтаксического оформления.

В устном разговоре часто бывает так, что говорящий высказывает какую-нибудь мысль, почти немедленно ее меняет, поясняет некоторыми деталями, подвергает сомнению или, рассудя вслух, начисто от нее отказывается. Тот же самый процесс эволюции мысли отражается во многих конструкциях, встречающихся в письмах.

«Виньетку бы не худо, даже можно, даже нужно, даже ради Христа сделайте.» (№ 147—брату Льву и П. А. Плетневу)

Первая мысль: полужелание, вторая: более определенное желание, 3-я—настоятельное требование, 4-я—уже слегка шутливая мольба.

«Здесь у нас молдованно и тошно, ах, Боже мой, что-то с ним делается—судьба его беспокоит меня до крайности.» (№ 35—Н. И. Гнедичу)

Употребив собственное слово «молдованно» по примеру ранее придуманного «кюхельбекерно», Пушкин сразу вспоминает о своем Кюхле—отсюда внезапный поворот мысли, который фиксируется в рамках одного предложения.

Примеров такой внезапной перемены мысли, а, чаще, поправок или дополнений к первоначальному сообщению можно найти очень много:

«Одна беда: слог и язык . . . Но знаете ли? и эта беда не беда.» (№ 542—М. П. Погодину) (отказ от собственного мнения). «кажется это не к добру. Впрочем, черт знает!» (№ 272—П. А. Вяземскому) (сомнение в своей правоте).

Яркую разговорную интонацию, а также почти физическую осязаемость присутствия автора, создает интереснейший прием, появившийся в поздних письмах: регистрация событий, происходящих в момент написания письма:

«Прощай. Кто-то ко мне входит. Фальшивая тревога: Иполит принес кофей . . . Опять тревога—Муханов прислал мне разносчика с пастилой. Прощай.» (№ 771—жене) «Вот едет ко мне Безобразов—прощай. Ух, насилу отвязался. Два часа сидел у меня.» (№ 1000—жене)

Паузы, создаваемые знаками препинания—это временны́е эллипсы. Во время этих пауз Пушкин что-то делает: встает, подходит к двери, пьет кофе, смотрит в окно, говорит с посетителем и т.д.

Разговорная интонация ясно звучит и в таких конструкциях, в которых как бы подразумеваются реплики невидимого собеседника. В нашей жизни это напоминает разговор по телефону, когда мы слышим только одного говорящего, но по его репликам догадываемся о том, что говорит его собеседник.

«Здесь нашел я Безобразова (что же ты так удивилась? не твоего обожателя, а мужа моей кузины Маргаритки.» (№. 1000—жене) «Можешь ли ты из онегинских денег дать Одоевскому пятьсот? нет? Ну, пусть меня дождутся—вот и все.» (№ 1197—жене)

Построение многих предложений часто бывает как бы ориентировано на интонирование, потому что при «глухом» чтении их смысл остался бы не совсем ясен.

«Как с ним связываться—довольно было с него легкого хлыста». (№ 28—П. А. Вяземскому)

Союзное слово «как», употребляется здесь в смысле «вместо

того, чтобы» и для того, чтобы понять смысл предложения, нужно произносить первую часть его со специальной модуляцией голоса.

«. . . просьбы о стихах рассердили меня (что я говорю *просьбы*, приказания, подряды на заказ).» (№ 853—жене)

На запятых в перечислении нужно делать длинные паузы и произносить каждое следующее слово с бо́льшим подъемом голоса.

Особой интонации требует несобственная прямая речь, которой не так часто, но пользуется Пушкин:

«Няня заочно у вас, Ольга Сергеевна, ручки целует-голубушке моей.» (№ 204—сестре)

Отметим такой тип ярко интонированных предложений, которые как бы включают сопроводительный физический жест:

«Но вот чем тебя рассержу: князь Шихматов, несмотря на твой разбор, и смотря на твой разбор, бездушный, холодный, наяутый скучный пустомеля . . . ай ай, больше не буду! не бей меня.» (№ 231—В. К. Кюхельбекеру)
«чихайте громче, еще громче.» (№ 18—Гнедичу)

Разговорно-бытовой, а особенно эмоционально-экспрессивной устной речи свойственно широкое употребление эллиптических предложений. Это, конечно, объясняется тем, что недостающие звенья эллипсов легко восполняются или словами из предыдущих фраз, или угадываются собеседником благодаря его осведомленности, или же восполняются интонацией.

Для данного исследования наиболее интересны эллипсы, пропущенные компоненты которых восполняются интонацией, иногда настолько яркой, что за ней угадывается жест:

«Карета моя хоть брось». (№ 770—жене)
«Жена не то, что невеста, Куда!» (№ 522—П. А. Плетневу)
«Ты спрашиваешь, какая цельу Цыганов? вот на! Цель поэзии—поэзия.» (№ 164—В. А. Жуковскому)

Совершенно исключительную роль в создании интонации играет пунктуация. Фактически, в корреспонденции Пушкина мы имеем дело с двумя системами пунктуации. Одна, вполне соответствовавшая формальным правилам, применялась Пушкиным в официальной переписке; другая, часто игнорировшая их, — в переписке личной. Оригинальность пунктуации в фонических письмах Пушкина отмечалась уже неоднократно, но, насколько мне известно, еще никогда не исследовалась.

Анализ постановки знаков препинания в фонических письмах выявляет, что их назначением было, по всей видимости, не только синтаксическое разделение предложений, но и графическое оформление интонаций и ритма живой, непринужденной разговорной речи.

Прежде всего бросается в глаза огромное количество знаков препинания и их разнообразие. Приведем некоторые статистические данные: фоническое письмо длиной около 200 слов может содержать около 70 знаков препинания, из них около 40 % — экспрессивных знаков (так для удобства и краткости мы называем вопросительные, восклицательные знаки, двоеточие и тире).

В официальной переписке на то же количество слов приходится в четыре раза меньше знаков препинания, а эмоциональных знаков нет вообще.

Это вполне естественно. В устной речи сложные предложения употребляются обычно редко. Чаще всего говорящий рубит их на короткие синтагмы, произвольно останавливаясь и прерывая мысль паузами. Те же явления наблюдаются и в дружеских письмах Пушкина, и такой паузой бывает прежде всего точка.

Современная Пушкину грамматика Греча рекомендовала употреблять точку там «где начинается новый смысл, не имеющий с предыдущим связи грамматической».[4]

В письмах Пушкина мы находим более ста случаев, когда точка не заканчивает, а прерывает мысль. Почти всегда дополнение к начальной мысли начинается с сочинительного союза *и, а* или *но*. Из письма М. П. Погодину:

«В утешение нашел я Ваши письма и Марфу. *И* прочел ее два раза духом. Ура!» (№ 542)

Точка приводит первое предложение к разрешительной интонации. После паузы новый подъем голоса с «и» создает порывистое движение и наполняет предложение новой энергией. Еще один пример:

«роюсь в старых книгах да орехи грызу. А ни стихов ни прозы, писать не думаю.» (№ 1096—жене)

Точка сигнализирует ступенчатость мысли. Благодаря ей первая мысль получает интонацию законченности; только потом, как бы спохватившись, Пушкин делает добавление, и оно звучит так же беспечно, как и первое сообщение. Без точки все предложение потеряло бы разговорную легкость.

Иногда точка разделяет тесно связанные по смыслу простые предложения, которые легко составили бы сложно-подчиненное или сложно-сочиненное предложение.

«от тебя благодеяние мне не тяжело—а от другого не хочу. Будь он тебе расприятель, будь он сын Карамзина.» (№ 220—В. А. Жуковскому)

Кстати, здесь само построение предложения чисто разговорное и требует совершенно определенной интонации.

Такую же роль паузы, прерывающей мысль, может играть точка с запятой:

«Баратынский говорит, что в женихах счастлив только дурак; а человек мыслящий беспокоен и волнуем будущим.» (№ 523— П. А. Плетневу)

Стараясь понять секрет ритма пушкинской прозы, литературоведы не раз обращали внимание на точки с запятой и запятые, членившие сложные предложения на интонационно законченные отрезки и создававшие между ними отчетливые паузы. Нетрудно заметить, что такие предложения состоят из отдельных коротких мыслей, нередко лишь отрывков мыслей, произвольно нанизанных на один синтаксический стержень, и роль запятых, точек с запятой и точек сводится, очевидно, к графическому оформлению ритма речи. Эта гипотеза подтверждается тем фактом, что и запятую, и точку с запятой и точку можно легко поменять местами.

«Теперь я ничего не пишу; хлопоты другого рода. Неприятности всякого рода: скучно и пыльно.» (№ 88—Льву)

«Я в деревне и надеюсь много писать, в конце осени буду у вас; вдохновения еще нет, покамест принялся я за прозу.» (№ 340—А. А. Дельвигу)

Если условно принять запятую за минимальную одномерную паузу, как это предлагалось в грамматиках Курганова и Греча, точку с запятой-за трехмерную, а точку-за четырехмерную, и читать эти отрывки со строгим соблюдением долготы пауз, то, по все вероятности, можно точно воспроизвести ритм устной речи Пушкина.

Точка с запятой может выступать в качестве удлиненной паузы там, где возникают трудно произносимые сочетания:

«Здесь жалеют о том, что я совсем, совсем упал; что моя трагедия подражание Кромвелю Виктора Гюго; что стихи без рифм не стихи; что замозваниц не должен был так неосторожно открыть тайну свою Марине.» (№ 560—П. А. Плетневу)

Кроме первого придаточного предложения, где между «о том» и «что» пауза сокращается до минимума, благодаря усиленному двойному «совсем», перед всеми остальными придаточными предложениями трехмерные паузы необходимы, потому, что спондей «*узна́л, что́*» «*Гюго́, что́*», «*стихи́, что́*», находящиеся на стыках длинных отрывков речи, сделали бы это предложение трудно произносимым. Такая пунктуация очевидно указывает на то, что все предложение было ориентировано на звук.

Предположение, что знаки препинания предназначались Пушкиным для графического оформления ритма, особенно подкрепляется их присутствием в тех местах, где, согласно формальным правилам пунктуации, никаких знаков не должно было бы быть.

Так, например, «лишние» запятые могут служить своего рода цезурой между равными ритмическими отрезками.

«Прекрасно, выражено сильно, и с красноречием сердечным.» (№ 175—А. А. Бестужеву)
4-х стопный ямб—цезура—4-х стопный ямб. Или:

«Кюхельбекерно мне, на чужой стороне.» (№ 48—брату Льву)

2-х стопный анапест—цезура—2-х стопный анапест.

Такие цезуры, т.е. интонационные а не синтаксические паузы, встречаются довольно часто, и именно они фиксируют ритм живой разговорной речи:

«Не жди от меня уж писем, до самой деревни.» (№ 847—жене)

Запятая указывает на ступенчатость мысли: сначала идет категорическое заявление, а потом смягченное добавление.

«В первых двух книжках Вы напечатали две капитальные пьесы Жуковского, и бездну стихов Языкова.» (№ 732—И. В. Киреевскому)

Запятая вносит, примерно, такой смысловой нюанс: Вы *не только* напечатали две капитальные пьесы Жуковского, *но* и бездну стихов Языкова.

Если еще отсутствие знаков препинания можно было бы отнести за счет небрежности Пушкина, то трудно объяснить той же небрежностью такие «лишние» знаки.

Особенное внимание в пунктуации писем обращают на себя вопросительные знаки, находящиеся внутри предложений. Они встречаются и в художественной прозе Пушкина, но только исключительно в прямой речи персонажей или в стилизованной авторской речи сказового типа. Несмотря на то, что они иногда попадаются в письмах корреспондентов Пушкина и в стилизованных под устную речь фельетонах в тогдашних журналах, они настолько многочисленны в письмах, что их можно рассматривать как собственно пушкинский метод графического оформления разнообразных оттенков вопросительных интонаций и ритма устной речи.

Для иллюстрации можно привести два коротких примера: 1. Интонация тревоги:

«И как тебе там быть? без денег, без Амельяна.» (№ 1001—жене) Если прочитать это предложение без внутреннего вопросительного знака, то оно будет звучать гораздо менее эмоционально. Второй пример: интонация изумления:

«Но какова наша цензура? признаюсь, никак не ожидал от нее таких больших успехов в эстетике.» (№ 35—Н. И. Гнедичу)

Само собой разумеется, что интонационные оттенки, вводимые вопросительным знаком, могут интерпретироваться по-разному:

«Что за дьявольщина? (озадаченность, возмущение, огорчение) неужели мы вразумили публику? (недоверие, радостное удивление) или сама догадалась голубушка? (насмешка, удовлетворение, удивление) и т.д.

Дело не в том, с *какой* интонацией можно произнести эти фразы —а в том, что здесь она неизменно требуется.

Типичной синтаксической конструкцией в дружеских письмах является так называемая цепь вопросов: несколько вопросительных синтагм, количество которых колеблется от трех до двенадцати:

«Что Всеволжские? что Мансуров? что Барков что Сосницкие? что Хмельницкие? что Катенин? что Шаховской? что Ежов? что граф Пушкин? что Семеновы? что Завадовской? что весь театр?» (№ 40—Я. Н. Толстому)

Подобные, даже менее длинные цепи вопросительных синтагм вносят нетерпение, нервность, иногда даже раздраженность.

Встречаются, но гораздо реже, и внутренние восклицательные знаки. Их роль, вероятно, можно сравнить с громкими аккордами внутри музыкальной фразы.

«Библию, библию! и французскую непременно.» (№ 117—Льву) «Не стыдно ли Кюхле напечатать ошибочно моего Демона! моего демона! после этого он и Верую напечатает ошибочно.» (№ 120—Льву)

Во втором предложении интонация восклицания и пауза совершенно необходимы.

Но все же наибольшую роль в процессе интонирования играет, конечно, *тире*. Точных правил его употребления в пушкинское время не было. В двух ведущих грамматиках тире вообще не упоминалось.

В грамматике Греча употребление тире рекомендовалось в четырех случаях:

«1) Между периодами, законченными точкой, для показания, что они не состоят в логической между собой связи.

2) Между речами двух лиц, когда сии лица не наименованы.

3) При опущении какого-нибудь слова.

4) При всяком неожиданном переходе речи.»[5]

В письмах современников Пушкина тире употреблялось редко, и, главным образом, в первых трех функциях. Четвертая функция тире, которая уже явно затрагивала проблему графического воспроизведения ритмомелодии устной речи, объяснялась весьма неопределенно и как бы представляла пишущему решать самому, какие именно переходы речи считать неожиданными. И в то время, когда современники Пушкина еще, по-видимому, не успели оценить широких выразительных возможностей тире, Пушкин сделал его своим излюбленным интонационным сигналом. О том, что он предназначал тире именно для этой цели, говорит тот факт, что оно совершенно не встречается в официальной переписке. С другой стороны, нет ни одного дружеского письма, в котором бы так или иначе не фигурировало тире.

Можно выделить более 20-и вариантов употребления тире в качестве интонационных сигналов (не считая случаев, соответствующих формальным правилам пунктуации), причем каждый из них повторяется десятки раз. Встречается более 150 случаев, когда тире заменяет законную с формальной стороны запятую. Если считать тире двумерной паузой, которой предшествует подъем голоса и задержка на последнем слове, то можно уловить тот оттенок интонации, который вносит тире по сравнению с вытесненной им запятой.

«Батюшка уехал из Петербурга[1го] июля—и я не получал об нем известия.» (№ 1228—Н. И. Павлищеву)

С запятой это предложение звучало бы как нейтральное сообщение; тире вносит в него интонацию досады или тревоги, иными словами живую экспрессию. Еще один пример:

«Это все мне нужно—потому что я люблю тебя—и ненавижу деспотизм.» (№ 10—П. Б. Мансурову)

Два тире внутри предложения придают каждой следующей за ним синтагме больше значимости и эмоции.

Однако, ярче всего роль тире проявляется тогда, когда оно стоит там, где никаким знакам быть бы не полагалось. Насчитывается около 120 таких случаев, и сама по себе эта цифра исключает возможность случайности такого «злоупотребления» тире. Иногда такие «лишние» тире можно сравнить с пометками, которые расставляет актер в тех местах текста, где ему из-за скопления длинных слов нужно «взять дыхание».

«С вашей вдохновенной деятельностью, с вашей чистой добросовестностью—вы произведете такие чудеса, что мы и потомство наше будем за вас Бога молить.» (№ 801—М. П. Пододину)

«Он называется главнокомандуюшим северных греческих войск —и уролномоченным тайного правительства.» (№ 19—В. Л. Давыдову)

В письмах 1821-23г часто встречаются сложные конструкции, расчлененные на несколько отдельных синтагм с помощью тире. Возникают паузы, создающие нервный перебойный ритм:

«На хлебах у Воронцова я не стану жить—не хочу и полно—крайность может довести до крайности—мне больно видеть равнодушие отца к моему состоянию—хотя письма его очень любезны.» (№ 58—брату Льву)

Когда Пушкин пользуется тире при перечислении, тогда возникают довольно типичные в устной речи паузы, когда говорящий старается припомнить все нужные предметы:

«Но надо подробностей—изложения его мнений—анекдотов разбора его стихов.» (№ 577—П. А. Плетневу)

Конечно, и здесь интерпретация пауз—хотя обычно в этом помогает содержание—может быть различной. Важно, однако, то, что тире неизменно нарушает повествовательный тон предложения и вносит какую-то внутреннюю эмоцию, следовательно, живой голос Пушкина.

Интересен случай, когда Пушкин пользуется тире просто для мистификации:

«Ради Бога, почитай ноэзию—доброй, умной старушкою. к которой можно иногда зайти, чтобы забыть на минутку сплетни ... (№ 16—брату Льву)

В первой части предложения, до тире, глагол «почитай» воспринимается как «уважай» или даже «читай немного», синтагма же «доброй умной старушкой» меняет его смысл на «считай» или «рассматривай».

«Лишнее» тире, как и ранее рассмотренные знаки препинания, часто сигнализирует процесс додумывания, дополнение или пояснение предыдущей мысли.

«Ради Бога, надень на него строгой муньштук и выезжай его— на досуге.» (№ 214—П. А. Вязамскому)
«Надоела мне печать—опечатками, критиками, защищениями, етс.» (№ 228—А. А. Бестужеву)

Часто «незаконное тире» создает драматическую (или шутливо-патетическую) паузу.

«Воронцов женится—на дочери К. А. Нарышкина». (№ 926— жене)
«В ней же первая персона Борис—Годунов!» (№ 223—П. А. Вяземскому)
«до 9 часов—читаю.» (№ 854—жене)

Последнее предложение наполняется благодаря тире почти осязаемым временем.

Но чаще всего тире служит предвестником акцентированной значимости следующей за ним синтагмы.

«Таким образом обязан я за все про все—друзьям моей славы— черт их возьми и с нею.» (№ 80—брату Льву)

Здесь благодаря тире ударным становится существительное «друзьям», и следующая синтагма «черт их возьми» подсказывает, что оно должно произноситься с иронией и злостью.

«но зато нет—ни саранчи, ни милордов Уоронцовых.» (№ 122—Д. М. Шварцу)

С тире отрицание «нет» почти звенит, полное радости и облегчения.

«. . . князь Федор и я будем следовать за тобой в лодке, и как-нибудь—выкарабкаешься.» (№ 862—П. В. Нащокину)

Здесь создается зрительная картина: человек, с усилием выкарабкивающийся на берег.

Можно найти значительное количество предложений и с «неадэкватными» знаками препинания. Это можно объяснить тем, что часто, когда сама структура предложения подсказывала нужную интонацию, Пушкин не считал нужным ставить эмоциональный знак препинания.

«Не давать ему за то ни / Моря ни капли стихов от меня.» (№ 120—Льву Пушкину)

Повелительное наклонение, выраженное инфинитивом всегда требует яркой восклицательной интонации, даже если на конце предложения нет восклицательного знака.

Остается отметить недостающие знаки препинания.

Чаще всего не достает запятых. Отсюда какой-то процент, может быть, и можно отнести за счет небрежности Пушкина, но чаще всего отсутствие запятой означает просто отсутствие паузы.

По той же причине Пушкин, по-видимому, не выделяет запятыми вводные слова и словосочетания.

«выгода конечно необъятная» (№ 293—Языкову)
«Я кажется писал тебе.» (№ 129—П. А. Вяземскому)
«кстати о стихах» (№ 103—П. А. Вяземскому)

Из 66 случаев употребления вводного слова «конечно» Пушкин выделяет его всего 6 раз, причем 4 раза в книжных конструкциях. В тех предложениях, где Пушкин выделял вводные слова знаками препинания, он, надо думать, выделял их интонационно, придавая им бо́льшую значимость.

Эта мысль подтверждается, например, различной пунктуацией явно по-разному звучащего сочетания «ради Бога».

1) «Ради Бога! слово живое об Одессе.» (№ 122—Д. М. Шварцу)

Восклицательный знак после «ради Бога» создает интонацию мольбы.

2) «ты смотри за ним—ради Бога! и ему случается завираться.» (№ 179—А. Вяземскому)

Благодаря тире—«ради Бога» звучит как дополнительное, усиленное, напоминание.

3) «Умоляю вас, ради Бога не приезжайте.» (№ 191—И. Ф. Мойеру)

«Ради Бога» произносится слитно с глаголом и имеет значение несколько более настоятельного «пожалуйста».

4) «Справься ради Бога об фонтане.» (№ 156—брату Льву)

Сочетание «ради Бога» проскальзывает незаметно. На его месте легко могла бы быть даже частица ка. «Справься-ка о фонтане.»

Значительно чаще Пушкин выделяет вводное слово «кажется», и выделение это большей частью вполне объяснимо, и во многих случаях необходимо для ясности смысла. Последнее происходит тогда, когда вводное слово «кажется» может быть принято за личный глагол.

«соединиться тайно—но действовать в одиночку, кажется, вернее». (№ 50—Вяземскому)

Без запятых «кажется» могло бы быть осмыслено как связка именного сказуемого при двух подлежащих, выраженных инфинитивом: соединиться, действовать кажется вернее.

В остальных случаях, выделенное, оно явно тормозит предложение, внося интонацию раздумья.

Интересно, что вопрос о пересмотре правил пунктуации

вводных слов был поднят совсем недавно. Профессор А. Б. Шапиро в своей книге «Основы русской пунктуации», в числе других реформ, рекомендует не выделять запятыми те слова, «которые выполняют исключительно функцию вводных слов (впрочем, конечно, пожалуйста и т.д.)»[5] Фактически этому принципу, подсказанному в наши дни простой целесообразностью, инстинктивно или намеренно следовал Пушкин.

Подведем итог: пунктуация фонических писем Пушкина функциональна. Выходя за рамки формальных правил она нередко была подчинена требованиям ритмомелодии устной речи, графически воспроизводя различные оттенки разговорных интонаций, и являясь одним из эффективных средств, создающих блестящий и неповторимый эпистолярный стиль Пушкина.

NOTES

1. Г. О. Винокур. *Культура языка.* (Москва, 1925).
2. И. Новиков—*Пушкин в изгнании.* (Москва, 1953) стр. 683.
3. Номера писем приводятся по П., 13, 14, 15, 16.
4. Н. И. Греч. *Практическая русская грамматика.* Изд. 7, (петербург, 1893) §605.
5. А. В. Шапиро. *Основы русской пунктуации.* (Москва. 1955г.) стр. 65-70.

PART THREE
Puškin's Narrative Poetry and Drama

"RUSLAN I LJUDMILA": NOTES FROM ELLIS ISLAND[1]

Walter Arndt
Dartmouth College

Immigrants arriving in the United States in this writer's time were not taken to Ellis Island any more. But one is told by those who were—whether from the old *Statendam*, the stately, now cremated *Queen Mary*, or the heirloom *Stavangerfjord*—that it was an experience calculated to cure one of the immigrant's "new world" syndrome: moist eyes, childish optimism, inflated expectations ("Ah, brave new world that has . . . *such people* in it?!"). It was a process designed to analyze your personality into its constituents, immediate and ultimate, flush your old-world social identity and cultural *amour-propre* into the gray harbor water, change your name if outlandish to the Man of Erin, run down your tree diagram to its Deep Structure, verify what went for your "total worth"—to leave you at last as fit raw material for that leached and lowly thing: a resident alien.

Russian-speaking readers of the English verse translation of Puškin's *Ruslan and Ljudmila* (the occasion of this article) may feel that they are given an Ellis Island view of the poem. Others may suspect what is nearly always true, that the translation has done little more for Puškin's puckish brainchild than give it resident-alien status. But in other hands *Ruslan and Ljudmila* never even reached Ellis Island. Oliver Elton lost the couple in mid-Baltic; a certain omnivore beyond the Spree had them expire on him of *Wassersucht* or Wagnerian pip. Perhaps it is as well, then, to accept the losses and to present here an introduction to the work — longer, by design, on comparative speculation than on pure philology or genetic research, and readily illustrated now by passages from the original or from the English echo-poem.

Ruslan and Ljudmila, which did for Puškin's career what *Die Leiden des jungen Werthers* did for Goethe's, is so wildly polyphyletic (as geneticists would say), so elusive a literary hybrid that a determined attempt to classify it might result in a label as terse as "a mock-romantic fairy-tale ballad parody of pseudo-Kievan sham-Chivalry." The poem was begun in 1817, before Puškin's graduation from the lycée at Carskoe Selo, and completed in draft on March 26, 1820. This was a few weeks before the twenty-year-old sybarite and brilliant literary sniper was packed off to the South on penal reassignment, having escaped Siberia through the intervention of high-placed friends.

The same day one of these, Vasilij Žukovskij, most illustrious poet of the era and Puškin's mentor and patron, gave Puškin his portrait with the much-cited inscription, "To a victorious pupil from a defeated master." This showed not only Žukovskij's unfailing generosity — he was after all a prime target of the graceful but irreverent lampoon — but also his literary judgment and insight. It was not long after this that his star as a poet was forever eclipsed by Puškin, and he turned — not for this reason so much as lured by new interests — to quite different literary pursuits, in which again he excelled.

The epilogue to the poem was written in the South in July 1820. Its rather mawkish strain of youth decayed and inspiration withered strongly suggests the hope that some influential reader might implore those in authority to pardon Puškin before brain fever or a decline should carry him off. As it turned out, such interventions were unsuccessful; but Puškin's "Southern exile" was not, on the whole, a desperate predicament, and it certainly proved one of his most productive periods.

Ruslan and Ljudmila was widely taken seriously by both admirers and detractors as the first native example of a "new romanticism" — as distinct from the preromantic and Gothic modes introduced to Russia earlier by Žukovskij and not generally so labeled. At the same time critics very plausibly discerned kinship with works not simply identifiable with romanticism, such as Wieland's three works on the theme of noble quests abandoned for the natural sensuous life, and his celebrated fairy tale in verse, *Oberon*; and of course, Ariosto's mock-epic. Such critics as were able to swim against the torrent of popular acclaim redoubled the strictures of literary conservatism which had met Žukovskij's work earlier: scandalously unbuttoned diction and a subject matter which combined chaotic structure with barbarity of taste.

A convenient way, as well as an amusing one, to understand the delight and, as it were, relief with which Puškin's poem was greeted by some, and the pained indignation it evoked from others, is to compare it with the work of Puškin's most immediate predecessor in its ostensible genre, Žukovskij. Within Žukovskij's work one should turn to the famous poem which was to some slight degree the direct target of Puškin's good-natured ridicule in *Ruslan and Ljudmila*. It will then be clearer, perhaps, that "The Twelve Sleeping Maidens" and all that Russia's imported romanticism up to then represented in terms of the poet's viewpoint, prosodic originality, and assumed state of public taste, was not being "programmatically" attacked by the twenty-year-old prodigy, as they might be in the name of French *raison* or in the spirit of the experimental realism of his thirties, or even on behalf of a more light-handed, native-flavored romanticism that he might have meant to launch. It was rather that the eighteenth-century scoffer conspired in him with the amateur historian and folklorist and with the man of taste allergic to solemn fustian to make fun of his mentor's fashionable "antiquing" of Russian poetry with mock-medieval wormholes and feudal verdigris.

This is most explicit at the point in Canto IV where after a graceful bow to Žukovskij and a genial plot summary of the soul-stirring "Twelve Maidens" Puškin confronts young Ratmir with a crenelated castle. This is, not accidentally, the only false "Western" prop in the poem. Unforced European notes, by contrast, abound in the chitchat which the detached singer intersperses between, and pertly sets off against, the mock-serious episodes of the fable. Maidens in white muslin, some gazing skyward, some chin on chest, commuted up and down the keeps in Žukovskij's poem. So they do, more briskly, in Puškin's, and one sings a (derisively trite) Lorelei ditty extolling the amenities of the castle and its inmates. But far from breaking their enchantment as Vadim had done, then freezing in chaste rapture before the head-maiden for some stanzas, then getting married in a derelict friary magically restored and refitted for the purpose, and finally running a sacred errand or two, Ratmir finds himself gently divested of his ironmongery and led by the assembled strength of seductive maidens into a Russian-cum-Oriental bathhouse and massage parlor. There, it is clear, wisps of vapor are his sole screen from caressing eyes, "cast down" but full of eager interest, and heaping armfuls of "all-but-nakedness" which throng about his couch to perform delightful ministrations with his increasingly fervent cooperation.

Yet Puškin, like his circle and most of the literary public, rightly stood in awe of Žukovskij's achievement and was aware of his historic role. In some moods, long after the period of *Ruslan and Ljudmila*, he accuses himself (1830) of puerile impudence for having aimed a squirt gun at his patron and friend:

. . . *Ruslan and Ljudmila* was favorably received on the whole. . . . Nobody even noticed that it is a frigid work. It was charged with being immoral because of a few sensuous descriptions, some lines which I deleted from the second edition:

O dreadful sight! The feeble wizard
Caresses with a wrinkled hand . . .

the introduction to I don't remember which canto:

In vain you nestled in the shadow, etc.

and because of the parody of "The Twelve Sleeping Maidens." For this last I deserved to be soundly reproved, as betraying a lack of aesthetic sensibility. It was inexcusable, particularly at my age, to parody a work of pristine poetry in order to please the mob. There were other criticisms which were fairly shallow. Is there a single passage in *Ruslan* which could be compared, where the ribaldry of its humor is concerned, to the pranks of, say, Ariosto, of whom I was constantly being reminded? Even the passage I deleted was a very toned-town imitation of Ariosto (Orlando, Canto V, oct. viii).[2]

But spontaneous modern taste, unwarped by comparison with Žukovskij's predecessors like Bogdanovič, would tend to judge that Puškin blamed himself needlessly. "The Twelve Sleeping Maidens," subtitled "An Olden Tale in Two Ballads," is, of all bleak auspices, of Saxon inspiration, the plot being lifted from *Die 12 schlafenden Jungfrauen* by Christian Heinrich Spiess,[3] a late eighteenth-century best-selling Gothic novelist and playwright. A three-word acknowledgment of this debt is followed by an untitled introductory poem in four octets, dated 1817, which is an (unacknowledged) close paraphrase or imitation of Goethe's "Zueignung," the poem musing on the resumption of his thirty-year-old labors on Faust which the old poet placed at the very head of the huge drama. The relevance of this translation to Žukovskij's poem is obscure.

Then, after some more epigraphs and dedications, follow over 150 monotonous stanzas of six identical iambic couplets. This stanza is derived by borrowing the static first quatrain of Bürger's famous "Lenora" stanza (cf. Puškin's "Bridegroom" and "Drowned Man") and repeating it ad infinitum; for there is nothing metrically to mark the onset of a new stanza from that of any internal couplet. The effect is deadening, as the involved story, unrelieved by a spark of humor or grace and sticky with religiosity, goes clacking along, tapock-tapock-tapock-tapock, tapick-tapick-tapickah, like wheels passing over the rail-gaps on a very steady local train.

But the chief tedium of this and other specimens of Drawing-Room Sepulchral, once the charm of absurdity has worn off, is its inherent lack of surprise, be it in narrative viewpoint, in incident, or in idiom. By sowing surprise with a lavish and mischievous hand, Puškin carves a deeper grave for the antecedent mode than by any digs of outright parody. The mode is so "square" (as we said in the sixties), so "straight" (as we shall presently stop saying) because its conventions rest on wish-fulfilling romantic assumptions about the age of chivalry, or a remote facsimile of it trimmed with outright fairy stuff. Knights, fairies, witches, rescued maidens, rejected suitors, have to behave in typecast ways to cater to the illusions, or at any rate the voluntarily suspended disbelief, of the public regarding the rectilinear morals and mores of feudal society. Poignant, unstylized tragedy, comic pratfalls, complexities of character, appealing evil, repellent virtue, humdrum humanity, did not fit into the mold, and injecting them would destroy its main escapist virtues—romantic distance in time and space, picturesque piety, moral simplicity, heroic identification, thaumaturgic excitement. For the fifteen years or so that Žukovskij and a few other prospectors were mining this vein, it was heady stuff, and the public developed a veritable addiction to it. But in keeping with the notorious telescoping of time scales in Russian literature of that period, the fashion was overripe by the second decade of the century and, instead of being followed by another foreign fad, perhaps still better russicized, it was followed by that unclassifiable, all-recasting phenomenon which was Puškin. And Puškin's cutting edge was *Ruslan and Ljudmila.*

Did Puškin then, with malice aforethought, forever unmagic these fairy lands forlorn by loosing a troupe of alien, complex, unbridled characters into the medium, and letting them gambol all over it? Did he, moreover, in his canto send-offs and asides personally laugh it to scorn? Not at all, nor should we assume that he had any such intention. His characters, too, are more than sketchy and start out, at least, as stereotypes.

The excitement in this story does not lie in any suspense about its outcome, hardly in even a momentary identification with hero or heroine, nor in any moral indignation at its human villains, who are pardonable or farcical—a sure sign of precocious realism. Instead, it lies in the teasing turns of the author's impish mind, the stylized intimacy with it to which we are admitted, the sure expectation of the joltingly unexpected; the delightful scandal of an overblown genre deflated by pert little similes from boudoir, barnyard, or nymphet's bower; and, more than anything, the infectious gaiety and effortless brilliance of the verse, which translate a gifted prank into the realm of aesthetic elation.

Something of the difference in form and spirit between Žukovskij's poem and Puškin's may emerge from just one juxtaposition of very short parallel passages—from Vadim's encounter with the redeemed Sleeping Maidens, and from Ratmir's with his unredeemed ones:

Žukovskij:

> And all that here to us is dim,
> To faith discovered only.
> Abruptly stood revealed to him,
> Blent in one image lonely.
> They gaze to Heaven, shedding tears,
> Devoid of speech with rapture;
> Then, lo, the group of maidens nears,
> Released from magic capture:
> Like stars shine forth reopened eyes,
> Alight with joy their faces,

With newly quickened beauty's prize,
With fresh redemption's graces.[4]

Puškin:

They spread rich fabrics of Iran,
Whereon reclines the weary Khan;
Fine wisps of steam about him loop;
Fond eyes cast down, the lovely troupe,
All eagerness to serve him, press
Their charming all-but-nakedness
About his couch, a playful group.
Above him, one of them is waving
The supple birch-twig's tender points,
His frame with fervent freshness laving;
Another cossets, silky palms
Perfumed with rose, his stiffened joints[5]

Fairness demands the acknowledgement that Žukovskij, too, or perhaps his model, the Philistine from Saxony, felt impelled to provide some decorously erotic relief, a brief peepshow or centerfold to quicken the stoutly virtuous reader's circulation and cheer him on that isometric rail journey. Vadim en route to the collective of cataleptic maidens has occasion to maim a giant and scoop in a freshly abducted princess of Kiev from him. They are presently caught in a dreadful thunderstorm in the forest, thoroughly soaked and knocked about against trees and cliffs, and take refuge in a cave. There Vadim is impelled to apply what we must assume are standard measures of chivalrous first aid, including mouth-to-breast resuscitation; and the princess, already stimulated no doubt by the earlier prospect of fate-worse-than-death, is silent but not unresponsive:

And to his bosom's safe repose
The young princess he presses,
He swabs away the rain that flows
From out her golden tresses.
His lips in gentle touch, he warms
The maiden breast with breathing,
And heat invests the chilly forms;
With silent tremors seething,
Beneath the touching lips they woke;

> An arm about him throwing,
> The quiet maiden never spoke
> But for her fingers' glowing.[6]

At such rare moments of proximate humanity on Vadim's part, however, a ghostly tolling comes from the distressed gentlewomen's far-off dorm, like the bell signaling that creative play-period is over, and Vadim resumes his pious quest with a start and perhaps an inaudible sigh.

Beyond such casual comparisons, which are less than fair or conclusive, we should make some attempt to account more fully for the astonishing success of Puškin's rather exotically blended confection. There are at least two, slightly farcical, "Byronic" devices appearing here, years before Puškin's acquaintance with Byron: the preclimactic suspension of the narrative, and authorial intrusion. But more than such devices in themselves, it is the fresh air of spontaneity and zest which breathes from these unshriven cantos, and the pleasantly unsettled feeling, akin to the rise of guilty but delicious laughter, which it induces from the start. This bubbles up in the sure anticipation, raised by faint hints in the initial diction, that musty romantic stereotypes will be infused with saucy, natural life, to play fast and loose with the conventions of the stodgy genre. These atmospheric elements alone not merely distinguish, but transubstantiate *Ruslan and Ljudmila* from any of the forms Žukovskij had transplanted to Russia from various Highland heaths, English churchyards, Rhinish blue-flower stands, and Saxon kitchen-plots of Western romanticism.

The antecedent mode chiefly relevant to *Ruslan and Ljudmila* and briefly sampled by us earlier may be termed the "folklore Gothic." This comprises highminded, moderately spine-tingling, often lachrymose verse romances or ballads, some redolent of a certain meretricious purity, a lily-browed pseudo-ingenuousness one is tempted to call Pre-Raphaelite or Wagnerian, or more broadly, decadent. For characters these often featured denizens — sacred, profane, or supernatural — of a book-derived feudal society set in as ill-defined an age of vassail, quest, and gadzooks as those tales of an avian entity American children call "Robin Hood." This milieu of romanticized chivalry, in West or East, had little to do with historical feudalism, and less with the Ukrainian principality of Kiev or the Russian duchies of the high middle ages or the living tradition of epic tales. But East-Slavic names and settings associated with these were at once adopted when the romantic ballad was naturalized by Žukovskij, starting with his first "Lenore" imitation (actually titled "Ljudmila") in 1808, and by his followers. These touches then took the place of the onomastic and toponymic links which, however tenuously and distantly, lent locale and lineament to the epigone form in Europe. Examples are the ancient Roland plots echoed in the fables of the Sicilian *pupi* bards to this day, and the slight flushes of life and color which filter even into Clemens Brentano's anemic lays through transfusions of blood and iron across seven hundred years from Picardy and Provence.

Žukovskij's masterly adaptations and, seldom, original ballads of the period from 1808 to 1820 did not alone account for this naturalized genre as such, but most probably for its immense vogue. And some of it, like some of the Scottish balladry and the rich German output of a century from Bürger to Count Strachwitz, Lulu v. Strauss u. Thorney, Fontane, C. F. Meyer, has the verve, mystery, and noble vigor which supplant tawdry historical reality and enchant the adolescent or romantic mind. Anchorites and wizards, knights and chatelaines, devils and damsels disported themselves against backdrops of Standard Western Chivalric or Slapdash Slavonic or more often a blend of both. Fable and motivation worked with strong color and contrast, inky guilt and snowy innocence, sin and retribution, betrayal or pitfall, and rescue by exploit or miracle. The language was consciously archaic, though by no means less limber or mellifluous for that. On the contrary, in keeping once more with the remarkable foreshortening of literary stages in this "catch-up" period, the language that had been a genuine and contemporary, if ponderous and over-rich, medium only a generation or two earlier in the hands of Deržavin and Shixmatov (and still was for Krylov), was already available to skillful hands as an optional resource for literary pathos or archaizing stylization.

A great many of the gross tangible elements of the Žukovskijan romantic ballad were retained by Puškin in *Ruslan and Ljudmila*. The effect of his brilliant dabbling in the genre was not assault and overthrow but infiltration and subversion from within with the subtle solvents of classicist sobriety and proto-realist debunking. One hastens to concede that *Ruslan and Ljudmila* is anything but sober and owlish; but its buoyant fancy and madcap parody are at least partially, and at least half consciously, *reductio ad absurdum* in the service of taste and measure. Abstract literary concepts are apt to creak piteously under the weight of metaphor. But the thought does suggest itself that classicism in him reached forward, and incipient realism reached back, to kill the consumptive genre with insidious kindness.

We have pointed to a quantum leap in the ease and vigor of poetic diction, and to a bracing suspense due to the minefield quality of the mock-epic mode. What else made *Ruslan and Ljudmila* different from its precursors? Half a dozen quite definable elements, not all new, went into the delicate mobile, and their harmonizing rather than jangling and collapsing in Puškin's hands helps account for the unforeseen *succès fou* of the poem, and for the gracious surrender inscribed by Žukovskij on the portrait he sent him on this occasion.

One of these elements was the panoply of Kiev and its court — as thoroughly mythistorical by then as Barbarossa's Kyffhäuser or King Arthur's war cabinet, but still evocative. Another was a dose of the romantic opulence and menace of Islamic and Mongol cultures — here purveyed by Scheherezade and perhaps Voltaire's second-hand Orient rather than by the bloody shades of Russian history, but blending in so well as actually to strengthen the "Russian scent" claimed in the lilting, misleading foreword. Still another was the elegant, rosy-pink yet thin-blooded *salon* carnality of Boucher and Watteau, echoed in verse by Parny and others, and sparingly injected into this poem by way of teasing suggestion only; partly for Puškin's own amusement, partly for the usual mock-epic purpose of comic incongruity as in the episode of Ratmir in the massage parlor. A fourth was a quasiromantic note of lyricism with delicate eighteenth-century pastoral echoes which is occasionally sounded, not in sentimental communing with nature or rapturous portraiture of landscape, but in gemlike, totally conventional miniatures, like jade and mother-of-pearl inlays of Fujiyama, such as Ljudmila's view of the arctic range from Černomor's castle; or in such golden-age motifs as the idyll of Ratmir and the fishermaiden, and the description of Černomor's glacier-guarded pleasaunce, which might have inspired Hilton's Shangri-La. Among still other shapes in the mobile are some genuinely evocative of the Russian fairy tale and heroic legend and the chapbooks of *Bova* ad *Eruslan*: Ruslan's name, some details of his quest, the magic sword and beard, the vanishing cap, the bleached bones of horses and warriors on the ancient battlefield, recalling the site of Oleg's death; the reek of barbarous Indo-European antiquity, redolent of Old Irish or East Slavic imagination, that hangs about the Head, though there is about it also a distinct aura of the Odyssey, of Aeolus combined with Polyphemus the Cyclops; and while the anticlimactic slap dispels it for the moment, it returns strongly with an admixture of pathos at the death scene.

Each of these quite disparate elements had a settled constituency in public taste; but they could only have been merged in the medium which Puškin alone commanded: light, swiftly paced, lucidly phrased verse that tasted of the present while moving gaily in a mythic past in a series of graceful stage sets which—blessed relief—one was not expected to take solemnly or milk for edification. Among the catalyzers of the fusion must surely be recognized the stance of humorous, tolerant detachment taken by the author from the outset—discounting the wide-eyed Folklorelei of the Prologue which he added eight years later, like a baby-food label on a can of firecrackers. In this atmosphere, the reader feels, it becomes graceless and pedestrian to raise considerations of time, space continuity, plausibility—and modesty.

The long afterglow, reaching well into the present, shed by Puškin's ambiguous masterpiece of 1820 is well documented by V. G. Belinskij's comments many years later. From his sober and somehow drab redoubt of realism and local color, he first judiciously praises Puškin with faint damns. Then his own first reading of *Ruslan and Ljudmila*—at nine? at fifteen?—surges up in his mind, he is bewitched again, and off he soars, ending in such a rainbow froth of rapture that one wonders what a "warm" poem would have done to him, if a "cold" one did this:

Not one of Puškin's works caused as much noise and outcry as *Ruslan and Ljudmila*. Some saw in it the finest product of creative genius, others a violation of all canons of poesy, an insult to sound aesthetic taste. Both opinions might now appear equally fatuous if one failed to place them in historical perspective, where it becomes clear that there was sense in both of them, and both were to some degree tenable and well founded.

Nowadays *Ruslan and Ljudmila* is no more to us than a fairy tale, void of any coloring of locale, epoch, nationality, and hence lacking verisimilitude; regardless of the fine verse it is written in, and the gleams of poetry that strike one at times, it is cold, by the author's own testimony. Hardly anyone is apt to contest this these days. Yet at the time this poem burst upon the scene, it was in fact bound to appear an uncommonly great work of art. Remember that until then an unconscionable respect was still accorded Bogdanovič's "Dušen'ka" and Žukovskij's "The Twelve Sleeping Maidens"; how wonderstruck the readers of that time must have been by Puškin's fairy poem wherein all was so new, so original, so alluring — the verse, which was quite without precedent, light, tuneful, harmonious, alive, buoyant; the diction, the bold brushwork, the vivid colors, the graceful capers of young fancy, playful *esprit*, the very freedom of the immodest but nonetheless poetic tableaus. . . .

When all is said and done, *Ruslan and Ljudmila* is the kind of poem which by its appearance marked an epoch in the history of Russian literature. As a fairy tale written when its time had come, it can even now stand as proof of the fact that our predecessors were not in error when they saw in it living revelation of the advent of a great poet in the Russian land.[7]

NOTES

1. This paper represents a later and somewhat modified version of the Introduction to the author's English verse translation of Puškin's *Ruslan and Ljudmila*, which appeared simultaneously with the Banff Conference (Sept. 1974) with Ardis Publishers, Ann Arbor.

2. P., 11, p. 144. This last reference is a little puzzling. The octave is part of Genevra's tale of her infatuation with a young courtier but is totally unrewarding for the seeker of titillation. It contains nothing more heating than the young lady's admission that she did her best to lure the gentleman to her bed.

3. Consider *Spiess*, 'roasting spit; pike'; whence probably *Spiesser*, 'militiaman; pawn,' then '*pošljak*, lowbrow, philistine'; cf. English piker.

4. *Polnoe sobranie sočinenij V. A. Žukovskogo* (St. Petersburg, 1902), p. 89.

5. P., 4, p. 53.

6. Žukovskij, op. cit., p. 85.

7. *V. G. Belinskij, Polnoe sobranie sočinenij* (Moscow, 1955), vol. 7, p. 102.

PUŠKIN'S MORAL REALISM AS A
STRUCTURAL PROBLEM

Victor Erlich
Yale University

The title of this paper may be no more misleading than most titles, but it is more cryptic than some. Its legitimacy, such as it is, will emerge, I trust, from what follows. At this point let me say only that by "moral realism" I mean a stance frequently associated with the mature Puškin, notably the recognition of the ineradicable and often tragic complexity of the human conflict, a distrust of simple and cheery answers. I will attempt to show that in at least two of Puškin's narrative poems this view has visible structural underpinnings or, to be a little more specific, that it is arrived at by querying and displacing the initial presentation of the given fictional universe. In arguing this point, I will be covering much familiar ground. For the student of Puškin there will be no surprises here, no new material or essentially novel interpretation but, perhaps, a somewhat different way of putting it.

Let us start from Puškin's first "Southern" poem, the admittedly derivative and relatively immature "Kavkazskij Plennik." Indebtedness of this work, indeed of Puškin's entire Southern cycle, to the Byronic Oriental tale has been amply documented, most reliably so by Viktor Žirmunskij.[1] So are the significant deviations from the Byronic canon, such as the relative downgrading of the hero, who in Byron always serves as a pivot, a driving force of the *agon*. Puškin himself provided an interesting gloss on this process in an 1822 letter to V. P. Gorčakov, quoted by both B. Eixenbaum and J. Tynjanov:[2] "Čerkesy, ix obyčai i nravy zanimajut bol'šuju i lučšuju čast' moej povesti i èto vse ni s čem ne svjazano i est' istinnyj *hors d'oeuvre*."[3]

The characteristically Romantic plotting devices were deliberately neglected: "Čerkes plenivšij moego russkogo mog byt' ljubovnikom ego izbavitel'nicy, mat', otec ee mogli by imet' každyj svoju rol', svoj xarakter; vsem ètim ja prenebrëg."[4] In his "Problems of Puškin's Poetics," Eixenbaum comments: "Romantičeskij geroj prevratilsja v detal' razvernuvšegosja pejzaža, istočnik kotorogo ne Bajron a Žukovskij (Poslanie k Voejkovu)."[5] (Even a cursory perusal of this descriptive epistle bears Eixenbaum out fully: the phraseological affinities here are so close that some of Puškin's sequences, such as his four-line description of the Caucasian moutain peak Elbrus, could be termed an echo of Žukovskij's corresponding passage, were it not a significant improvement upon the latter.)[6]

Let us pause briefly before Part I of "Kavkazskij Plennik," which is clearly at issue here. The narrative proper is preceded by a thirteen-line introduction to the Circassian "customs and mores," a compact summary of an old-timers' bull session:

> В ауле, на своих порогах,
> Черкесы праздные сидят.
> Сыны Кавказа говорят
> О бранных, гибельных тревогах,[7]

The survey lists the characteristic pastimes of the fierce, intrepid mountaineers; it speaks of victories won by dint of courage and cunning, of the risks and rewards of warfare. The "exoticity" of the way of life into which the reader is being ushered is pointed out by the use of two "foreign" words: "uzden'" (chieftain) and "šaška" (saber). The latter, it is true, is perfectly intelligible in Russian, but both are supplied with footnotes.

As many will recall, the peaceful chat about warlike exploits is interrupted by an event which triggers the poem's meager plot—the intrusion of an outsider, literally propelled into the scene on a lasso ("na arkane"). For some 160 lines the narrative focuses on the young Russian's plight, on his hopes of freedom so cruelly dashed and the lovely Circassian maid's response to him and his predicament, only to yield for the remainder of Part I to a pageant of the Circassian mores. The ethnographic strain, briefly featured at the very outset, reasserts itself in an extended sequence which projects the rugged magnificence of Caucasian scenery and the indomitable vigor of its inhabitants in a diction both eloquent and concise, a diction which, as Puškin himself shrewdly recognized, is the strongest asset of the poem. For a while the *hors d'oeuvre* does steal the show:

> Но европейца всё вниманье
> Народ сей чудный привлекал.
> Меж горцев пленник наблюдал
> Их веру, нравы, воспитанье,
> Любил их жизни простоту,
> Гостеприимство, жажду брани,
> Движений вольных быстроту,
> И легкость ног, и силу длани;[8]

It is hardly necessary to insist that the speaker's stance is not entirely "objective." In fact, Puškin's statement that "all this bears no relation to anything" ought to be taken with a grain of salt. What we are being treated to is not simply an ethnographic digression but a skillfully localized celebration of the "simplicity," spontaneity, and vitality of the *Naturmensch*. The underlying myth of the noble savage—a recognizable Romantic or pre-Romantic notion—could scarcely be deemed unrelated to the literary genre exemplified by "Kavkazskij Plennik," or the tradition which helped shape it. Yet in one sense Puškin's dictum is certainly valid: outside of serving as an implicit repudiation of the less simple and vital world which the young Russian left behind in pursuing the will-of-the-wisp of freedom—"Svoboda! On odnoj tebja ešče iskal v podlunnom mire!"—the pageant bears no direct relation to the plot. Due to the nature of the situation, no dramatic clash between the two cultures is allowed to occur; the captive is reduced to the role of the passive if appreciative, indeed admiring, spectator of his captors' war games. The value-laden descriptive sequence remains a static piece of décor. Such drama or melodrama as is generated here is confined to the somewhat conventional encounter between the beautiful Circassian and the predictably burned-out Russian

captive. No opportunity is provided to test the Romantic stereotype of the natural man which informs the exotic set piece.

This is emphatically not the case with "Cygany," a poem whose
half-epic, half-dramatic structure encompasses many characteristic
themes and devices of Puškin's Southern period even as it reaches
beyond it. We will recall that the first scene of "Cygany" is likewise
a vivid tableau of an exotic way of life:

> Цыганы шумною толпой
> По Бессарабии кочуют.
> Они сегодня над рекой
> В шатрах изодранных ночуют. . . .[9]

As in "Kavkazskij Plennik," the initial presentation of the alien
ethos has an unmistakably favorable bias. Once again straight
description is intermingled with explicit or implicit value judgments.
The insistence on conveying the "quality of life" — the distinctive
virtues of the Gypsy community — occasions not only the use of
emotionally loaded epithets, but, in one instance, a curiously
abstract simile:

> Как вольность, весел их ночлег
> И мирный сон под небесами.[10]

The implication of moral superiority of "their" way of life to
"our" staid and constricting sophistication is still more pronounced
in the second scene, which portrays the Gypsies on the move, and
thus provides a dynamic sequel to the cozy opening passage. As the
tattered throng noisily and gaudily hits the road, the discordant
timbre of the proceedings — the absence of that *strojnost'* (harmony)
which Puškin otherwise valued so highly — is parlayed into a triumph
of spontaneity over deadening convention:

> Всё скудно, дико, всё нестройно;
> Но всё так живо-неспокойно,
> Так чуждо мертвых наших нег,
> Так чуждо этой жизни праздной,
> Как песнь рабов однообразной.[11]

Needless to say, this emotionally loaded pageant is no *hors d'oeuvre*. Because of Aleko's ill-fated project the Gypsy ethos as reality and as appearance is drawn into the vortex of the drama. The outsider—incidentally, not necessarily a Russian, but a European of a murky and indeterminate provenance—enters the scene in the wake of a brief descriptive prelude, not as a captive, but of his own volition. Let me rephrase: since the view of passion that will be expounded here makes a man gripped by it less than a free agent, it would be more accurate to say that the outsider enters propelled by an inner motive—love for a Gypsy maiden and an irresistible attraction for her world. "He wants to be like us, a Gypsy," Zemfira states pithily.[12]

This boldly utopian attempt at a cultural metamorphosis ends in an unmitigated disaster—a double murder and the assassin's banishment from the paradise regained. The contrast between the serenity of the overture and the unrelieved grimness of the finale is ironically pointed up by phraseological convergences. The poem's opening lines,

Цыганы шумною толпой
По Бессарабии кочуют.

are echoed with a symmetrical ominousness in an immediate sequel to the old Gypsy's much-quoted verdict:

Сказал, и шумною толпою
Поднялся табор кочевой.[13]

The key terms of the tribal leader's cordial welcome extended to the stranger,

Будь наш, привыкни к нашей доле,
Бродящей бедности и воле. . . .[14]

recur in a totally different context—that of the already mentioned act of expulsion:

Ты не рожден для дикой доли,
Ты для себя лишь хочешь воли. . . .[15]

Finally, if in the opening passage the phrase "tattered tents" is associated with "freedom" and "gaiety,"

> Они сегодня над рекой
> В шатрах изодранных ночуют.
> Как вольность, весел их ночлег

in the Epilogue, these same "tents" become receptacles of "tormenting dreams":

> Но счастья нет и между вами,
> Природы бедные сыны!
> И под издранными шатрами
> Живут мучительные сны,[16]

Should the ending of "Cygany" be thus construed as an outright negation of its beginning, a total repudiation or debunking of the tattered pastoral? As usually with Puškin, things are not as simple as that. To be sure, something has gone tragically wrong. The Gypsy concept of freedom (*volja*) has turned out to be totally incompatible with Aleko's. The delusion of cultural mimicry as a sheer act of will has been exploded. Yet within the Gypsy community the gentle code announced in the first two scenes of the poem has stood up well enough under the strain. The calm dignity of the old Gypsy's response to the bloody outrage shows that the values celebrated in the opening sequence have been properly internalized. Moreover, as a number of critics have pointed out, the threat did come from the outside. In the scheme of the poem, writes John Bayley, "Aleko must be the sole disruptive element in the Gypsies' pastoral innocence."[17] It is his "tormenting dreams"—his jealousy and vengeance-filled nightmares—that wreck the peace of the humble Gypsy tents.

But the somber moral of the Epilogue, reminiscent of Greek tragedy—G. Fedotov has spoken of "antičnyj tragizm"[18]—cannot be disposed of so easily. For if Aleko's *crime de passion* epitomizes the "civilized" man's inability to shed his skin and divest himself of the age-old ballast of fatal "passions," his disastrous intrusion upon the peace-loving sons of nature may well suggest the vulnerability of the "nomadic shelters" to the storms that rage around them, or, more broadly, the precariousness and marginality of the Gypsy pastoral. It might imply further that, however admirable

and internally consistent this model of behavior might be, it is
bound to remain a noble aberration, a movable oasis of gentleness
and meekness in the world of assertive and unreconstructed egos,
of possessiveness and passion.

There is also, it seems to me, the hidden cost of Gypsy tolerance.
Let us recall the Old Gypsy's confession, made to Aleko on the
eve of the catastrophe: the residue of his love for Mariula, who one
day had walked out on him and his little daughter, has been years
of quiet grief, of unrelieved loneliness.[19] (Free-love casualness
seems to have been in this instance a one-way street!) To be sure,
resignation, hurt borne in silence, is a more humane response than
murder, but it too is a far cry from "happiness," from the easy-
going, carefree stance which the opening scenes have led us to
expect. In sum, there are no easy solutions, no safe havens, no
escape from pain, loss, conflict. There is no place to hide:

И всюду страсти роковые,
И от судеб защиты нет.[20]

Ultimately, the Rousseauist myth of the Golden Age embedded in
the poem's descriptive ethnographical *donnée* has been neither de-
bunked nor validated by the plot. Rather it has been sharply called
into question and significantly qualified. The initial statement has
proved largely misleading, if not totally deceptive. "Truth" has
emerged as a more complex, more sobering, indeed more somber
affair than the set piece, which serves as a prelude to the story and
as a "thesis" of its moral dialectics.

Let us now reach across nearly a decade of Puškin's career and
shift from his last "Southern" poem to that masterful St. Petersburg
tale, "Mednyj vsadnik." The differences as to setting and theme
need not be insisted upon. In "Cygany" we are being introduced
to a totally alien milieu, a world whose fascination lies precisely
in its visual and moral exoticism. The Prologue to "The Bronze
Horseman" projects and celebrates the speaker's habitat and the
focus of his national identity and pride. Yet in both cases a dramatic confrontation is preceded by an extended description of a
social organism, a collective entity, a distinctive human project, a
description whose ideological and literary antecedents are easily
identified and thus "conventional."

The celebrated Prologue moves from a brief evocation of Peter the Great and his vision through the miracle of the "young proud city's" spectacular rise into a full-throated paean of praise of "Peter's creation" as perceived and savored by the speaker—its stately beauty, its nightly revels, and finally the stirring magnificence of its martial displays.[21] As the "thunder and smoke" of the most accomplished brand of patriotic rhetoric in the language sonorously take over, a "private," lyrical tribute to the poet's beloved city shades off into a "public" apotheosis of St. Petersburg as a symbol and warrant of Russia's imperial might:[22]

> Люблю, военная столица,
> Твоей твердыни дым и гром,
> Когда полнощная царица
> Дарует сына в царский дом,
> Или победу над врагом
> Россия снова торжествует,
> Или, взломав свой синий лед,
> Нева к морям его несет
> И, чуя вешни дни, ликует.[23]

The tone is confident, triumphant, not to say arrogant. It remains so through the closing lines of the sequence which announce the finality of Peter the Great's conquest, even as they bid the "vanquished elements" to make their peace with it:

> Вражду и плен старинный свой
> Пусть волны финские забудут
> И тщетной злобою не будут
> Тревожить вечный сон Петра![24]

It is this confidence that will be challenged as soon as the ensuing "sorrowful" tale gets under way. Yet other components of the Prologue's vision, too, will be put to an acid test.

Once again a dramatic shift in moral perspective that occurs in the course of the narrative is reflected in vocabulary. A comparison of Peter the Great's first appearance in the opening lines of the Prologue with the demeanor of his "bronze double" (R. Jakobson) in Part II, on the threshold of the fatal encounter between the ill-matched protagonists yields continuity as well as contrast. Thus the line "stojal on, dum velikix poln" is matched in the later and more ominous image by "kakaja duma na čele! kakaja sila v něm sokryta!" Yet in the same passage the statesmanlike act of "hacking a window through to Europe" is metamorphosed into a "fatal will" which founded the city *under* the sea. Let us note the significant difference between the Prologue's benign and constructive notion of a firm beachhead *by* the sea, or on the sea level—"nogoju tvërdoj stat' *pri more*"—and the high-handed arbitrariness of building a city "*pod morem*"— beneath the sea level,[25] and thus exposing its lowly inhabitants to the intermittent wrath of the repressed but not quite tamed "elements."

The dramatic conflict which dominates "The Bronze Horseman" has been identified repeatedly as that between *raison d'état* or "historic necessity" on the one hand, and the ordinary individual's claim or right to personal happiness on the other. Yet if the central theme of the poem has seldom been at issue, the critics' attempts to pin down the tenor of the poem have diverged widely. Some, notably Belinskij, have argued that in spite of the author's undeniable compassion for the individual victims of Peter's grand design, the "historic necessity" is ultimately vindicated.[26] Others, e.g., D. Merežkovskij, felt that on balance the poem sided with the human, all too human, rather than the superhuman, as it challenged in Evgenij's behalf the arrogance of power.[27] In an otherwise thoughtful essay, V. Brjusov maintained that in an implicit polemic with Mickiewicz, Puškin was forswearing a militantly rebellious stance, a direct challenge to despotism, only to opt for a more "realistic" but still libertarian stance—a belief in the gradual erosion of tyranny and an ultimate triumph of freedom.[28]

It is astounding that so intelligent a student of Puškin as Brjusov could have misjudged so thoroughly the essential thrust and structure of Puškin's moral vision. Whatever his politics in 1833 may have been, "Mednyj vsadnik" cannot be reduced to such a comfortingly pat, mildly "liberal" message. The conflict at the heart of Puškin's Petersburg tale, like all tragic conflicts, is never resolved; indeed, in the context of the poem it appears unresolvable. The rival claims are impossible to adjudicate, not only because they are irreconcilable, but also because they are incommensurate, Paraša's death or Evgenij's ordeal can no more cancel the austere harmony or the imperial grandeur of "Peter's creation" than can the latter meaningfully justify the wanton destruction of human life and of "ordinary" human dreams. The competing truths remain equally valid, equally unassailable within their respective realms.

What is then the function and the status of the Prologue? What is in retrospect the validity of the image of Peter the Great and his handiwork that emerges from this, the most famous set piece in Russian literature?

In one sense the speaker's confident prediction has been borne out. The rage of the elements failed to shake the seat of the empire; Peter the Great, or, rather, his "bronze double" has remained throughout intact and immune to the threat:

> И, обращен к нему спиною,
> В неколебимой вышине,
> Над возмущенною Невою
> Стоит с простертою рукою
> Кумир на бронзовом коне.[29]

Yet Evgenij's plight forces upon the reader a question for which the rhetoric of the Prologue has scarcely prepared him: What price glory? Once again the story serves to query the donnée, to press beyond the facade by revealing the pitfalls and the risks, in brief, the exorbitant cost of the much-publicized venture and dramatizing the unreliability of moral commonplaces, of stereotyped views of reality.

It has been previously noted that in his receptiveness to ideas, however disparate and incompatible, Puškin was not averse to toying with clichés. In his lyric verse he sometimes seems to try ideas for size, to sound them off, as it were, to explore their aesthetic and verbal potentialities. (Thus, a cliché "I dolgo budu tem ljubezen ja narodu/čto čuvstva dobrye ja liroj probuždal"—found its way into his self-apotheosis "The Monument.[30]")

It has been my contention here that in his narrative poems Puškin tended to use a set of images embodying a moral commonplace—a relatively simple and readily available proposition or preconception—as an enabling act, a launching pad of a drama, as a thesis to be tested, challenged, and crucially modified, if not entirely repudiated. He knew that art did not need to spurn les idées reçues, that it could well afford to incorporate them provided it was ready to transcend them.

NOTES

1. *Bajron i Puškin* (Iz istorii romantičeskoj poemy) (Leningrad, 1924).
2. See especially B. Eixenbaum, "Problemy poètiki Puškina," *O poèzii,* (Leningrad, 1969) and Ju. Tynjanov, "Puškin," *Arxaisty i novatory,* (Leningrad, 1929), p. 256.
3. P., 13, 52.
4. Ibid.
5. Op. cit. p. 26.
6. In Žukovskij's "K Voejkovu" we read:
   "И в сонме их гигант седой/Как туча Эльборус двуглавый/ Ужасною и величавой/Там все блистает красотой." Zukovskij, *Polnoe sobranie sočinenij* (St. Petersburg, 1902), vol. 2, p. 39. And now Puškin:
   "И в их кругу колосс двуглавый/В венце блистая ледяном/ Эльбрус огромный, величавый/Белел на небе голубом . . ." (P., 4, p. 98).
7. Op. cit., p. 93.
8. Ibid., p. 99.
9. Ibid., p. 179.
10. Ibid.
11. Ibid., p. 182.
12. Ibid., p. 180.
13. Ibid., p. 202.
14. Ibid., p. 180.
15. Ibid., p. 201.
16. Ibid., pp. 203–204.
17. John Bayley, *Pushkin* (Cambridge University Press, 1971), p. 103.
18. G. P. Fedotov, "Pevec imperii i svobody," *Novyj grad* (New York, 1952), p. 257.
19. P., 4, pp. 194–195.
20. Ibid., p. 204.
21. P., 5, pp. 136–137.
22. Ibid., p. 137.
23. Ibid.
24. Ibid., p. 135.
25. Ibid., pp. 135 and 147, respectively.
26. "Sočinenija Aleksandra Puškina," V. Belinskij, *Sočinenija* (Moscow, 1950) p. 628.
27. Quoted in V. Brjusov, "Mednyj vsadnik," *Moj Puškin* (Moscow-Leningrad, 1929), pp. 64–65.
28. Ibid., p. 82.
29. P., 5, p. 142.
30. Op. cit., v. 3, p. 424.

THE EUDAEMONIC THEME IN PUŠKIN'S "LITTLE TRAGEDIES"

Richard Gregg
Vassar College

I shall begin by quoting with minimal commentary from speeches made by the protagonists of each of Puškin's four "little tragedies," namely, the Baron, Salieri, Don Juan, and Walsingham.

Moved to feverish excitement by the prospect of again beholding his beloved gold, the Baron opens the famous soliloquy that constitutes all of the second scene of *The Covetous Knight* with these words:

> Как молодой повеса ждет свидания
> С какой-нибудь развратницей лукавой
> Иль дурой, им обманутой, так я
> Весь день минуты ждал, когда сойду
> В подвал мой тайный, к верным сундукам
> *Счастливый день!*[1]

> (emphasis added)

Then, having dilated at length on the imagined power which his wealth has procured for him and on the almost sensual joys which the unlocking of his trunks yields ("Vot moë blaženstvo!"[2] he cries), he continues in a kind of megalomaniac rapture:

> Я царствую! . . .Какой волшебный блеск!

178

> Послушна мне, сильна моя держава;
> *В ней счастие*, в ней честь моя и слава!³
>
> (emphasis added)

Such is the happiness of the first of the protagonists.

As he had done in *The Covetous Knight*, Puškin gives to the protagonist of *Mozart and Salieri* a long and psychologically revealing opening soliloquy. For the most part this speech is devoted to Salieri's description of the laborious apprenticeship of his early years and to the "winter of his discontent" which the ascendancy of Mozart has brought on. But Salieri's difficult beginnings on one hand, and the pangs of jealousy which are now tormenting him, are set off by a brighter period in between, when his sacrifices to the Muse had at last been crowned by artistic success and popular recognition:

> Усильным, напряженным постоянством
> Я наконец в искусстве безграничном
> Достигнул степени высокой. Слава
> Мне улыбнулась; я в сердцах людей
> Нашел созвучия своим созданьям.
> *Я счастлив был.* . . .
>
> (emphasis added)

This is, it will be noted, an idea which is echoed in passing by Mozart himself, when in his final speech he confides to Salieri:

> Нас мало избранных, счастливцев праздных,
> Пренебрегающих презренной пользой,
> Единого прекрасного жрецов.⁵

Although in their temperament and attitudes the two musicians are opposed in almost every respect, on one point they seem to agree: that to possess exceptional artistic gifts is to possess the means to happiness.

In the third drama of the group, *The Stone Guest*, the same motif receives more insistent treatment. In Scene 3 Don Juan, having finally extorted from Dona Anna a promise that she will receive him in her rooms alone, exults to his manservant:

> Милый Лепорелло!
> *Я счастлив!* . . . «Завтра—вечером, позднее . . .»
> Мой Лепорелло, завтра—приготовь . . .
> *Я счастлив,* как ребенок![6]

(emphasis added)

And a moment later

> *Я счастлив!*
> Я петь готов, я рад весь мир обнять.[7]

(emphasis added)

These exuberant outbursts are, it will be noted, essentially a confirmation of what he had earlier in the same scene assured Dona Anna herself:

> Давно или недавно, сам не знаю,
> Но с той поры лишь только знаю цену
> Мгновенной жизни, только с той поры
> И понял я, *что значит слово счастье.*[7]

(emphasis added)

Although *a priori* the pestilential atmosphere that reigns in the last of these plays might seem to rule out the theme under consideration, it occupies in fact a crucial position therein. For it is about two-thirds of the way through *Feast During the Time of the Plague* that the Master of Ceremonies, having been called on to deliver a "bacchic song," recites instead a "hymn in honor of the plague,"[9] the second and third stanzas of which read:

> Есть упоение в бою,
> И бездны мрачной на краю,
> И в разъяренном океане,
> Средь грозных волн и бурной тьмы,
> И в аравийском урагане,
> И в дуновении Чумы.
>
> Всё, всё, что гибелью грозит,
> Для сердца смертного таит
> Неизъяснимы наслажденья—

Бессмертья, может быть, залог!
И счастлив тот, кто средь волненья
Их обретать и ведать мог.[10]

(emphasis   added)

No one familiar with the "little tragedies" will be surprised by
the wide differences in the tone and dramatic function of these
passages. What is striking is that at a crucial moment in each play
the hero not only specifically addresses himself to the theme of
human happiness, but by his own example suggests what, for him,
happiness is. It is this that I have called the eudaemonic theme.[11]

These explicit references do not, however, take the full measure
of the theme of happiness in the "little tragedies." For related to the
eudaemonic idea either by way of reinforcement or through direct
and pointed opposition—the graphic principle of the repoussoir
could be invoked here—is a trio of ancillary motifs which recur
in all four plays. Of these the most prominent are the antithetical
motifs of the *banquet* (or *convivial gathering*) and *poison* (or *disease*).
Thus, in *The Covetous Knight* the banquet, though figurative, is
nonetheless concrete: "Xoču sebe segodnja pir ustroit'"[12] gloats
the Baron as he feasts his eyes on his gold; whereas the poison is the
deadly philter which the Jew tries to sell Albert in Scene 1. In
Mozart and Salieri the convivial gathering is the dinner of the two
musicians at "The Golden Lion"; while the poison is the lethal
dose which Salieri administers to his rival. Contrary to expectations,
the feast in *The Stone Guest* is not where Da Ponte and Tirso de
Molina placed it, namely, at the end, but rather in Scene 2, which
represents Laura's after-theater party for her friends; while the
motif of disease is touched on at the beginning when the Don speaks
of the morbid fascination of the late Dona Ineza, who with her
weak voice and "deathly pale" (*pomertvely*) lips was like "one
diseased."[13] As for the final play of the group the two antithetical
motifs are not only explicit in the "feast" and the "plague" of the
title; they are, as we shall see, the necessary conditions for the
unfolding of the entire dramatic action.

This is not all, however. For there is yet a third motif common
to all four plays, which, like the disease/poison theme, is related
antithetically to the eudaemonic idea, namely that of the *unwanted
guest* or *trouble-fête*. In the last of the quartet—to reverse our order
of approach—the *trouble-fête* is the Priest, who near the end of the

play breaks in on the revelers and casts over the proceedings the shadow of his stern and oppressive morality. In the penultimate drama the motif repeats itself twice. Fof if the Don, who breaks into Laura's rooms after the party and kills Don Carlos, is undeniably an uninvited guest of sorts, the authentic claimant to this title is, plainly, the Stone Commander in Scene 4. In *Mozart and Salieri* this figure is embodied by Salieri who terminates the convivial meal with nothing less than murder. Finally, in *The Covetous Knight* the Baron's "feast" is troubled twice: by the paranoid fear that on his death his son will break into his vaults (unwanted guest indeed!) and by his memory of the gnawing remorse which his greed had once caused:

> . . . Совесть,
> Когтистый зверь, скребущий сердце, совесть
> *Незваный гость*, докучный собеседник.[14]

(emphasis added)

Bearing this constellation of recurrent motifs in mind, I would like to take a different tack and propose that these four thematically linked plays, when arranged in the order which Puškin had specified,[15] form an entity whose separate parts may be defined in terms of *generic modifications* of tragedy, and which, when viewed as a whole, may be seen to possess a coherent and definable "shape."

To begin at the beginning: to my knowledge no one has yet disputed the tragic stature of *The Covetous Knight*. Nevertheless, it could be plausibly argued that the plot of this drama is ironic, not tragic, in essence. In itself the fact that the miser has through the ages been a satirical, not a tragic, figure cannot perhaps weigh too heavily in favor of this argument. Puškin's genius was no doubt great enough to elevate even the contemptible vice of greed to the status of *hamartia* had he so wished. But did he in fact do so?

To pose this question is not to disparage the magnificence of the Baron's soliloquy. Replete with passion, hubris, self-deception, and gnawing suspicions, it is plainly the stuff of which tragedy is made. But a tragic soliloquy is not synonymous with tragedy. And what the play as a whole presents is a heroic speech lodged in nonheroic surroundings, a soliloquy whose tragic amplitude contrasts sharply with what has preceded and what follows.

Basically, the play may be said to unfold dialectically. In Scene

1 we see the astringent effects of the father's avarice on his son, who, grown querulous, self-pitying, and obsessed by his need for money, is scarcely a heroic figure. In Scene 2 the action shifts to the Baron, whose hallucinatory vision of limitless power possesses somewhat paradoxically a tragic size lacking in his son's imprecations and complaints. Lastly, in Scene 3 antithesis and thesis, son and father meet for the first time. But the result of this encounter is not the magnification of the Baron's heroic size, but its diminution. Far from putting his vision of omnipotence to a test commensurate with its grandeur, he slanders his son behind his back and then exchanges insults with him in front of the Duke. Far from being granted a moment of tragic anagnorisis, he remains unseeing to the end. Far from being caught up in a necessary catastrophe for which the whole play has been a preparation (the fates of Salieri and Don Juan are instructive examples of such tragic inevitability), he is toppled suddenly and without warning—by a stroke. Finally, the whole stance of the Baron in this final scene is at striking variance with his previous demeanor. Before his trunks of gold he believes himself all-powerful: "Cto, ne podvlastno mne?"[16] he rhetorically inquires; and later: "Mne vsë poslušno—ja že ničemu."[17] Confronted in Scene 3, however, with actual people rather than chimeras, the omnipotent ruler turns out to be a courtier who, convoked by his lord for an accounting, squabbles meanly and inconclusively with his son and must then listen to a reprimand from the Duke who, it is pertinent to note, is a model *raisonneur* drawn from neoclassical satiric comedy.

Pure satire, of course, *The Covetous Knight* most emphatically is not. But if generations of critics have been right in asserting that a characteristic effect of irony—hence of satire, too—is meiosis, we have not taken the full measure of this play until we recognize the ironic ingredients in which it is so rich.

Despite certain structural similarities which it shares with its predecessor,[18] *Mozart and Salieri* is a vastly different kind of play. Simpler, shorter, more dynamic, it tends to concretize those motifs which were inconclusively or abstractly treated in *The Covetous Knight*. Thus, the banquet and the *trouble-fête* which are figurative in the first play become literal in the second; the poison is not merely discussed, it is lethally administered; the physical clash between the antagonists is not averted, but consummated. This relative dynamism is further reinforced by the temperamental and ideological polarity of the antagonists. For Mozart and Salieri differ from one another so deeply and so extensively that—a little like Turgenev's Don Quixote and Hamlet, or Nietzsche's Apollo and Dionysus—they seem to sum up and embrace all the possibilities in a given sphere, namely the artist's attitude toward his art. A generation later in England, Matthew Arnold was in a celebrated and seminal essay[19] to distinguish between the open, free, tolerant, and pluralistic spirit of Hellenism on one hand, and the intense, narrow, introverted, and monistic spirit of Hebraism on the other, and exhort his countrymen to partake more of the former. In pitting an extroverted, playful, spontaneous, and life-embracing genius against a dour, brooding, and self-disciplined Puritan on the other, Puškin is not only embodying in his art—and in terms of art—Arnold's antinomy, he is, by making the embodiment of "Hebraism" a murderer, anticipating Arnold's prejudices as well.

It is true of course—and by no means inconsistent with what has just been said—that Mozart is not simply the embodiment of Arnoldian "sweetness and light" any more than Salieri is simply a cruel distortion of Hebraism. Indeed it is an important paradox of his play that the at times almost childish gaiety of Mozart makes the better man and the greater genius seem less complex, less interesting, and ultimately a less tragic character than his rival. But this does not alter the fact that with one possible exception[20] no work of Puškin's mature years presents so sharp a contrast between moral good and evil as does this play. And if we recall that it is characteristic of the melodramatic plot to depict, in the words of one distinguished critic, "goodness beset by badness, a hero beset by a villain,"[21] and further, that melodramatic plots are apt to abound with wicked confessions, dark omens, and acts of diabolical villainy, it is obvious that *Mozart and Salieri* with its innocent victim, his archvillainous adversary, its sinister Man in Black, its plotting, and its poison has certain affinities with a dramatic genre related to, but not identical with, tragedy, namely melodrama.

However one may choose to rank *The Stone Guest* among its congeners as an achieved work of art, there can be little doubt that in design and scope it is the most ambitious play of the group, the "biggest," if you will, of the "little tragedies." This fact is not only due to its greater length, its larger cast, and its more complex plot; it stems also from the character of the hero himself. Unlike the Baron and Salieri, who must "share the limelight" with major rivals, Don Juan dominates the proceedings to such an extent that his presence is felt even during those brief moments (*viz.*, the beginning of Scene 2) when he is absent from the stage. Moreover, unlike them, he is almost bafflingly complex: a philanderer, who is by turns cruel and compassionate, murderous and tender, cynical and moralistic, intoxicated with life and drawn to death. He is so protean and iridescent (*divers et ondoyant*) that perhaps the only formula that can subsume his contradictions is a voracious — one is tempted to say omnivorous — *appetite for life*. Finally, alone among the four protagonists, Don Juan passes through the full gamut of tragic experience: supremely confident and hubristic at the outset, he launches on a deliberate and determined action leading inevitably to a catastrophe which is self-willed, conclusive, and complete. In sum, if one play of the group aspires to what might be called "high" or "grand" tragedy, *The Stone Guest* is, I would submit, that play.

More than its congeners *The Feast During the Time of the Plague* is a play of atmosphere; less than its congeners it makes use of plot to sustain interest; alone among the group it develops an action which is determined almost as much by the demands of protocol (the ceremony of the feast) as by the spontaneous and unpredictable impulses of the characters. Although emotions often run high, the play contains no violence; although death is present throughout, no one dies; although relationships are revealed, only one is significantly altered.[22] Indeed, structurally speaking, this play, or fragment from a play, may be described as a sequence of relatively loosely joined songs and speeches reflecting the speakers' various relations to a single terrifying fact.

Such a description is not intended to obscure the dramatic development or the moral conflicts that emerge. For it must be clear that as we move from the tight-lipped stoicism of the Young Man to the tearful nostalgia of Mary, and on to the clash between the latter and the bellicose Louisa, we are following a gradient of rising emotional intensity which culminates in the quasi-blasphemous "hymn to the plague" sung by the Master of Ceremonies himself. And when immediately thereafter the Priest intrudes and rebukes the revelers; and Walsingham, having at first stood his ground, ultimately shows the impact which his adversary's words have had on him by declining to rejoin his companions, it is clear that the "Dionysian" moment has passed.

To point out the presence of a dramatic development is not, however, to affirm tragic stature. And that play which has no purposeful hubristic hero, which exemplifies no tragic flaw, which has no catastrophe, and whose very plot is rudimentary and inconclusive—such a play can be called a tragedy only by stretching the term beyond its traditional limits. And while the business of pasting labels on the fluid forms of literature is not always rewarding and the label I propose is imprecise, it may be useful to recall that a theatrical form in which the lyrical element is emphasized at the expense of dramatic intensity, in which the characters tend to represent a single aspect of the human personality (e.g., the Priest, Mary, Louisa), and in which a stylized or ceremonial dimension is prominent is called a *masque*.[23] An authentic masque *A Feast During the Time of the Plague* most certainly is not. But in trying to assess the differences that separate this play from full-blown tragedy, it is instructive to note that many of them may be subsumed under the concept of the masque or lyrically colored closet drama.[24]

Bearing in mind the generic peculiarities of these plays, we can now stand back and survey the group as a whole. And what emerges is that "definable shape" which I have already proposed by way of hypothesis. Starting with the asperities of *The Covetous Knight*, which, with its deflated and mean-spirited hero, its thwarted antagonist, and its occasional satirical touches,[25] partakes of the ironic plot, we move to the quicker, more "transitive" action of *Mozart and Salieri* which, with its relatively black-and-white characterizations and its more lurid plot accessories, makes for tragedy tinged with melodrama. Whereupon we ascend to the "high tragedy" (as I have chosen to call it) of *The Stone Guest*, in which a passionate and apparently amoral hero boldly reaches out, risks all, and, even as he seems to be on the verge of a moral conversion, brings full and unequivocal ruin upon himself. Then, having reached this moment of maximal intensity, we fall back into the muted, lyrical diminuendo of the masquelike *Feast During the Time of the Plague*.

To this I will make two supplementary observations. If in trying to define the "shape" of this group of plays, we had, instead of investigating their generic properties, asked the simple question: which of these heroes engage our emotions and sympathies (*uvlekaet nas*) most fully (a criterion of obvious relevance in gauging tragic intensity)—we would find ourselves plotting a similar asymmetrical curve. With the cold and solipsistic Baron it is, for all the splendor of his rhetoric, virtually impossible to identify. Though more wicked perhaps, Salieri is also more sympathetic: we can, after all, understand his envy even as we deplore its manifestations; and when he weeps for the dying Mozart we weep for both victor and victim. As for *The Stone Guest*, the exuberantly amoral and animally high-spirited Don Juan sweeps us willy-nilly off our feet, much like the women he woos. Lastly, in Walsingham we recognize the sanest, least passionate, and most morally admirable of our protagonists. And it is partially, perhaps, precisely because of these *reasonable* virtues that he is unable to quicken our pulses to the same degree as the flamboyant Don.[26]

Finally, if, as I have suggested, these dramas describe a curve of rising and falling tragic intensity, the congruity of their settings is worth noting. From the north European locale of *The Covetous Knight* (not for nothing do we speak of irony as being *cold*) we move southward to the Vienna of the more dynamic *Mozart and Salieri*, then on to the semitropical setting of Madrid in the third and climactic play.[27] only to retreat to the cooler climes of England for the less cathartic action of *The Feast During the Time of the Plague*.

Heretofore we have been concerned with two apparently un-related ideas: first, the recurrence in these plays of the eudaemonic theme with its attendant motifs of feast, poison, and *trouble-fête*; secondly, the theory that this "experiment in dramatic studies" (the phrase is Puškin's[28]) describe, when viewed as a whole, that unbalanced curve of gradual rise and more precipitous decline which may be seen as a paradigm of the typical dramatic action. I would now like to propose that these ideas are related; specifically, that the nature and fate of the Good Life in these plays can be connected to the *kind* of tragedy (or nontragedy) which each embodies.

To begin (again) at the beginning: the first stage of this progression is *The Covetous Knight*, which may be said to depict the *preclusion* of eudaemonia. This occurs twice. On the obvious level the Baron's avarice denies Albert the Good Life by denying him those amenities without which he cannot live like his peers. More subtly, by fostering in the Baron the illusion that money is all, it has *ipso facto* denied him, too, the possibility of knowing authentic happiness. For we do not have to wait for the anguished fears that assail him at the end of the soliloquy to realize that the feverish and transitory bliss which this monomaniac recluse feels is not the Good Life but its ugly caricature. As for the kind of happiness denied, it is symptomatic of the preoccupation which satire has traditionally

shown with antisocial behavior that the Good Life denied both
father and son is dependent on social integration. For if the father's
greed has prevented his son from joining the society of his peers,
it has turned himself, once a "true, brave knight"[29] into a harmful
parasite of that same society.

If eudaemonia is precluded in the first play, in the second it is
destroyed. Unlike the Baron and his son, both Mozart and Salieri
have, as the passages quoted above make clear, experienced happiness in their lives. Nor is it to disparage the satisfactions of social
integration to suggest that service to the Muse is a purer, more dis-
interested sphere of activity than the life of a courtier. And it is in the
gratuitous destruction of this good activity that we can see the link
between the genre (tragedy tinged with melodrama) and the nature
and fate of eudaemonia. For what is the murder of the happy,
childlike Mozart but "goodness beset by badness" — to repeat
Bentley's useful formula.

Whether or not Don Juan's ultimate conception of happiness (love
for Donna Anna) is in point of fact ethically superior to the happiness which Albert vainly seeks or which Mozart is cruelly deprived
of is a matter I shall leave to the moralist. What is certain is that
since the Middle Ages romantic love, later sanctified by the Christian institution of marriage, has in the literature of the western
world been the most universally acknowledged form of earthly
happiness, the great secular *summum bonum*.[30] This being so, it
should not surprise us that the third and climactic tragedy presents
as the goal of the hero's eudaemonic quest neither Society nor Art,
but Woman.

The question is: which woman, and why?

Although during the course of the play we learn a good deal
about the Don's amours both past and present (Dona Ineza, the
blue-eyed blondes of the north, Laura) the word "happiness" —
which is invoked seven times in all[31] — is used with reference to
one woman only, Dona Anna.

Although the sincerity of the Don's love for Dona Anna has
recently been questioned by several distinguished Slavists,[32] and
while there are undeniably vestiges of the old *ars amoris* in his
wooing of the widow,[33] there is, I believe, good reason to prefer
the traditional view that his intentions are, ultimately at least,
"honorable." A detailed rebuttal of the "revisionist" theory does
not fall within the purview of this paper. Suffice it to suggest that

the man who on being granted a rendezvous with a woman jubilates to his lackey that he is "happy as a child" and wants to "hug the whole world"; who is so consumed by his jealousy of her deceased husband that he endangers the success of his suit by needlessly revealing his true identity, and risks (and loses) everything by challenging his "rival" to attend the nocturnal tryst;[34] that the man who, alone at night in the chambers of the woman of his desires consents to depart with no more than a "cold" kiss for his pains; who on the apparition of the terrifying statue draws close to this woman;[35] and who, finally, has her name on his lips at the most solemn and dreadful moment of his life—that such a man, far from being an unreconstructed lecher, is as the play draws to a close, in the process of falling sincerely, even virtuously, in love.

But who then is Dona Anna that the greatest lover of Spain perishes for love of her? Momentarily the answer cannot but perplex us. For she is neither more or less than the stereotypic Perfect Wife as conceived by a Superior Male.[36] Not only does she combine the predictable virtues of beauty, devoutness, and fidelity ("*Vdova dolžna i grobu byt' verna*,"[37] she piously intones),[38] she is also endowed with those small feminine foibles which the stronger sex is supposed to find irresistible. She is charmingly *egocentrical*: "I ljubite davno už vy menja?"[39] she cannot resist inquiring, even as she is indignantly rejecting him. She is *coy*: "Podite proč'—vy čelovek opasnyj/ . . . ja slušat' vas bojus'"[40] she exclaims as he presses his suit. She is *curious*: "Vy mučite menja./Ja strax kak ljubopytna . . ."[41] she cries as he is tantalizing her with his disclosure. She is *flirtatious*: "Kakoj vy neotvjazčivyj: na, vot on,"[42] are the words with which she bestows her farewell kiss on him. To measure the distance that separates Dona Anna from a woman of authentic originality and depth of character one need only try to imagine Tat'jana exclaiming to Onegin during their last encounter: "Kakoj vy neotvjazčivyj!"

Such then is Dona Anna. And if we wonder how the sophisticated and worldly-wise Don Juan can possibly fall in love with this pretty, shallow, conventionally virtuous widow, the answer is surely that she is pretty, shallow, and conventionally virtuous. It was after all Puškin himself who, having led a Don Juanesque life for years, was as he was writing these lines determined to settle down to "bourgeois" (the word is his)[43] domesticity and was fond of quoting Chateaubriand's aphorism: "Il n'y a de bonheur que dans les voies communes."[44] And if it be objected that his proclaimed fondness for the commonplace could not possibly extend to his choice of a wife, one need only look at the fiancée he was then so ardently wooing, a woman quite as pretty, shallow, and conventional as Dona Anna. After the exotic beauties of the north, after the decadent charms of Dona Ineza, after the gifted but promiscuous Laura, Don Juan has discovered what might be called the banality of virtue, or better yet: the virtue of banality. And his tragedy is that even as he is making this discovery, the figure of the Stone Commander, a complex symbol simultaneously suggesting an avenging nemesis and the punishing superego, destroys him.

In the last of our plays the centrality of Walsingham's "hymn to the plague" is so plain, its eloquence so powerful, and its quasi-Nietzschean message so appealing, that one is tempted to agree with those Soviet critics who see in it the life-affirmed moral of the play.[45] But does this view square with the action taken as a whole? For it should not be forgotten that the same Walsingham who praises the plague and denounces the jeremiads of the Priest is ultimately forced to ask the latter in tones of near entreaty:

> Зачем приходишь ты
> Меня тревожить? Не могу, не должен
> Я за тобой идти: я здесь удержан
> Отчаяньем, воспоминаньем страшным,
> Сознаньем беззаконья моего
> И ужасом той мертвой пустоты,
> Которую в моем дому встречаю.[46]

Plainly it is not the life-affirming principle that detains Walsingham at the revelers' banquet, but a sense of despair which, it transpires, stems from his belief that his liaison with a prostitute has barred his "fallen spirit" from any communion with true goodness.[47] In the last of these plays, as in the first, a self-deceived protagonist eloquently claims to enjoy a happiness which proves to be transient and false.

But if the ubiquitous plague has denied earthly happiness to all the characters, it has not extinguished in all of them a remembrance of that condition. Wearing the persona of "Jenny," Mary is evidently recalling her own youth when she sings:

> Было время, процветала
> В мире наша сторона:
> В воскресение бывала
> Церковь Божия полна.[48]

And later, without the persona, she says of her maidenhood:

> Мой голос слаще был в то время; он
> Был голосом невинности.[49]

These souvenirs of piety and innocence prefigure in turn Walsingham's recollection of his deceased wife:

> Меня когда-то
> Она считала чистым, гордым, вольным—
> И знала рай в объятиях моих. . . .[50]

The symbolic prototype of this lost paradise where love between the sexes could be "pure" is of course the Eden of Genesis, where conjugal love, virtue, and pleasure were parts of an indivisible, happy whole. But in the death-obsessed and guilt-ridden world of the revelers (a world to which man's post-lapsarian condition is the obvious prototype and analogue) a disassociation of virtue and pleasure has occurred. One may practice the former—as does the priest—or cultivate the latter—as do with varying degrees of success the rest of the cast—but one cannot possess both. One can, in short, no longer know the Good Life.

And it is here that we can see the link between the fate of eudaemonia which the play describes and the kind of drama which it exemplifies. For if the Good Life on earth has been forfeited by all the characters, and if as a result they must resort to reminiscences, hymns, sermons, and songs to allay (but not remove) their suffering, then tragic action in the traditional sense is all but impossible. Rather than do active battle against a painful reality, the revelers use their songs and speeches as refuges from it. And these refuges *are* in a sense the play. If, in short, a universal fact (the plague) has induced a certain homogeneity of *mood*, a common activity (the ritual of the feast) confers a certain air of *ceremony*. Working in cooperation the two eponymous elements, plague and feast, thus produce those atmospheric and ritualistic qualities which, as already noted, one commonly associates with a masque.

Wary of the dangers that schematizations entail, we may nonetheless summarize the theme of happiness in the "little tragedies" as follows: in the first play happiness is conceived of as social integration, and it has been precluded; in the second it has been realized through artistic activity which is destroyed by an external force; in the third it is realized through a woman's love and is destroyed by largely internal (i.e., self-destructive) forces;[51] in the fourth it is the attribute of an anterior paradisiacal innocence which has been forfeited. Moreover, corresponding to these eudaemonic variations is that generic evolution from ironic tragedy to melodramatic tragedy to full or "high" tragedy and finally to masquelike pseudotragedy, which, with its pattern of rising and falling dramatic intensity, may be said to recapitulate the archetypal tragic action.

From what has been said it should not be inferred that the negation of the Good Life is the only theme which unites the "little tragedies." Death, decadence, the "ruling passion" are, as the studies of Blagoi, Seeley, and others have shown, also important unifying themes. Nor, in noting the overall "shape" of this group of plays, have I sought to imply that only a sequential reading can do them artistic justice. In allowing them to be published separately,[52] Puškin indicated that he thought otherwise. Nevertheless, the original plan to include them in one volume and in a specified order is a fact; the abandonment of this plan may well have been prompted by personal rather than artistic considerations; and the restoration of the "original" order (*habent sua fata libelli*) is now a universal editorial practice. Under the circumstances, the "archaeological" investigation which I have attempted here is, I think, not only licit; it is overdue.

NOTES

1. P., 7, p. 110.
2. Ibid., p. 112.
3. Ibid.
4. Ibid., p. 124.
5. Ibid., p. 133.
6. Ibid., p. 159.
7. Ibid.
8. Ibid., p. 157.
9. It is noteworthy that although Walsingham explicitly denies that the has composed the "bacchic song" (130) requested of him, in many ways his "hymn" is unquestionably Dionysian in spirit.

10. P., 7, p. 180.
11. It is not my purpose here to explore the autobiographical ramifications of this theme. Suffice it to say that, as Anna Axmatova has pointed out, Puškin's correspondence at the time of the writing of the "little tragedies" reveals a clear and continuing preoccupation with the idea of happiness ("*Kamennyj gost'* Puškina," *Puškin: Issledovanija i materjaly,*" 2 [1958], p. 191).
12. P., 7, p. 112.
13. Ibid., p. 139.
14. Ibid., p. 113.
15. A mock cover or title page designed for this volume by Puškin himself has survived. It bears the title "Dramatičeskie Sceny." Other "alternative" titles indicated on the same sheet are "dramatičeskie očerki," "dramatičeskie izučenija," and "opyt dramatičeskix izučenij." Attached to this sheet is another one on which Puškin indicated the table of contents: "I Okt[avy] II Skupoj III Salieri IV D. Guan V Plague. (reproduced in *Puškin: Polnoe sobranie sočinenij*, ed. D. P. Jakubovič et al. [Leningrad, 1935], VII, 98, 377).
16. P., 7, p. 110.
17. Ibid., p. 111.
18. Both plays are constructed on the principle of an agon or duel between two characters — one essentially good, the other essentially evil. In both plays the evil character is the protagonist; in both plays the good character is victimized.
19. "Hebraism and Hellenism," in *Culture and Anarchy* (1869).
20. I have in mind the opposition of the villainous Švabrin and the virtuous Grinev in *The Captain's Daughter*.
21. Eric Bentley, *The Life of the Drama* (New York, 1972), p. 200.
22. Namely Walsingham's shift in attitude toward the Priest.
23. Cf. Northrup Frye's definition of a masque as a "species of drama in which music and spectacle play an important role and in which the characters tend to be or become aspects of human personality rather than independent characters" (*Anatomy of Criticism: Four Essays* (New York, 1968), p. 366). I take Frye's "spectacle and music" to be related to, though not identical with, the ceremonial and lyrical aspects which I mention.
24. Many but not all. One important difference which separates this play from full-fledged tragedy and which cannot be subsumed under the concept of the masque is its somewhat fragmentary nature.
25. Tomaševskij has noted in the exchange between the Baron and Albert in Scene 3 a direct borrowing from Molière's *L'Avare* ("'Malen'kie tragedii' Puškina i Mol'er," *Puškin: Vremennik Puškinskoj Kommissii,*" I (1936), 115–125).

26. The reason that Walsingham's fate moves us less than the Don's does not, of course, lie merely in the former's reasonableness. The simple fact that the latter perishes, while Walsingham does not is of obvious importance here.
27. It is noteworthy that in this, the most passionate of the four dramas, one of the characters (Laura) gratuitously compares the warm Madrid night to the colder weather of Paris (P., 7, p. 148), almost as if it were Puškin looking back to the North European setting of his first play.
28. See Note 30.
29. P., 7, p. 116.
30. The two classic studies of the emergence of the cult of romantic love in Western civilization are C. S. Lewis' *The Allegory of Love* and Denis de Rougemont's *Love in the Western World*.
31. I am including its grammatical variants (*sčastliv, sčastlivec*, etc.)
32. E.g., Charles Corbet, "L'Originalité du *Convive de Pierre*," *Revue de Littérature Comparée* (Paris, 1955), XXIX, 48–71; Frank Seeley, "The Problem of *Kamennyj Gost'*," *The Slavonic and East European Review*, 41 (1962–63): 345–367.
33. This has been eruditely demonstrated by Seeley, op. cit.
34. It is not being suggested that jealousy is the only motive for these irrational acts. Insolence, cruelty, and a desire for self-punishment may also be involved. It is, however, my view that the psychological need to exorcise the "ghost" of Don Alvar is the most satisfying *single* explanation for his bizarre behavior.
35. Otherwise the statue would not be prompted to say: "Bros' ee" (P., 7, p. 171).
36. Seeley, op. cit., makes a very similar point when he calls attention to the "ordinariness" of Dona Anna.
37. P., 7, p. 164.
38. It could be argued that by Scene 4 her virtues appear to be anything but impregnable; but, of course, there is no way of knowing what *might* have happened. In terms of the *données* she does in fact remain a virtuous woman to the end.
39. P., 7, p. 157.
40. Ibid.
41. Ibid., p. 166.
42. Ibid., p. 170.
43. *The Letters of Alexander Puškin*, ed. J. Thomas Shaw (Bloomington and Philadelphia, 1963), vol. 2, p. 459.
44. Ibid.
45. E.g., D. Blagoj, *Tvorčeskij put' Puškina* (Moscow, 1967), pp. 664–667.
46. P., 7, p. 182.
47. Ibid., p. 183.

48. Ibid., p. 176.
49. Ibid., p. 178
50. Ibid., p. 183.
51. See Note 34.
52. Op. cit.

THE PLACE OF "DOMIK V KOLOMNE" IN PUŠKIN'S CREATION

William Harkins
Columbia University

Critics have either passed by Puškin's "Domik v Kolomne" in silence, as if embarrassed to deal with it, or have been much, perhaps excessively, intrigued with it. But no one, if we except Modest Gofman's work with the text[1] or Jurij Semjonow's survey monograph and commentary,[2] has made a large-scale study of the poem. Even the Russian Formalists, who found in "Domik" a rare example of an entire work that could serve to illustrate that device to which they gave the name of *obnaženie priëma* ("laying bare the device"), failed to devote any real study to this neglected work. Especially neglected is the question of the place "Domik" should rightly have in Puškin's development and in his whole creation.

No doubt "Domik" is an embarrassing work to deal with. An anecdotal incident serves as the basis of the plot: a young girl, Paraša, lives with her widowed mother in a little house in Kolomna, a part of Petersburg along the River Fontanka. Paraša shows exemplary industry in managing the household, and though she dreams of romance when she reads the novels of Emin or sits up to watch the moon at night, there is no evidence that she flirts with any of the soldiers who pass her house. The family's aged cook dies; a new one must be found, in a hurry and cheap. Paraša comes home with a girl, Mavruša, who proves singularly inept for her post. One Sunday at church the widow is seized by the sudden fear that Mavruša may take advantage of their absence to rob them blind; she returns home at all speed—to find the new cook shaving! The man rushes away and is never seen again. At this point (omitting in his usual concise manner to refer to any relation between Paraša and the supposed Mavruša), Puškin drops the tale, and refuses to supply a moral, but then, in an afterthought, he comes up with a double one:

> Вот вам мораль: по мненью моему,
> Кухарку даром нанимать опасно;
> Кто ж родился мужчиною, тому
> Рядиться в юбку странно и напрасно:
> Когда-нибудь придется же ему
> Брить бороду себе, что несогласно
> С природой дамской . . .Больше ничего
> Не выжмешь из рассказа моего».[3]

Thus the plot, based on the motif of transvestite disguise, is a thin one, and the poet underlines the letdown which attends discovery at the end by his refusal to draw any serious lesson from the incident. It is true that the details of daily life of Paraša and her mother are more promising, suggesting a "new realism," if we may call it that, of everyday life of the middle classes. But these details are interrupted by Puškin's everlasting ironic mockery and by continual digressions, and in the end the whole is rather thin, less promising in its use of realistic detail, perhaps, than the similar details, this time concerning life on the country estate, from the earlier comic poem, "'Graf Nulin."

More promising, it would seem, is the poet's long, metapoetic introduction which so appealed to the Formalists. Quoting the final two stanzas (the second of which I myself have just quoted) Viktor Šklovskij cites the poem as an example of a work from which no conclusion, ideological, moral, or whatever, can be drawn, and adds (possibly in exaggeration) that the same ending might have been added (but why wasn't it, then?) to Puškin's Onegin. For Šklovskij, "Domik" is an example of an "almost subjectless art," and it is "one of the most striking examples of a case where a work is almost entirely filled with a description of the device with which it is constructed."[4] And Tynjanov commented that the octave verse of "Domik" was used by Puškin to create a new, "debased" and "prosaicized" epos at odds with the established form of the iambic tetrameter poetic narrative.[5]

So fascinated have the critics been with the metapoetic part of the work that they have frequently resurrected and reprinted several rather topical stanzas, critical of the journals of the day, which Puškin had written along with the rest of the poem but which he decided to leave out in the first published edition of 1833; one factor in his decision may have been the fact that one of the journals criticized by Puškin, Del'vig's Literaturnaja gazeta, had ceased to appear in 1831.

Not counting these omitted stanzas, the metapoetic introduction to the poem covers the opeining eight and one-half stanzas; there is also other metapoetic and metaliterary matter spread through the remainder of the forty stanzas of the poem, to the extent that we might count a good half of the poem as metaliterary. The principal subject of this metaliterary matter is verse itself; in the famous opening line, "Četyrestopnyj jamb mne nadoel",[6] Puškin turns his back on that very verse form that had served as the staple of his poetry up to that time. In what follows he describes his new preference (a change marked, of course, in the verse of "Domik" itself) to the ottava rima, a form that was a prosodic tour de force requiring triple rhymes in alternation. As critics have long since shown, the form was borrowed by Puškin from similar narrative poems with metapoetic passages by Byron, Musset, and especially by Barry Cornwall.[7] We must beware, of course, of taking Puškin literally in this introduction; though ostensibly he is "fed up" here with the four-foot iamb, still he did return to it in his poetic masterpiece, Mednyj vsadnik. And, though he had never written octaves before "Domik," the fact is that he already had considerable experience with both iambic pentameter and with triple rhymes, both masculine and feminine, in his early "Gavriiliada," as well as others of his earlier narrative poems. But the octaves of "Domik" lead nowhere, seemingly, in the work of the later Puškin, struggling to remake himself a prose writer; at any rate, there are no octaves to follow. Thus Puškin seems to play with his reader, to promise what he has no intention of delivering, for the sake of a comic irony.

Yet we must beware of taking these implications too literally. For "Domik" is one of the first works of a period of rhythmic experimentation that characterizes Puškin's last poetry. We may divide this experimentation into two types: (1) a "folk" type, embracing a whole series of attempts either to suggest or to develop the rhythmic patterns of folk poetry; these are found in the *Skazki* and the *Pesni zapadnyx slavjan*, as well as in a few other poems. The second pattern consists in the introduction of regular, formal, iambic patterns little used or unused by Puškin earlier: the *ottava rima* in *Domik*, and the hexameter in *Andželo*. These experiments may seem likewise to lead nowhere, but they are important at least in establishing an effort to find new ways in poetry. In the end, of course, prose won out, and the sole late masterpiece in verse, *Mednyj vsadnik*, is in a practiced form, the once supposedly repudiated iambic tetrameter.

In the metaliterary introduction there is other matter not concerned with metrics; in the eighth and ninth stanzas the poet renounces classicism in the following terms:

> Парнасский иноходец
> Его не обогнал бы. Но Пегас
> Стар, зуб уж нет. Им вырытый колодец
> Иссох. Порос крапивою Парнас;
> В отставке Феб живет, а хороводец
> Старушек муз уж не прельщает нас.
> И табор свой с классических вершинок
> Перенесли мы на толкучий рынок.
>   Усядься, муза; ручки в рукава,
>   Под лавку ножки! не вертись, резвушка!
> Теперь начнем.[8]

This renunciation of classicism is so striking that we may overlook the much less explicit digs at the expense of romanticism that are buried in the middle of the poem. Puškin's heroine, Paraša, reads sentimental romances; her favorite author is Emin; she is described, in what seems to be a parody of the poet's own Tat'jana, as gazing at the moon at night. But more decisive is the digression concerning Countess X, in real life the Countess Strojnovskij, a great beauty who had sold herself to an old husband to redeem her family from poverty. Puškin had evidently seen her in Kolomna when he himself lived there. The subject of her personal tragedy no doubt tempted the poet, but he turns from it in favor of the much more mundane story of his new heroine, Paraša. The comparison of the two is notable:

> . . . она была несчастна.
> Блаженнее стократ ее была,
> Читатель, новая знакомка ваша,
> Простая, добрая моя Параша.[9]

This opposition of romanticism and a debunking antiromanticism was to continue throughout the last work of Puškin, especially in his prose. But we also find it in *Mednyj vsadnik*, where the ordinary, down-to-earth hero, Evgenij, is opposed to the idealized mythic hero, Peter. *Onegin* contains rich examples of the same apparently ambivalent opposition. But it is in "Domik" itself that this opposition of the romantic and realistic, the idealized and the real, the everyday and the exotic, comes most clearly, and here the opposition is even "laid bare" as a basic device. If we trace it through Puškin's work, we will find its origins not only in *Onegin*, but in Puškin's earlier comic poem, "Graf Nulin," where the poet rejects the conception of his heroine as ready for an adulterous affair in favor of a practical, everyday, commonsensical, ethical attitude, just as in the same poem he puts down the French romantic poets Lamartine and D'Alencourt, who were just then beginning to be imitated in Russian by Puškin's contemporaries.

"Graf Nulin" resembles "Domik" in yet another respect: the anecdotal basis of its humorous plot. Without going into the question of the actual origins of these anecdotes (both are fundamentally obscure), it is probably safe to assume that both stories derive from real life, as did the more celebrated anecdotes that Puškin supposedly related to Gogol'. If we compare "Graf Nulin" and "Domik" with Puškin's earlier comic poem, the *Gavriiliada*, we find in *Gavriiliada* another subject in a sense also anecdotal, but here the anecdote is not taken from real life and is treated in the high style of the mock epic; because of this elegant, elaborate treatment the anecdotal basis of the plot is almost totally obscured. Moreover, the humor of "Gavriiliada" is based more on character types than on anecdotal situation: God is an old lecher, Gabriel a young rake, Joseph an impotent old man who no longer cares, and so on. Only Mary, the heroine, has a more fluid and substantial character, though she does not really come off, it must be added.

In "Graf Nulin" there are traces of the high style, especially in the very funny passage where Nulin attempts to make his way in the dark to the heroine's bedroom; these traces are presumably inspired by the classical origin of the subject (the name of Tarquin is even mentioned in this passage), as well as by the influence of Shakespeare's poem, *The Rape of Lucrece*, which Puškin had just been reading. But, in spite of these fragmentary epic strands, the real quality of "Graf Nulin" is a rough-and-ready treatment of everyday life, the details of which are comic because they are bathetic and vulgar, if none the less real. In "Domik v Kolomne" there is also a brief recollection of the high mock-epic style, but only in the metaliterary introduction, where the Muse is preemptorily dismissed.

In their anecdotal conception "Graf Nulin" and "Domik" are tied most closely to Puškin's last manner. *The Tales of Belkin* are all anecdotal, and in *Mednyj vsadnik* the element of anecdote is considerable, if not, of course, total. We should define the term; for my purposes here I am using the word to denote a narrative with a brief action, a strong turn or *pointe* at the end, and minimal characterization, not to speak of character development. *Mednyj vsadnik* possesses all these attributes with the possible exception of the sharp *pointe*; it would have one, to be sure, in the statue's sudden pursuit of the fleeing Evgenij, but this is partly veiled by the reader's hesitation to accept the event as a real one, external to Evgenij's consciousness, as well as by the anticlimax that follows: the discovery of Evgenij's dead body. We might perhaps dispute whether the fact of Evgenij's madness represents "character development" in the ordinary sense, but there can be no dispute over the fact that the other characters in the poem, the widow and her daughter, are left almost totally uncharacterized, while Evgenij himself is depicted largely in negative terms: his complete lack of distinction and his dreams of a peaceful family existence free from want.

The name Paraša also seems to connect these three works, "Graf Nulin," "Domik," and *Mednyj vsadnik*, In "Graf Nulin" Paraša is the mistress's confidante and, perhaps, the master's concubine: she is young, lively, rough and ready, has a sharp tongue and is ever ready for a flirtation. In "Domik" she is a widow's daughter, energetic and active at the tasks of household management, while her mother drowses or plays solitaire. In *Mednyj vsadnik* she is likewise a widow's daughter, Evgenij's fiancée, who is drowned when the great flood of 1824 washes away their island cottage. This is all we know about her. The characters are, of course, not precisely the same, but obviously in the combination of the widowed mother and daughter who live in a small house (one called *domik* in both poems) something has passed from "Domik v Kolomne" into *Mednyj vsadnik*. The name Paraša is metrically accommodating; it has the same amphibrachic form that the name Evgenij, a favorite of Puškin's possesses. It hardly supplies significant rhymes: in "Graf Nulin" it is rhymed only once, with *vaša*; in *Mednyj vsadnik* only once, with *naša*; in "Domik" only once, but with two words because of the pattern of triple rhymes: with *naša* and with *kaša*; the last rhyme is semantically significant, of course, since it implies the girl's familiarity with and efficiency in executing the rather vulgar household chores. Perhaps the poet employed the name in *Mednyj vsadnik* as a kind of shorthand associated with the combination of widow and daughter: this combination would imply defenselessness, of course, a defenselessness that is countered in "Domik" by the daughter's industry, efficiency, and self-reliance, but for which there is no counter in *Mednyj vsadnik*: there the mother and daughter are helpless victims of fate.

Not unrelated are the poet's amazement and irritation, in "Domik", when out for a stroll he observes that the little house where the widow and Paraša had once dwelt is missing, replaced now by a new three-storied mansion, and Evgenij's horror, after the flood, when he roams the main street of the island and finds no trace of his financée's cottage. Both changes are the work of fate, and though this theme has no further echo in "Domik" save for the poet's futile, unanswered question ("Živy li oni?—I čto že?"[10]) still it does foreshadow the theme of the working of blind fate in *Mednyj vsadnik*.

In "Graf Nulin" the setting is the country, but "Domik" is set, of course, in Kolomna, that part of Petersburg on the bank of the Fontanka, where Puškin himself had lived until his exile to the South in 1820, and where, it would seem, he had heard the anecdote which was the basis of the story action in "Domik." In *Mednyj vsadnik* the widow and her daughter dwell on one of the small islands in the River Neva, but Evgenij lives in Kolomna. The flood occurred in 1824, when Puškin was in the South; he did not return to the capital until 1826, so that Kolomna must have remained that part of Petersburg with which he preserved the closest and most intimate association. Moreover, was there perhaps not a personal association: between himself and Evgenij—and between Peter and Alexander or Nicholas? Alexander was the sovereign who had exiled him to the South. That monarch in fact appears in the poem:

В тот грозный год
Покойный царь еще Россией
Со славой правил. На балкон,
Печален, смутен, вышел он
И молвил: «С божией стихией
Царям не совладеть». Он сел
И в думе скорбными очами
На злое бедствие глядел.[11]

Were it not for the shift of scene from country to city, we could completely identify the genre of "Domik" with that of the earlier poem, "Graf Nulin." Both are based on anecdotes, very likely on actual incidents. Both have traces of mock-epic style, but only traces; and in "Domik" the epic line is firmly and finally rejected. Both use details of everyday life for humor, color, and picturesqueness. Both have simple, direct story lines, complicated only by Puškin's ironic digressions. "Graf Nulin" lacks, to be sure, the elaborate metapoetic introduction to "Domik," but still it has its share of metaliterary elements: the criticism of the Paris theater and of French poetry at the supper scene; the poet's speculations as to how the heroine should answer her guest's ardent advances, and so on. Both poems end with irreverent and irrelevant morals. The chief innovation in "Domik," then, at least in its narrative part, is the introduction of the city itself, and this is new for Puškin. With the exception of *Onegin*, which begins and ends in the city, it is hardly possible to find an earlier example of a work by Puškin that is set in the city, and there is in fact relatively little of the city atmosphere in that poem, and almost none at the end. "Domik" is, in fact, the first of a series of later works in which Puškin attempts to make poetry of city life and atmosphere. Following "Domik," to this same series belongs the uncompleted poem, "Ezerskij" and its ultimately completed variant, the *Rodoslovnaja moego geroja,* and, finally, *Mednyj vsadnik* itself. Among Puškin's prose tales there is the single story "Grobovščik," ("The Coffin Maker") in *The Tales of Belkin*, written, by the way, during the same autumn as "Domik", as well as "Pikovaja dama". What, we may ask, besides the city setting, do the three poems have in common: "Domik," "Ezerskij," and *Mednyj vsadnik*? What they have in common is an ordinary hero, one deprived of conventionally heroic characteristics. Such a character could of course exist in the country as well, at least in a comic avatar, e.g., "Graf Nulin," but the city was ultimately a more organic setting for such a figure, since the ordinary hero could draw significance from his status as symbolic representative of the faceless masses of the city's population. In "Domik" there is no hero, but an ordinary heroine, presumably one of gentle birth in view of her (admittedly petty) court connections. In "Ezerskij" there is a hero from a great aristocratic family fallen to the low estate of a *kolležskij registrator*, a humble rank in the civil service. In *Mednyj vsadnik* we have a petty clerk, also of aristocratic origin, who longs for his own rather banal and philistine happiness, a longing not unlike that implied to Paraša in "Domik" when she reads novels by Emin or when she gazes at the moon.

Poetry of city life is a much later discovery than poetry of the country, both in the narrative poem and in the lyric. Folk poetry and folk tales likewise illustrate the absence of conventions for describing the city and for dealing with city life. In an approach to a poetic narrative of the city Puškin at first makes tentative and, in a sense, abortive efforts: in "Domik" he fleshes out a comic anecdote with a long introduction ostensibly preoccupied with metrical problems (but, more importantly, with questions of literary style). In the course of the poem he leaves us several nuggets of real poetry of city life, replete with an actual sense of locale and a tangible atmosphere. "Ezerskij" is a second attempt, even more abortive, since the poem was not finished; here the city setting is associated in the poet's mind with an ordinary hero who springs from honorable and aristocratic origins. Was it not himself Puškin had in mind when he wrote this? For "Ezerskij" parallels the poet's *Moja rodoslovnaja*, written just two years before in 1830, and both poems seem to reflect Puškin's preoccupation with his own aristocratic origin.

Many commentators have remarked the possible identification of Ezerskij and of Evgenij in *Mednyj vsadnik* with the poet himself: both heroes have in common with Puškin their ancient noble lineage.[12] To identify the transvestite Mavruša of "Domik" with Puškin is more difficult, though this was done by Ermakov in his rather crude Freudian study of Puškin in the 1920s.[13] The argument is perhaps not entirely groundless: Ermakov's most solid support is an alleged slip of the pen made by Puškin in the rough draft of the poem: for Paraša he writes the name of his would be bride, Nataša. But there would seem to be little point in pursuing the argument here, and at most it remains an intriguing suggestion.

"Domik" can be viewed, then, as a turning point for its author, away from classicism as well as romanticism, toward a poetry of everyday life and of the little man. It is not perhaps so important as it might at first seem that the poem is comic and ironic: the bridge to the serious poems "Ezerskij" and *Mednyj vsadnik*, is apparent. Likewise, there is a turning away from the country to the city in which Puškin lived, and a deliberate attempt to exploit the atmosphere of city life for the sake of making poetry. What "Domik" does not prepare us for in *Mednyj vsadnik*, of course, is what we might wish to call the symbolic or mythic dimension of that poem. But this is perhaps unprecedented in all Puškin's poetry.

NOTES

1. M. L. Gofman, ed., "Domik v Kolomne," Petrograd, 1922.
2. Jurij Semjonow, "Das Häuschen in Kolomna" in der poetischen Erbschaft A. S. Puškins, Acta Universitatis Upsaliensis, Studia Slavica Upsaliensea, Vol. 3, Uppsala, 1965.
3. P., 5, p. 93.
4. Viktor Šklovskij, *Literatura i kinematograf* (Berlin, 1923), pp. 16.–17.
5. Jurij Tynjanov, "O literaturnoj èvoljucii," *Arxaisty i novatory* (Leningrad, 1929), pp. 30–47.
6. P., 5, p. 83.
7. See Valerij Brjusov's introduction to "Domik v Kolomne," in *Puškin*, ed. S. A. Vengerov (St. Petersburg, 1909), vol. 3, pp. 88–91.
8. P., 5, p. 85.
9. Ibid., p. 89.
10. Ibid., p. 85.
11. Ibid., p. 14.
12. Most recently in John Bayley, *Pushkin* (Cambridge, 1971), pp. 150–151.
13. I. D. Ermakov, *Etjudy po psixologii tvorčestva A. S. Puškina* (Petrograd, 1923), pp. 17–38.

PUŠKIN'S "FEAST DURING THE PLAGUE" AND ITS ORIGINAL: A STRUCTURAL CONFRONTATION

Victor Terras
Brown University

The fame of *Pir vo vremja čumy* ("Feast During the Plague") would seem to be out of proportion with its merit if it is to be judged by the fact that it is essentially a translation of parts of a single scene from John Wilson's drama *The City of the Plague*. John Wilson (1785–1854), better known under his pen name Christopher North, is important in English literature as a critic. As a poet he is wholly second-rate. I shall quote George Saintsbury's opinion of his poetry, with which I cannot but agree, because it is relevant to my own argument regarding Puškin's *Pir*:

His poems are now matters of interest to very few mortals. It is not that they are bad, for they are not; but they are almost wholly without distinction. He came just late enough to have got the seed of the great romantic revival; and his verse work is rarely more than the work of a clever man who has partly learnt and partly divined the manner of Burns, Scott, Campbell, Coleridge, Wordsworth, Byron, and the rest.[1]

It is significant that Russian critics have from the very beginning tended to ignore or to minimize the fact that *Pir* is not an original work.[2] Thus, Belinskij wrote:

Pir vo vremja čumy, a fragment from Wilson's tragedy *The City of the Plague*, is one of Puškin's mysterious works. It is generally known that *The Covetous Knight* is an original work of his and that he called it a fragment from Shenstone's tragicomedy, *The Covetous Knight*, in order to find out, as is said, what effect it might have on our public. It may be that Wilson is simply a brother of Shenstone's, though it is rumored that both Wilson and his play are for real. Be as it may be, if only Wilson's play is as good as the fragment translated by Puškin, it is an undisputable fact that this Wilson has written a great work. It may also be that Puškin only used the idea, expressing it after his own fashion, and as a result created a marvelous poetic work, not a fragment, but a whole and complete work.[3]

Dostoevskij, in his celebrated *Discourse on Puškin*, exclaims:

What profound, fantastic images in that poem *Pir vo vremja čumy*! Yet in these fantastic images England's genius appears. This wonderful song about the plague, sung by the hero, and Mary's song with the lines

> And the voices of our children
> In a noisy school were heard —

are English songs, this is the sorrow of British genius, these are his tears, his tragic premonition of his future.[4]

It is only natural that the interest of Russian critics has been focussed in these two songs, for they are essentially Puškin's own creation. Both have become a part of Russian literary mythology. Thus V. Ja. Brjusov's cycle *Neiz"jasnimy naslažden'ja* (1911) bears the epigraph:

> Все, все, что гибелью грозит,
> Для сердца смертного таит
> Неизъяснимы наслажденья.

A poem of the same year, "Moej Dženni" ("To My Jenny"), bears the epigraph:

> А Эдмонда не покинет
> Дженни даже в небесах.

Mary Gray's song must have been a serious preoccupation of Brjusov's that year, for he sponsored a contest for the best poem on the theme of these lines. Marina Cvetaeva was one of the winners.[5]

The facts regarding the genesis of Puškin's *Pir* are simple. During his stay at Boldino in the fall of 1830 the poet had with him a volume entitled: *The Poetical works* of Milman, Bowles, Wilson and Barry Cornwall. Complete in one volume. Paris, 1829. The volume contains Wilson's *City of the Plague* (1816), from which Puškin translated a portion of Act I, scene 4. Puškin's work was published under the title *Pir vo vremja čumy* (Iz Vil'sonovoj tragedii *The City of the Plague*) in *Al'ciona: Al'manax na 1832 god*, izdan baronom Rozenom (St. Petersburg, 1832), pp. 19–32. It had been passed by the Censor on November 20, 1831. The manuscript is extant, along with some variants, neither being particularly revealing of Puškin's creative process.[6]

Before discussing *Pir* as a work of art in its own right, one must view its relationship with Wilson's drama and Puškin's other "little tragedies": the first to determine Puškin's contribution to the effect of his one-act play, the second because it seems that the merit of *Pir* is enhanced by the cumulative effect of the other plays, with all four sharing certain important thematic, philosophic, and structural traits. The following chart shows the mechanical correspondence between Puškin's text[7] and Wilson's original.

Lines 1–25 faithful translation;
26–31 somewhat shortened and simplified (eight lines in the original);
32–71 Mary's song, essentially Puškin's own work;
72–137 faithful translation;
138–173 Walsingham's song, essentially Puškin's own work;
174–196 faithful translation; but Wilson's line, "The Devil pays his tithes—yet he abuses him," has remained untranslated after line 189.
197–207 somewhat abridged (by 1 1/2 lines); at this point 17 lines (exchange between Priest and Fitzgerald ["Young Man"]) have been left out by Puškin.
208–236 faithful translation; at this point 6 lines (belonging to Walsingham) have been omitted by Puškin;

237–238   faithful translation; Puškin has added: Пир
продолжается. Председатель остается по-
гружен в глубокую задумчивость.

Puškin's active role is then threefold: (1) he has selected a single
scene from Wilson's three-act play and presents it as a one-act play;
(2) he acts as a "cutter" and adds some minor effects, in particular
the concluding remark: "The President remains deeply absorbed
in thought"; (3) he has written his own text for the two songs.

Puškin uses the meter of the original, but it happens to be the
meter of his other little tragedies anyway. Walsingham's song,
though different in its strophic form, is in rhymed iambic tetrameter
in both Puškin and Wilson. Wilson's version of Mary's song is in
amphibrachic tetrameter (with some irregularities, including frequent anacrusis). Puškin's meter, trochaic tetrameter, would seem
to clash somewhat with its description in the dialogue: *unylo i
protjažno*, a faithful translation of "most sad, most slow."

A comparison of Puškin's and Wilson's iambic pentameter reveals that the Russian poet was not at all influenced by the rhythm
of the original, as the statistical tabulations compiled by Tomaševskij show that *Pir* falls well within the statistical curves of Puškin's
original works.[8] Also, the distribution of apparent pauses shows
that Puškin's pentameter leans toward a regular caesura much more
strongly than does Wilson's:

	Pause (caesura) after syllable							
	?	3	4	5	6	7	8	no pause
Wilson (185 lines)	—	3	36	29	34	27	3	53
Puškin (161 lines)	3	8	65	34	25	12	7	7

While in Puškin's pentameter 62 percent of all lines have a clear-
cut caesura after the fourth or fifth syllable, the corresponding
percentage in Wilson is only 35 percent. In this respect, then,
Puškin's verse is more "organized" than Wilson's. In addition,
Puškin's verse is, so far as I can see, also richer in sound patterns

and syntactic figures that make for poetic organization. I counted:

	Puškin (161 lines)	Wilson (185 lines)
Alliteration*	72	32
Repetition	20	10
Formulaic expressions	13	6

* Three or more alliterating words in a line, or two different alliterating pairs are counted as one.

In addition, I counted in Puškin: assonance—11, inner rhyme—8, anaphora—3, grammatical parallelism—26, inversion—6, antithesis—2, "one word line"—4. Of 161 lines in *Pir*, only 28 have no special organizing features (besides meter, caesura, and rhythm), while a great majority of Wilson's lines have only meter (and rhythm, of course) to give them structure. Nevertheless, it is my subjective impression that the English text sounds more intensely like "poetry" than does the Russian text.

As a translator, Puškin does a creditable though by no means flawless job. There are these outright mistranslations:

Line 17   Хотя красноречивейший язык/Не умолкал еще во прахе гроба
The grave did never silence with its dust/A tongue more eloquent

Line 101   Крикливых северных красавиц
... these crying beauties of the north

Line 111   Ужасный демон
Приснился мне: весь черный, белоглазый . . .
Он звал меня в свою тележку. В ней
Лежали мервые—и лепетали
Ужасную, неведомую речь . . .
I saw a horrid demon in my dream!
With sable visage and white-glaring eyes,
He beckoned on me to ascend a cart
Filled with dead bodies, muttering all the while
An unknown language of most dreadful sounds.

(Here Puškin has overlooked the position of the comma, which suggests that "muttering all the while" refers to the Negro, not to the dead bodies.)

Line 221   ... старик, иди же с миром;
                Но проклят будь, кто за тобой пойдет.
                Beloved old man, go thy way in peace,
                But curst be these feet if they do follow thee.
Line 189   Here Puškin leaves a rather strong line, "The Devil pays his tithes—yet he abuses him," untranslated, conceivably because he could not understand it. But then, too, this line anticipates the exchange between the Priest and Fitzgerald, with bitter and blasphemous words on the latter's part. Certainly blasphemy with outright mention of the Scriptures (the hundredth psalm) would have had no chance to be passed by the Censor.

There is another detail which may have caused the omission of the exchange between the Priest and Fitzgerald. The lines

> Why! We can pray
> Without a priest—pray long and fervently
> Over the brimming bowl. Hand him a glass

tie in with Scene 3 of the same act, in which a participant in the "feast" describes it as what is easily recognized as black mass and willful sacrilege.[9] The recurring motif of rebellious and agressive atheism which dominates Wilson's play certainly was not apt to meet with approval on the part of Nicholas I.

As for the point at which Puškin's translation breaks off, it is obviously determined by the inner logic of Puškin's own idea. To this we shall return later.

The two songs clearly are more important for Puškin's play than they are for Wilson's (which contains a number of other lyric inserts). Blagoj emphasizes the symmetry and polarity of these songs, which is underlined, he says, by certain external factors quite absent in the original: In *Pir* Mary's song (40 lines) comes after 31 lines of dialogue, and is followed by another 62 lines of dialogue; then, Walsingham's song (36 lines) and another 65 lines of dialogue. The respective figures for Wilson's scene are 32–64 (Mary's song)—64–90 plus 4 × 6 lines of refrain (Walsingham's song)—177. The two songs act as structural foci in Puškin's one-act play, something which they cannot be in Wilson's drama and which they are not even in the scene in question.

Blagoj also sees the two songs as bearing the basic idea (*osnóvnoj pafos*) of the play: "the triumph of a lofty human spirit over death, accomplished by the eternally feminine through self-effacing, self-sacrificing love (Mary's song) and by the eternally virile through a fearless challenge of death (Walsingham's "Hymn in Honor of the Plague")."[10] Nothing of this kind is present in Wilson's two songs. Mary's song in *The City of the Plague* is a lengthy and tearful description of the ravages of the plague in her native Scotland, without any pointed message or personal touch.[11] Puškin's last two stanzas are not even implied in Wilson's version of Mary's song:

> Если ранняя могила
> Суждена моей весне—
> Ты, кого я так любила,
> Чья любовь отрада мне,—
> Я молю: не приближайся
> К телу Дженни ты своей;
> Уст умерших не касайся,
> Следуй издали за ней.
>
> И потом оставь селенье.
> Уходи куда-нибудь,
> Где б ты мог души мученье
> Усладить и отдохнуть.
> И когда зараза минет,
> Посети мой бедный прах;
> А Эдмонда не покинет
> Дженни даже в небесах!

However, the sentiment contained in these stanzas is certainly present elsewhere in *The City of the Plague*. Its heroine, Magdalene, is the very symbol of self-sacrificing womanhood. When she knows that she has been stricken, her first thought is not of herself, but of those she loves:

> *Magd.* Too well am I acquainted with the Plague,
> And all its fatal symptoms. I beheld
> The slumb'rous weight upon my eyes, the dim
> Blue shade that ever more must leave my cheeks—
> My lips are touched by death—before the hour

Of earliest morning—the small midnight hour,—
O Heaven protect my faithful Isabel,
And waft her safe, as on an angel's wing,
To that sweet Lake which I must see no more!
(Act III, Scene 2)

In fairness to Wilson, Magdalene, like some of his other characters, has some surprisingly disquieting and intriguing traits which
belie the romantic stereotype which she seems to be at first glance.
Her self-sacrificing care for the victims of the plague turns to bla-
tant, spine-chilling necrophilia toward the end:

Lo! I his bride am here,
And I will kiss his lips, even if the worm
Should be my rival. I will rest my head
Upon his breast, than icy tombstone colder!
Ay! the grave shall be my happy nuptial-bed
Curtained with black walls of the dripping clay.
(Act III, Scene 4)

There are indications of this theme earlier in the play.[12] In fact, it
would appear that Magdalene loves so she could die with her lover:

We shall die
Like two glad waves, that, meeting on the sea
In moonlight and in music, melt away
Quietly 'mid the quiet wilderness!
(Act III, Scene 3)

In comparison with these disquieting traits, the feelings of Puškin's
Jenny are wholesome and straightforward—wholly unromantic,
I daresay.

Puškin's hymn to the Plague likewise differs radically from Wilson's. The latter's "Song" sings the praises of the plague, that most
efficient of all killers, that great equalizer, the revealer of ultimate
truth, Death *par excellence*. Walsingham's "Song" is certainly
symbolic of the play as a whole, whose message can only be: the
old die, and so do the young; the wicked die, and so do the virtuous;
those who have something to live for die, and those who have not;
those whose death makes sense die, and those whose does not. In
short, the plague dramatizes the absurdity of death.[13] Puškin's
"Hymn," meanwhile does not deal with death at all. Rather, it
avoids the issue by pointing at the fascination of mortal danger—not
death.

Again, the psychological phenomenon in question is brought out frequently and prominently in Wilson's play:[14]

> *Voice.* Heed not that foolish wretch—go on, go on,
> I love to feel my hair stand up on end,
> And my heart beat till I can hear its sound.
>
> (Act II, Scene 3)

There exists a rather clear dichotomy in Wilson's play between characters who love life:

> Thou lovest life with all its agonies:
> Buy poison, and 'twill lie for years untouched
> Beneath thy pillow, when thy midnight horrors
> Are at their worst. Coward! thou canst not die!
>
> (Act I, Scene 2)

and those who are attracted by death, such as Magdalene. Thus, an ambivalent attitude toward mortal danger is well motivated.

The one line in Puškin's "Hymn" which strikes an irrational note is:

> бессмертья, может быть, залог!

It suggests that fascination with mortal danger may be caused by a subconscious awareness that death is a bridge to eternal life. Once more, this thought is also present in *The City of the Plague*:

> This frame of dust, this feeble breath,
>   The Plague may soon destroy;
> We think on Thee, and feel in death
>   A deep and awful joy.
>
> (Magdalene's "Hymn," Act II, Scene 2)

And once again, Wilson has given this theme a more complete, and more profound, treatment. To be sure, the concluding lines of his play:

> Hush! sob not—for they now are Spirits in Heaven!

are well prepared for throughout the play. But there is also this other, intriguing, and terrifying view:

Who could deny, with that unearthly sound
Tolling through his brain, that something in the grave
Exists more horrible than worms and darkness!
It may be that wild dreams inhabit there,
And disembodied thoughts! Despair — remorse —
And with his stifled shrieks — Insanity!
Half-conscious all the while that the curse of God
Must be eternal, struck into the grave.

(Act III, Scene 4)

All in all, Puškin has very skillfully cut out from Wilson's arch-romantic, ambivalent, contradictory creation a vignette that serves his own purposes admirably. Among the themes important in Wilson's drama, but not in Puškin's, are a Karamazovian attack on the divine order,[15] a dialogue between atheism and faith,[16] the theme of the world's absurdity, the theme of time madly accelerated or wholly meaningless,[17] the theme of the leveling effect of death,[18] or summarily: the theme of death as a "limiting situation."

While *The City of the Plague* is a kind of *danse macabre*, a panorama of death, the theme and structure of *Pir* are obviously much narrower and more focused. It would seem that theme and structure of *Pir* will have to be discussed against the background of the other little tragedies. Conversely, *Pir*, a relatively simple piece, may facilitate or at least support the interpretation of the other little tragedies.

The influence of Barry Cornwall's dramatic sketches is a key to the interpretation of Puškin's little tragedies. Barry Cornwall's introduction to several of his pieces suggests that he saw them as "expressions of natural emotion,"[19] meaning in today's language: statements of archetypal psychological situations. If the same is true of Puškin's little tragedies, the relationship between these dramatic fragments and tragedy is that of the novella and the novel. It can be safely assumed that a single, well focused, psychological theme is present in each fragment and that all its details are aimed at enhancing the single effect planned, much as E. A. Poe, in his "Philosophy of Composition," demanded for the novella.[20]

What is the theme of *Pir*? Tomaševskij, in his commentary to *The Stone Guest*, says: "Like the other 'little tragedies' of Puškin, this piece develops characters invented by Puškin, who are connected with one another by the idea of 'the pleasures of life' (inspiration, love, wealth)."[21] If this is so, *Pir* will have to be a piece about the pleasure of "living dangerously."

Some Soviet critics, led by D. D. Blagoj, read an optimistic, life-affirming message into all of the little tragedies in general, and into *Pir* in particular.[22] If this interpretation is correct, Puškin's version is radically different from Wilson's original whose positive message (if we are to believe it) is wholly based on a Christian faith in the afterlife. There are, however, some facts which seem to refute such interpretation. Each of Puškin's plays, and so *Pir*, contains a transition from defiance to defeat. In *Pir*, this circumstance is emphasized by Puškin's addition to the text of the original: "The President remains absorbed in deep contemplation." This is a far cry from his defiant hymn to the plague.

Anna Axmatova's interpretation of *The Stone Guest*,[23] to the effect that this play is a projection of Puškin's personal preoccupations, is both plausible and easily transferred to the other plays. It is strongly supported by the fact that Puškin's Don Juan is a poet. So is of course the hero of *Pir*. Even more important is Axmatova's suggestion that Puškin is both Don Juan and Commendador: seducer and jealous husband. If this is so, Puškin can be both Mozart and Salieri, as Nadežda Mandelštam has recently suggested. In a way, too, he is not only Albert, but also expresses some of his deepest insights into contemporary life through the old Baron, as S. Rassadin suggests.[24]

Pir almost certainly owes its existence to the cholera epidemic which forced Puškin to spend the autumn of 1830 at Boldino. Certainly he who had written "Pod nebom golubym strany svoej rodnoj" could understand Walsingham's bravado with the wound of his young wife's death still open. The duality of Walsingham's soul is by all means Puškin's. It is, however, somewhat different from what it is like in Wilson's play. Wilson's Walsingham is quite complex and contradictory, perhaps incredibly so. In spite of the sobering experience in Act I, Scene 4 he goes on to kill Fitzgerald in a nocturnal duel. His perversely excessive grief at his mother's death (which we witness in Puškin's version) becomes understandable only in the light of a strange, matricidal nightmare experienced by Frankfort, whose double Walsingham is. Puškin's Walsingham makes more sense.

In Axmatova's interpretation, rather as in Tomaševskij's, the theme of *The Stone Guest* is human happiness, or rather, its elusiveness. Don Juan must perish when, for the first time in his life, he believes to have happiness within his grasp and when life has become precious. Similarly, the grasp for happiness by the heroes of the other little tragedies is frustrated in every case. Surely *Pir* is no exception and Walsingham's intoxication with death and danger ends in a hangover.

We are now ready to ask: what was Puškin trying to do in *Pir*, and what did he accomplish? Vladimir Solov'ev, in a recent article,[25] suggests that Puškin's little tragedies are indeed "antidramas" (*antip'esy*), as Puškin said himself, in that they are really dramatic studies in which a subjective, reflective element is superimposed upon the objective, dramatic action. Solov'ev's view is corroborated by the fact that at the time in question Puškin was finishing the "anti-novel" *Evgenij Onegin*, writing the "anti-*poema*," "Domik v Kolomne," and the "anti-stories" of *The Tales of Belkin*. As Solov'ev further points out, *Pir* is a fragment of a work which is itself fragmentary, an "antifragment," as it were. The obvious inference from this is that in his *Pir*, Puškin saw an opportunity to create a whole and to give a focus where there were none in Wilson's play.

As Dostoevskij pointed out in his famous analysis of "Egyptian Nights," a piece which is formally a fragment, i.e., ostensibly open-ended, may still be artistically a perfect whole. In fact the "fragment" may be the ideal form for delivering a certain message. This is precisely true of Puškin's *Pir*.

The City of the Plague (implying a panorama) has become *The Feast during the Plague*, implying a polarity and so a focus. The effect of the contrast (somber, half-deserted city, death cart: gay revelry in one street) is greatly enhanced as its effect is not diluted by other scenes, as it is in Wilson's play. The two songs, as pointed out earlier, present a polarity (which appropriate music would enhance). Walsingham's inner conflict (despair in his heart, defiance on his lips) is very much in the center of attention and is underscored by supporting details (Louisa, the exchange between Fitzgerald and the old priest).

Pir is a neatly structured and well focused study in human emotion, which contrasts with Wilson's unstructured and unfocused work. Its basic idea is analogous to that of the other three little tragedies. In each of them a would-be "superman" places himself above all moral law, only to be unmasked as a mere pretender. He who aspires to be godlike, only gets to be diabolic, as R. L. Jackson has recently demonstrated so convincingly for *Mozart and Salieri*.[26] This is essentially how D. Darskij saw *Pir* back in 1915.[27]

The Devil is present in *Pir*, as the Priest likens the revelers to a band of devils who:

> With shouts of devilish laughter dragged away
> Some hardened atheist's soul unto perdition.

As noted earlier, the Priest's outcry is well motivated in Wilson's play, because the orgy has been earlier described as a black mass. This motif is, of course, absent in Puškin's version.

Without a doubt everything that Puškin has done serves to eliminate the irrational, the chaotic, the abysmal—the "romantic," in a word. These are precisely the qualities that Wilson is credited—or charged—with by his critics: "reckless, audacious and luxuriant in diction, at times startling with gleams of profound insight, but often utterly obtuse, perverse, defiant of courtesy, good taste, and good sense."[28] Consistently with the other little tragedies, a "romantic" theme is taken up in *Pir* and artfully resolved in a rational and moral, antiromantic manner. In each case human *hubris* is defeated. It may be mentioned in this context that even in *Boris Godunov* Puškin had chosen to follow Karamzin's rational and moralizing conception of that theme rather than opting for the "romantic" tragedy of an innocent Boris Godunov.

NOTES

1. George Saintsbury, *Essays in English Literature 1780–1860*, 2nd ed. (London, Percival, 1891), p. 277.
2. Anna Axmatova is an exception to the general rule when she says that "*Pir* is a simple translation." See A. A. Axmatova, "*Kamennyj gost'* Puškina," *Puškin: Issledovanija i materialy*, II (Moscow, Leningrad, AN SSSR, 1958), p. 193.
3. V. G. Belinskij, *Polnoe sobranie sočinenij*, 13 vols. (Moscow, AN SSSR, 1953–59), 7:555–556.
4. Quoted from F. M. Dostoevskij ob iskusstve (Moscow, Iskusstvo, 1973), p. 365.
5. See commentary in Valerij Brjusov, *Sobranie sočinenij v semi tomax* (Moscow, Xudožestvennaja literatura, 1973–), III, 605.
6. See P., 7, pp. 317–318 and P., 17, pp. 51–52.

7. P., 7, pp. 173–184.
8. See B. V. Tomaševskij, *O stixe* (Leningrad, 1929), p. 243.
9. Here is a part of the passage in question:

> With drunken guilt, I mocked my Saviour's name
> With hideous mummery, and the holy book
> In scornful fury trampled, rent, and burned.
> Oh! ours were dreadful orgies!—At still midnight
> We sallied out in mimic grave-clothes clad,
> Aping the dead, and in some churchyard danced
> A dance that ofttimes had a mortal close.
> Then would we lay a living Body out,
> As it had been a corpse, and bear it slowly
> With what at distance seemed a holy dirge,
> Through silent streets and squares unto its rest.
> One quaintly apparelled like a surpliced priest
> Led the procession, joining in the song;—
> A jestful song, most brutal and obscene,
> Shameful to man, his Saviour, and his God.
>
> > (*The Works of Professor Wilson,*
> > ed. Professor Ferrier [Edinburgh
> > and London, Wm. Blackwood,
> > 1858], vol. 12, p. 99)

Quotes and references will be from this edition.

10. D. D. Blagoj, *Tvorčeskij put' Puškina (1826–1830)* (Moscow, Sovetskij pisatel', 1967), p. 666.
11. See. N. V. Fridman, "Pesnja Meri," *IAN* 33 (1974):242–253.
12. See Act II, Scene 2: "I know well/That they who love their friends most tenderly/Still bear their loss the best . . ." (p. 118); ibid. "We think on Thee, and feel in death/A deep and awful joy" (p. 124).
13. The idea of the world's absurdity is very much on Wilson's mind, for example: Act III, Scene 4: "Laugh on—laugh on—for all the world is nought/But emptiness and mockery" (p. 167).
14. Other examples: Act I, Scene 3: "We knew that we were lost, yet would we pluck/The flowers that bloomed upon the crater's edge,/Nor feared the yawning gulf" (p. 100); Act I, Scene 4: "Before an action fearless men look pale,/And fling away their smiles; but once engaged,/They scoff at death with gleesome mockery" (p. 110).
15. Thus, Fitzgerald exclaims:

God cares, forsooth, for us His worshippers!

Yet though we perish thousands in one night,
And like the brutes are buried, still we call Him
Lord—Priest, and Father, and still hope to rise
Even from the crowded pit where we lie smothered
Like bees in brimstone,—to rise beautiful,
And soar to God's throne, spirits glorified! (p. 142)

16. One such exchange immediately follows the passage translated by Puškin (pp. 109–110).

17. Particularly in the exchange between Frankfort and Wilmot, Act I, Scene 1, started by Frankfort's words: "and the Plague/Mocks in his fury the slow hand of time."

18. For example:

> —One little month—and all thy earthly part
> Mouldered away to nothing—darkly mixed
> With a great city-churchyard's dismal mould!
> Where sleep, in undistinguishable dust,
> Young, old, good, wicked, beauteous and deformed,
> Trodden under feet by every worthless thing
> Human and brute! (p. 171)

19. See Barry Cornwall, *Dramatic Scenes* and other poems (London, C. and J. Ollier, 1819), p. iv.

20. It may be mentioned that Dostoevskij had claimed exactly this much for another "fragment" of Puškin's, "Egyptian Nights," in his "Reply to *The Russian Herald*" (1861).

21. A. S. Puškin, *Polnoe sobranie sočinenij v desjati tomax*, 3rd ed. (Moscow, Nauka, 1964), vol. 5, p. 616.

22. Blagoj, op. cit., pp. 659–667.

23. Axmatova, op. cit., pp. 185–195.

24. St. Rassadin, "Nevol'nik česti," *Novyj Mir* 50 (1974), iv:247–259.

25. Vladimir Solov'ev, "'Opyt dramatičeskix izučenij' (K istorii literaturnoj èvoljucii Puškina)," *Voprosy Literatury* (1974) 5, pp. 128–158.

26. Robert Louis Jackson, "Miltonic Imagery and Design in Puškin's *Mozart and Salieri*: The Russian Satan," in *American Contributions to the Seventh International Congress of Slavists* (The Hague and Paris, Mouton, 1973), 2:256–264.

27. D. Darskij, *Malen'kie tragedii Puškina* (Moscow, 1915), pp. 69–72.

28. *Chamber's Cyclopaedia of English Literature* (Philadelphia and New York, J. B. Lippincott, 1938), vol. 3, p. 246. The statement refers to Wilson's critical prose, but is valid for his thought at large.